FIA

MA1
MANAGEMENT INFORMATION

INTERACTIVE TEXT

BPP Learning Media is the sole **ACCA Platinum Approved Learning Partner –
content** for the FIA qualification. In this, **the only MA1 study text to be reviewed by
the examiner:**

- We **highlight** the **most important elements** in the syllabus and the key skills
  you will need

- We **signpost** how each chapter links to the syllabus and the study guide

- We **provide** lots of **exam focus points** demonstrating what the examiner will
  want you to do

- We **emphasise key points** in regular **fast forward summaries**

- We **test your knowledge** of what you've studied in **quick quizzes**

- We **examine your understanding** in our **exam question bank**

- We **reference all the important topics** in our full index

BPP's **Practice & Revision Kit, i-Pass** and **Interactive Passcard** products also
support this paper.

FOR EXAMS FROM FEBRUARY 2013 TO JANUARY 2014

First edition March 2011
Second Edition August 2012

ISBN 9781 4453 9962 1
Previous ISBN 9781 4453 7301 0
eISBN 9781 4453 9238 7

British Library Cataloguing-in-Publication Data
A catalogue record for this book is available from
the British Library

Published by

BPP Learning Media Ltd
BPP House, Aldine Place
142-144 Uxbridge Road
London W12 8AA

www.bpp.com/learningmedia

Printed in the United Kingdom by

Polestar Wheatons
Hennock Road
Marsh Barton
Exeter
EX2 8RP

Your learning materials, published by BPP
Learning Media Ltd, are printed on paper
obtained from traceable sustainable sources.

We are grateful to the Association of Chartered
Certified Accountants for permission to
reproduce past examination questions. The
suggested solutions in the exam answer bank have
been prepared by BPP Learning Media Ltd.

©
BPP Learning Media Ltd
2012

Contents

Helping you to pass – the ONLY MA1 study text reviewed by the examiner!

BPP Learning Media – the sole Platinum Approved Learning Partner - content

As ACCA's **sole Platinum Approved Learning Partner – content**, BPP Learning Media gives you the **unique opportunity** to use **examiner-reviewed** study materials for exams from February 2013 to January 2014. By incorporating the examiner's comments and suggestions regarding the depth and breadth of syllabus coverage, the BPP Learning Media Interactive Text provides excellent, **ACCA-approved** support for your studies.

The PER alert!

To become a Certified Accounting Technician or qualify as an ACCA member, you not only have to pass all your exams but also fulfil a **practical experience requirement** (PER). To help you to recognise areas of the syllabus that you might be able to apply in the workplace to achieve different performance objectives, we have introduced the '**PER alert**' feature. You will find this feature throughout the Interactive Text to remind you that what you are **learning in order to pass** your FIA and ACCA exams is **equally useful to the fulfilment of the PER requirement**.

Your achievement of the PER should be recorded in your online *My Experience* record.

Tackling studying

Studying can be a daunting prospect, particularly when you have lots of other commitments. The **different features** of the Text, the **purposes** of which are explained fully on the **Chapter features** page, will help you whilst studying and improve your chances of **exam success**.

Developing exam awareness

Our Texts are completely **focused** on helping you pass your exam.

Our advice on **Studying MA1** outlines the **content** of the paper, the **recommended approach to studying** and any **brought forward knowledge** you are expected to have.

Exam focus points are included within the chapters to highlight when and how specific topics might be examined.

Using the Syllabus and Study Guide

You can find the syllabus and Study Guide on page ix of this Interactive Text.

Testing what you can do

Testing yourself helps you develop the skills you need to pass the exam and also confirms that you can recall what you have learnt.

We include **Questions** – lots of them – both within chapters and in the **Exam Question Bank**, as well as **Quick Quizzes** at the end of each chapter to test your knowledge of the chapter content.

Chapter features

Each chapter contains a number of helpful features to guide you through each topic.

Topic list		Tells you what you will be studying in this chapter and the relevant section numbers, together with the ACCA syllabus references.
Introduction		Puts the chapter content in the context of the syllabus as a whole.
Study Guide		Links the chapter content with ACCA guidance.
Fast Forward		Summarises the content of main chapter headings, allowing you to preview and review each section easily.
EXAMPLE		Demonstrates how to apply key knowledge and techniques.
Key Term		Definitions of important concepts that can often earn you easy marks in exams.
Exam Focus Point		Tell you how specific topics may be examined.
Formula		Formulae which have to be learnt.
PER Alert		This feature gives you a useful indication of syllabus areas that closely relate to performance objectives in your Practical Experience Requirement (PER).
Question		Gives you essential practice of techniques covered in the chapter.

Chapter Roundup   A full list of the Fast Forwards included in the chapter, providing an easy source of review.

Quick Quiz   A quick test of your knowledge of the main topics in the chapter.

Exam Question Bank   Found at the back of the Interactive Text with more exam-style chapter questions. Cross referenced for easy navigation.

Studying MA1

How to Use this Interactive Text

Aim of this Interactive Text

> To provide the knowledge and practice to help you succeed in the examination for Paper MA1 *Management Information.*

To pass the examination you need a thorough understanding in all areas covered by the syllabus and teaching guide.

Recommended approach

(a) To pass you need to be able to answer questions on **everything** specified by the syllabus and teaching guide. Read the Text very carefully and do not skip any of it.

(b) Learning is an **active** process. Do **all** the questions as you work through the Text so you can be sure you really understand what you have read.

(c) After you have covered the material in the Interactive Text, work through the **Exam Question Bank**, checking your answers carefully against the **Exam Answer Bank**.

(d) Before you take the exam, check that you still remember the material using the following quick revision plan.

    (i) Read through the **chapter topic list** at the beginning of each chapter. Are there any gaps in your knowledge? If so, study the section again.

    (ii) Read and learn the **key terms**.

    (iii) Look at the **exam focus points**. These show the ways in which topics might be examined.

    (iv) Read the **chapter roundups**, which are a summary of the **fast forwards** in each chapter.

    (v) Do the **quick quizzes** again. If you know what you're doing, they shouldn't take long.

This approach is only a suggestion. You or your college may well adapt it to suit your needs. Remember this is a **practical** course.

(a) Try to relate the material to your experience in the workplace or any other work experience you may have had.

(b) Try to make as many links as you can to other papers at the Introductory and Intermediate levels.

> For practice and revision use BPP Learning Media's Practice and Revision Kit, iPass and Passcards.

What MA1 is about

The aim of this syllabus is to build a knowledge and understanding of the principles and techniques used in recording, analysing and reporting costs and revenues for internal management purposes. It covers management information, cost recording, costing techniques, source documents, comparisons and spreadsheets.

Approach to examining the syllabus

Paper MA1 is a two-hour paper. It can be taken as a written paper or a computer based examination. The questions in the computer based examination are objective test questions – multiple choice, number entry and multiple response. (See page xiv for frequently asked questions about computer based examinations.)

The written examination is structured as follows:

	Number of marks
50 compulsory multiple choice questions of two marks each	100

Syllabus and Study guide

Syllabus

AIM

To develop knowledge and understanding of providing basic management information in an organisation to support management in planning and decision-making .

RATIONALE

The syllabus for paper MA1, Management Information, introduces candidates to basic costing principles and techniques and the tools with which to use these principles and techniques
The syllabus starts by introducing business organisations and the specific role of management accountant within the organisation. The next section deals with cost classification followed by the identification of sources of information and coding, to ensure that cost information is properly classified. The syllabus then introduces basic techniques for recording costs followed by how to provide information.

It finally introduces candidates to spreadsheets as an important tool in supporting cos and management accounting.

MAIN CAPABILITIES

On successful completion of this paper, candidates should be able to:

A   Explain the nature and purpose of cost and management accounting

B   Identify source documents in a costing systems and correctly code data

C   Classify costs by nature, behaviour and purpose

D   Record costs for material, labour and expenses

E   Provide information on actual and expected costs

F   Use the spreadsheet system in Microsoft excel

RELATIONAL DIAGRAM OF MAIN CAPABILITIES

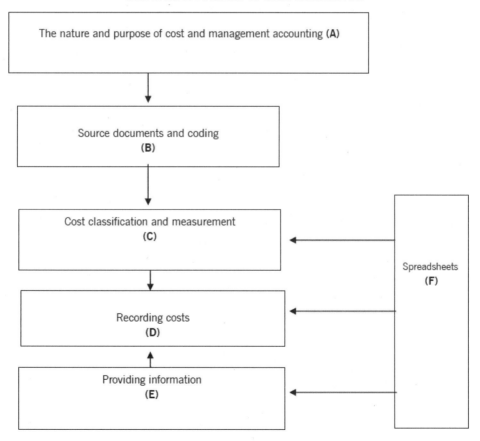

DETAILED SYLLABUS

A   The nature and purpose of cost and management accounting

1.   Nature of business organisation and the accounting systems

2.   Nature and purpose of management information

B   Source documents and coding

1.   Sources of information

2   Coding system

C   Cost classification and measurement

1.   Cost classification and behaviour

2   Cost units, cost centres, profit centres and investment centres

D   Recording costs

1.   Accounting for materials

2.   Accounting for labour

3.   Accounting for other expenses

4   Accounting for product costs

E   Providing information

1   Information for comparison

2   Reporting management information

F   The spreadsheet system

1   Spreadsheet system overview

2   Using computer spreadsheets

3   Presenting information in spreadsheets

APPROACH TO EXAMINING THE SYLLABUS

The syllabus is assessed by a two hour computer-based or paper based examination. Questions will assess all parts of the syllabus and will include both computational and non computational elements. The examination will consist of 50 two-mark questions.

Study Guide

A THE NATURE AND PURPOSE OF COST AND MANAGEMENT ACCOUNTING

1. Nature of business organisation and accounting systems

a) Describe the organisation, and main functions, of an office as a centre for information and administration.[K]

b) Describe the function and use of a manual of policies, procedures and best practices.[K]

c) Identify the main types of transactions undertaken by a business and the key personnel involved in initiating, processing and completing transactions.[k]

d) Explain the need for effective control over transactions.[K]

e) Explain and illustrate the principles and practice of double-entry book-keeping.[s]

f) Describe and illustrate the use of ledgers and prime entry records in both integrated and interlocking accounting systems.[s]

g) Identify the key features, functions and benefits of a computerised accounting system.[k]

2. Management information

a) State the purpose of management information.[K]

b) Compare cost and management accounting with external financial reporting.[k]

c) Distinguish between data and information.[k]

d) Describe the features of useful management information.[K]

e) Describe and identify sources and categories of information.[K]

f) Explain the limitations of cost and management accounting information.[K]

g) Describe the role of a trainee accountant in a cost and management accounting system. .[K]

B SOURCE DOCUMENTS AND CODING

1. Source documents

a) Describe the material control cycle (including the concept and calculation of 'free' inventory, but excluding control levels and EOQ) and the documentation necessary to order, receive, store and issue materials.[k]

b) Describe the procedures and documentation to ensure the correct authorisation, analysis and recording of direct and indirect material costs.[k]

c) Describe the procedures and documentation to ensure the correct authorisation, coding, analysis and recording of direct and indirect labour and expenses.[k]

d) Describe the procedures and documentation to ensure the correct analysis and recording of sales.[k]

2. Coding system

a) Explain and illustrate the use of codes in categorising and processing transactions.[s]

b) Explain and illustrate different methods of coding data. (including sequential, hierarchical, block, faceted and mnemonic).[K]

c) Identify and correct errors in coding of revenue and expenses.[S]

C COST CLASSIFICATION AND MEASUREMENT

1. Cost classification

a) Define cost classification and describe the variety of cost classifications used for different purposes in a cost accounting system, including by responsibility, function, behaviour, direct/indirect.[s]

b) Describe and illustrate the nature of variable, fixed and mixed (semi-variable, stepped-fixed) costs.[s]

c) Describe and illustrate the classification of material and labour costs. [s]

d) Prepare, and explain the nature and purpose of, profit statements in absorption and marginal costing formats. [s]

e) Calculate the cost and profit of a product or service. [S]

2. **Cost units, cost centres, profit centres and investment centres**

a) Explain and illustrate the concept of cost units. [K]

b) Explain and illustrate the concept of cost centres. [K]

c) Explain and illustrate the concept of profit centres. [K]

d) Explain and illustrate the concept of investment centres. [K]

e) Describe performance measures appropriate to cost, profit and investment centres (cost / profit per unit / % of sales; efficiency, capacity utilisation and production volume ratios; ROCE / RI, asset turnover) . [s]

f) Apply performance measures appropriate to cost, profit and investment centres. [S]

D **COST ACCOUNTING**

1. **Accounting for materials**

a) Distinguish different types of material (raw material, work in progress and finished goods) [K]

b) Describe and illustrate the accounting for material costs. [s]

c) Calculate material requirements making allowance for sales and product/material inventory changes (control levels and EOQ are excluded) . [S]

d) Explain and illustrate different methods used to price materials issued from inventory

(FIFO, LIFO and periodic and cumulative weighted average costs) . [s]

2 **Accounting for labour**

a) Describe and illustrate the accounting for labour costs (including overtime premiums and idle time) . [s]

b) Prepare an analysis of gross and net earnings. [s]

c) Explain and illustrate labour remuneration methods. [s]

d) Calculate the effect of changes in remuneration methods and changes in productivity on unit labour costs. [s]

3 **Accounting for other expenses**

a) Explain the process of charging indirect costs to cost centres and cost units and illustrate the process of cost apportionment for indirect costs (excluding reciprocal service) . [s]

b) Explain and illustrate the process of cost absorption for indirect costs . [s]

4 **Accounting for product costs**

a) Job costing
   (i) Describe the characteristics of job costing [K]
   (ii) Calculate unit costs using job costing. [s]

b) Batch costing
   (i) Describe the characteristics of batch costing. [K]
   (ii) Calculate unit costs using batch costing. [S]

c) Process costing
   (i) Describe the characteristics of process costing. [K]
   (ii) Calculate unit costs using process costing. [S] (note: split of losses into normal and abnormal is excluded)
   (iii) Describe and illustrate the concept of equivalent units for closing work in progress. [s]
   (iv) Calculate unit costs where there is closing work-in-progress. [S].
   (v) Allocate process costs between finished output and work-in-progress. [S]

(vi) Prepare process accounts.[S]

E   PROVIDING MANAGEMENT INFORMATION

1   Information for comparison

a)   Explain the purpose of making comparisons.[K]

b)   Identify relevant bases for comparison: previous period data, corresponding period data, forecast/budget data.[S]

c)   Explain the forecasting/budgeting process and the concept of feed forward and feedback control.[K]

d)   Explain and illustrate the concept of flexible budgets.[S]

e)   Use appropriate income and expenditure data for comparison.[S]

f)   Calculate variances between actual and historical/forecast data which may or may not be adjusted for volume change (note: standard costing is excluded).[S]

g)   Identify whether variances are favourable or adverse.[S]

h)   Identify possible causes of variances.[S]

i)   Explain the concept of exception reporting.[K]

j)   Explain factors affecting the decision whether to investigate variances.[K]

2   Reporting management information.

a)   Describe methods of analysing, presenting and communicating information.[K]

b)   Identify suitable formats for communicating management information according to purpose and organisational guidelines including: informal business reports, letter and email or memo.[S].

c)   Identify the general principles of distributing reports (e.g. procedures, timing, recipients) including the reporting of confidential information.[K]

d)   Interpret information presented in management reports.[S]

F.   THE SPREADSHEET SYSTEM

1.   Spreadsheet system overview

a)   Describe a spreadsheet system.[K]

b)   Explain the role of spreadsheets in management accounting.[K]

c)   Describe advantages and limitations of spreadsheets.[K]

2   Using computer spreadsheets

a)   Identify what numerical and other information is needed in spreadsheets and how it should be structured.[S]

b)   Describe the process of entering and editing information.[K]

c)   Describe and illustrate formatting tools.[S]

d)   Identify and use a wide range of formulae to meet calculations requirements (addition, subtraction, multiplication, division and average) .[S]

e)   Describe and correct errors in formulae.[s]

f)   Describe how data from different sources are linked and combined.[K]

g)   Describe how spreadsheet files are stored and retrieved.[K]

3   Presenting information in spreadsheets

a)   Describe and illustrate methods of summarising and analysing spreadsheet data (including sorting, ranking and filter).[K]

b)   Describe and interpret charts and graphs (bar, line, pie and scatter) .[S]

c)   Describe how to present and format information to meet particular needs.[S]

d)   Describe how to print information including page layout.[K]

The Computer Based Examination

Computer based examinations (CBEs) are available for the first seven FIA papers (not papers FAU, FTX or FFM), in addition to the conventional paper based examination.

Computer based examinations must be taken at an ACCA CBE Licensed Centre.

How does CBE work?

- Questions are displayed on a monitor

- Candidates enter their answer directly onto the computer

- Candidates have two hours to complete the examination

- When the candidate has completed their examination, the final percentage score is calculated and displayed on screen

- Candidates are provided with a Provisional Result Notification showing their results before leaving the examination room

- The CBE Licensed Centre uploads the results to the ACCA (as proof of the candidate's performance) within 72 hours

- Candidates can check their exam status on the ACCA website by logging into myACCA

Benefits

- **Flexibility** as a CBE can be sat at any time

- **Resits** can also be taken at any time and there is no restriction on the number of times a candidate can sit a CBE

- **Instant feedback** as the computer displays the results at the end of the CBE

- Results are notified to ACCA within 72 hours

CBE question types

- Multiple choice – choose one answer from four options

- Multiple response – select more than one response by clicking the appropriate tick boxes

- Multiple response matching – select a response to a number of related statements by choosing one option from a number of drop down menus

- Number entry – key in a numerical response to a question

The January 2012 issue of ACCA *Student Accountant* magazine contains an article on CBEs. Ensure that you are familiar with this article.

http://www.accaglobal.com/content/dam/acca/global/PDF-students/2012s/sa_jan12_cbe.pdf

For more information on computer-based exams, visit the ACCA website.

http://www.accaglobal.com/en/student/Exams/Computer-based-exams.html

Tackling Multiple Choice Questions

MCQ's are part of all FIA exams. They form the paper-based exams and may appear in the CBE.

The MCQs in your exam contain four possible answers. You have to **choose the option that best answers the question**. The three incorrect options are called distracters. There is a skill in answering MCQs quickly and correctly. By practising MCQs you can develop this skill, giving you a better chance of passing the exam.

You may wish to follow the approach outlined below, or you may prefer to adapt it.

Step 1	Skim read all the MCQs and identify what appear to be the easier questions.
Step 2	Attempt each question – **starting with the easier questions** identified in Step 1. Read the question **thoroughly**. You may prefer to work out the answer before looking at the options, or you may prefer to look at the options at the beginning. Adopt the method that works best for you.
Step 3	Read the four options and see if one matches your own answer. Be careful with numerical questions as the distracters are designed to match answers that incorporate common errors. Check that your calculation is correct. Have you followed the requirement exactly? Have you included every stage of the calculation?
Step 4	You may find that none of the options matches your answer. • Re-read the question to ensure that you understand it and are answering the requirement • Eliminate any obviously wrong answers • Consider which of the remaining answers is the most likely to be correct and select the option
Step 5	If you are still unsure make a note and continue to the next question
Step 6	Revisit unanswered questions. When you come back to a question after a break you often find you are able to answer it correctly straight away. If you are still unsure have a guess. You are not penalised for incorrect answers, so **never leave a question unanswered!**

After extensive practice and revision of MCQs, you may find that you recognise a question when you sit the exam. Be aware that the detail and/or requirement may be different. If the question seems familiar read the requirement and options carefully – do not assume that it is identical.

The January 2012 issue of ACCA *Student Accountant* magazine contains an article on how to answer MCQs. Ensure that you are familiar with this article.

http://www.accaglobal.com/content/dam/acca/global/PDF-students/2012s/sa_jan12_mcq.pdf

BPP
LEARNING MEDIA

part

A

The nature and purpose of cost and management accounting

Businesses come in all shapes, sizes and forms. There are manufacturers, retailers, wholesalers and providers of services such as accountants and solicitors. However, whatever the function of the business, all require an effective and efficient system of administration and accounting.

Business organisation and accounting

TOPIC LIST	SYLLABUS REFERENCE
1 Office organisation and functions	A1(a)
2 Policy manual	A1(b)
3 Main types of transactions of a business	A1(c)
4 Control over transactions	A1(d)
5 Double entry bookkeeping – basic principles	A1(e)
6 Cost ledger accounting	A1(f)
7 Computerised accounting systems	A1(g)

Study Guide	**Intellectual level**
A **The nature and purpose of cost and management accounting**	
1 **Nature of business organisation and accounting systems**	
(a) Describe the organisation, and main functions, of an office as a centre for information and administration.	K
(b) Describe the function and use of a manual of policies, procedures and best practices.	K
(c) Identify the main types of transactions undertaken by a business and the key personnel involved in initiating, processing and completing transactions	K
(d) Explain the need for effective control over transactions.	K
(e) Explain and illustrate the principles and practice of double-entry book-keeping.	S
(f) Describe and illustrate the use of ledgers and prime entry records in both integrated and interlocking accounting systems.	S
(g) Identify the key features, function and benefits of a computerised accounting system.	K

1   Office organisation and functions

The **office** in an organisation is a centre for information and administration.

The most common functions in an office are **purchasing**, personnel **(human resources)**, general **administration**, **finance** and **sales** and **marketing**.

1.1 Office functions

There are a number of areas or functions to be administered and managed within a business. For example, the 'head office' of say a manufacturing, retailing or service business may cover the following areas:

- Purchasing
- Personnel/human resources
- General administration
- Finance
- Selling and marketing

Whether a business manufactures products or sells 'bought in' products, there will be a large purchasing function, either purchasing raw materials for manufacture or purchasing finished goods for resale. The function of the purchasing department will be to ensure that the business purchases from suppliers providing the best overall deal in terms of price, service, delivery time and quality. The purchasing department will also be responsible for ensuring that only necessary purchases are made by the business.

Any business that employs a significant number of people is likely to have a personnel function or human resources function as it is often called in larger organisations. This area of the office will be responsible for the hiring and firing of staff, for training of staff and for the general welfare of the employees.

General administration functions are very wide-ranging but might include secretarial support, dealing with telephone queries and arranging matters such as rent of properties.

The finance function is also very wide-ranging. On a day to day level the accounts department will deal with sending invoices to customers, receiving invoices from suppliers, payment of suppliers, receiving money from customers and making other payments such as purchases of non-current assets and payment of employees. The higher levels of management in the accounting function may also be responsible for management of the cash balances and for the overall financing of the organisation.

The selling and marketing function will deal with all aspects of taking sales orders, advertising, and any sales personnel.

1.2 Organisation charts

Organisation charts are a traditional way of depicting the various roles and relationships of the formal structure. They are a simplified and standardised way of showing:

(a) The units (eg departments) into which the organisation is divided and how they relate to each other

(b) Formal communication and reporting channels

(c) The structure of authority, responsibility and delegation

(d) Any problems in these areas, such as excessively long lines of communication, lack of co-ordination between units or unclear areas of authority.

The most common form of organisation chart is the vertical organisation chart, which illustrates the flow of authority downwards through the different levels of the organisation, and the pyramid shape of many organisations. (We will look at various examples in Section 6 of this chapter.) Different types of organisation may, however, be depicted in different ways.

A simple example is shown below for a small company where the personnel function is covered by general administration.

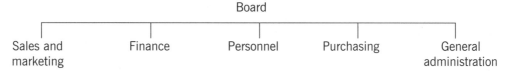

1.3 Functional departmentation

Functional organisation involves setting up departments for people who do similar jobs. Primary functions in a manufacturing company might be production, sales, finance, and general administration. Sub-departments of marketing might be selling, distribution and warehousing.

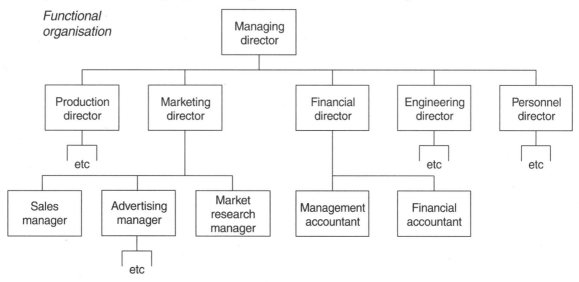

1.4 Geographical departmentation

Where the organisation is structured according to geographic area, some authority is retained at Head Office but day-to-day operations are handled on a territorial basis (eg Southern region, Western region). Many sales departments are organised territorially.

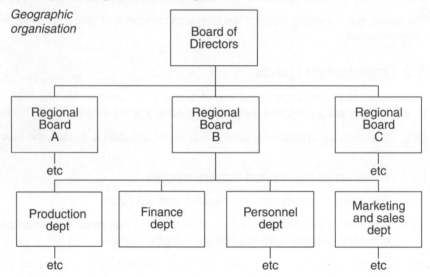

1.5 Product/brand departmentation

Some organisations group activities on the basis of **products** or product lines. Some functional departmentation remains (eg manufacturing, distribution, marketing and sales) but a divisional manager is given responsibility for the product or product line, with authority over personnel of different functions.

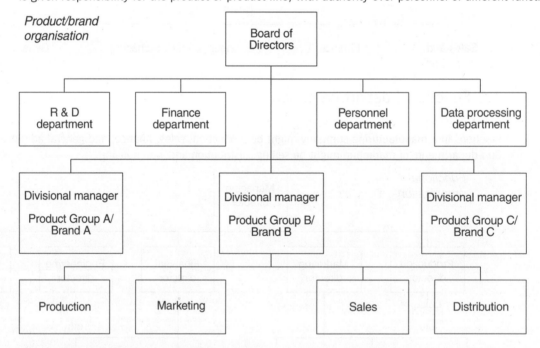

1.6 Centralisation / decentralisation

In many organisations administrative functions are carried out at head office as much as is possible. When this is the case, the administration function is said to be **centralised**.

A **centralised** administration department involves as many administrative tasks as possible being carried out at a single central location, such as head office.

Advantages of a centralised administration office include the following.

(a)   Consistency – for example the same account codes are likely to be used no matter which part of the organisation submits an invoice. Everyone uses the same data and information.

(b)   Decisions are made at one point and so are easier to co-ordinate.

(c)   It gives better security/control over operations and it is easier to enforce standards.

(d)   Head office is in a better position to know what is going on. Senior managers in an organisation can take a wider view of problems and consequences.

(e)   Decisions are made that benefit the organisation as a whole, rather than just the local office, as could happen with a decentralised administration office.

(f)   Senior management can keep a proper balance between different departments or functions - eg by deciding on the resources to allocate to each.

(g)   Quality of decisions is (theoretically) higher due to senior managers' skills and experience.

(h)   Crisis decisions are taken more quickly at the centre, without need to refer back, get authority etc.

(i)   There may be economies of scale available, for example in purchasing computer equipment and supplies.

(j)   Administration staff are in a single location and more expert staff are likely to be employed. Career paths may be more clearly defined.

(k)   Standardisation of policies, systems, procedures and documentation.

(l)   Specialised staff can be used.

(m)   Duplication of services can be avoided.

Advantages of a decentralised administration office include the following.

(a)   Local offices do not have to wait for tasks to be carried out centrally
(b)   No reliance on head office. Local offices are more self-sufficient
(c)   A system fault or hold-up at head office will not affect the organisation at a local level
(d)   Procedures may be tailored to suit local offices
(e)   Decisions are made by people with knowledge of local situations. Geographically dispersed organisations should often be decentralised on a regional/area basis
(f)   Decisions can be made more quickly because no need for head office approval
(g)   Local managers are able to make their own decisions, which may help motivate them
(h)   More opportunities for junior managers to take on responsibility – important since job challenge and entrepreneurial skills are highly valued in today's work environment
(i)   There may be greater continuity between functional to general management, which may enable junior managers to make the transition to senior management more smoothly
(j)   Top managers are free to focus on matters affecting the organisation as a whole, and are not overly burdened or stressed with local concerns
(k)   Easier to identify separate spheres of responsibility, which may result in improved controls, performance measurement and accountability

When administrative tasks are carried out at various separate locations, the administration function is said to be **de-centralised.** This may be appropriate when there is a large geographical spread between local offices or where substantially different activities are performed in separate locations.

QUESTION

The purchasing department

Which of the following is not a function of the purchasing department?

A   Ensuring that only required goods are purchased
B   Ensuring that suppliers used give the best price
C   Paying suppliers' invoices
D   Negotiating discounts with suppliers

ANSWER

C   Normally the accounts department will pay suppliers' invoices

2 Policy manual

A **policy manual** should help to ensure that all personnel follow procedures and best practices

As you will be starting to realise in any reasonable sized business there will be a lot of different transactions and roles being carried out by many different people in the organisation. As with any entity, in order for the management to keep control of the activities there will have to be some form of rules and procedures.

For example there must be authorisation policies for the purchase of non-current assets, procedures for choosing new suppliers, procedures for accepting new customers, limits on business expenses etc.

In smaller organisations where only a handful of individuals are involved in the transactions of the business such procedures and best practices can be communicated orally by management. However in larger organisations where there are very many people carrying out functions possibly at a number of different geographical locations then a more formal procedure is needed to ensure that the correct procedures and practices are followed.

This often takes the form of a policy manual which will set out the required procedures for all of the various functions of the business. Every employee will be expected to have read the areas relevant to their functions and the policy manual should always be readily available for easy reference.

Although a policy manual is to be recommended as a form of control over the activities of employees care must be taken that strict adherence to the rules does not create inflexibility and in cases of doubt a more senior member of the staff should be consulted.

3 Main types of transactions of a business

The main types of transactions that most businesses enter into are **sales**, **purchases**, **paying expenses**, **paying employees** and purchasing **non-current assets**.

It was mentioned earlier that businesses come in all shapes and forms however there will be a number of types of transactions which will be common to most businesses:

- Making sales
- Making purchases
- Paying expenses
- Paying employees
- Purchasing non-current assets

For each of these functions we will consider the key personnel involved in initiating, processing and completing the transaction.

3.1 Making sales

In a **retail organisation sales** made **on the shop floor**. However in a **manufacturing organisation** there will normally be a **sales and marketing function** whose responsibility is to market the organisation's products and take orders from customers. Often the day to day responsibility for taking orders will be with the **salesmen and women**. This may be done over the telephone or may be via personal visits to customers or potential customers.

If a sale is being made to an **existing customer**, provided that customer has **not exceeded their credit** balance then the procedure will be for the sales person to take **details of the order** and pass those details to the stores department for despatch and to the accounts department for invoicing of the customer.

However **if the sale is to a new customer** then a more senior level of management will have to be involved because if the sale is to be on credit, **the credit status of the new customer must be determined** and a decision made as to whether sales on credit should be made to this customer.

Once the goods have been despatched to the customer, responsibility then passes to the accounting function to invoice the customer for the goods and to ensure that payment is received.

3.2 Making purchases

The making of purchases will initially be started by either the purchasing department or the stores department. The need for the purchase of more goods will be recognised by, for example, the stores manager when he realises that an item of inventory is running low. He will then complete a **purchase requisition which must be authorised** and then the purchasing function will determine the most appropriate supplier on the basis of price, delivery and quality. An order will be placed by the purchasing function and the goods will normally be received by the stores department.

After this, **responsibility then goes to the accounting department** which will await the arrival of the invoice for the goods from the suppliers, will check that the invoice is accurate and for goods that have in fact been received and then **in due course pay the amount due to the supplier**.

3.3 Paying expenses

Organisations will incur a variety of expenses such as rent and rates, insurance, telephone bills, energy bills, advertising expenses etc. In some cases these will be incurred by a specific department of the business such as the marketing department entering investing in an advertising campaign or alternatively the receipt of the telephone bill will be part of the general administration of the business.

When bills for expenses are received they will be passed to the accounting function which will check that the expense has been incurred or is reasonable and then will process the expense for payment.

3.4 Paying employees

Every week and/or every month the **employees of the business must be paid**. For this process to take place there are a lot of calculations to be made and a lot of paperwork to be filled out. In larger organisations there will be payroll department which will deal with this otherwise it will be the responsibility of the payroll clerk in the accounting function.

The payroll function will determine the **gross pay** for each employee, based upon a variety of different remuneration schemes (see Chapter 6), and then will calculate the statutory and other deductions that must be made and will then calculate the net pay due to the employee. Finally the payroll function must then organise the method of payment to the employees.

3.5 Purchasing non-current assets

From time to time an **organisation will need to purchase non-current assets**. These are assets that are to be used in the business for the medium to long term rather than being purchased for resale. This will include items such as machinery, cars, computer equipment, office furniture etc.

In order for the purchase of non-current assets to be put in motion the manager of the department which requires the asset must firstly fill out a **purchase requisition**. As most non-current assets are relatively

expensive this will probably have to be **authorised** by more senior management. Once the requisition has been authorised the **purchasing function** will then find the most **appropriate supplier** for the assets.

Once a purchase order has been placed the details will then be passed to the accounting function which will then process and pay the invoice when it is received. It will be necessary to verify or check that employees and payments are valid during this process, this is covered in the following section.

QUESTION

Business personnel

Which of the following personnel in an organisation would **not** be involved in the purchase of materials?

A   Credit controller
B   Stores manager
C   Accounts clerk
D   Purchasing manager

ANSWER

A   The credit controller deals with credit customers not the purchase of materials

---

4   Control over transactions

In order for management to control the transactions of the business there must be a system of **authorisation** of transactions in place.

As you may have noticed in the last section any transaction that a business is involved in will tend to involve a number of different people within the organisation. You will have also noticed the requirement for transactions to be authorised.

The management of a reasonably large business cannot have the time to personally be involved in every transaction of the business. However in order to keep control of the sources of income of the business and the expenditure that the business incurs it is important that transactions are authorised by a responsible member of the management team.

In particular this means that management must have control over the following areas:

(a)   Sales on credit made to new customers. If a sale is made on credit the goods are sent out with a promise from the customer to pay in the future therefore the management of the business must be as certain as they can be that this new customer can, and will, pay for the goods. This means that the credit controller must be happy that the new customer has a good credit rating and is fairly certain to pay for the goods.

(b)   Purchases of goods or non-current assets and payments for expenses. This is money going out of the business therefore it is essential that these are necessary and valid expenditures so a responsible official must authorise them.

(c)   One of the largest payments made by most organisations is that of the wages bill for their employees. It is essential that only bona fide employees are paid for the actual hours that they have worked therefore authorisation of the payroll is a very important part of any business.

5 Double entry bookkeeping – basic principles

The basic principle of **double entry bookkeeping** is that for every debit entry there must be a corresponding credit entry.

Debit entries in ledger accounts are increases in assets or expenses and decreases in liabilities and income.

Credit entries in ledger accounts are increases in liabilities and income and decreases in assets and expenses.

In later chapters we will be dealing with the accounting entries for materials, labour and expenses. Therefore, in this chapter we remind ourselves of basic double entry bookkeeping and give an overview of how this is used in cost accounting.

You may have covered double-entry bookkeeping in earlier studies. You should remember that one of the basic principles of double entry is that for every debit entry there is an equal and opposite credit entry. Remember also that the owner of the business is treated as a separate entity to the business itself and the amount that the owner puts into the business is a special payable of the business known as capital. These two points together mean that the accounting equation will always be:

Assets – liabilities = Capital + profit – drawings

For cost accounting purposes we will be concerned largely with the sales of goods, purchases of materials, the payment of wages and the treatment of expenses. So here is a brief reminder of the basic double-entry that you are likely to come across.

Sales of goods

DEBIT   Bank/receivables
CREDIT   Sales

Receipts from receivables

DEBIT   Bank
CREDIT   Receivables

Purchases of materials

DEBIT   Materials control
CREDIT   Bank/payables

Payment of payables

DEBIT   Payables
CREDIT   Bank

Payment of wages

DEBIT   Wages expense
CREDIT   Bank

This is for the net wages – the full picture is slightly more complicated and this will be dealt with in Chapter 6.

Payments of expenses or overheads

DEBIT   Expenses/overheads
CREDIT   Bank/payables

If in doubt with double entry remember the following rules:

Debit entry: increase in an asset
                decrease in a liability
                increase in an expense
                decrease in income

Credit entry: increase in a liability
                decrease in an asset
                increase in income
                decrease in an expense

QUESTION   Double entry

Which of the following is the correct double entry for a sale on credit?

A   DEBIT   Payables
        CREDIT   Sales

B   DEBIT   Sales
        CREDIT   Payables

C   DEBIT   Receivables
        CREDIT   Sales

D   DEBIT   Sales
        CREDIT   Receivables

ANSWER

C

EXAM FOCUS POINT

A question on double entry in the costing system is highly likely in the exam.

6 Cost ledger accounting

Transactions are initially recorded in **books of prime entry**, which are totalled and the totals posted to the ledger accounts.

Cost accounting is the accumulation of costs for inventory valuation in order to meet the requirements of external reporting and also for internal profit measurement. In other words it produces information for both financial accounting and management accounting.

Again from your earlier studies, you may remember that in practice a business will not enter every individual transaction into the ledger accounts. Instead each type of transaction will be recorded initially in its own primary entry record or book of prime entry. The daily totals from these books are then posted into the ledger accounts. The ledger accounts will only contain the totals from the day books, so to find individual transactions one has to look to the day books.

As a reminder the main types of transaction and their related books of prime entry are given below:

Sales invoices sent out   –   Sales day book
Credit notes sent out   –   Sales returns day book

Purchase invoices received   –   Purchases day book
Credit notes received   –   Purchases returns day book

Cash/cheque receipts   –   Cash received book
Cash/cheque payments   –   Cash payments book

Petty cash receipts/payments –   Petty cash book

QUESTION

Double entry

Which of the following is not a book of prime entry?

A   Petty cash book
B   Journal
C   Non-current asset register
D   Purchase returns day book

ANSWER

C

An **integrated system** is one which combines the cost accounting and financial accounting functions in one system of ledger accounts.

An **interlocking system** has a separate cost ledger for the cost accounting function and a separate financial ledger for the financial accounting function.

From the summaries of transactions in the day books, double entry bookkeeping takes place. For example, in the sales day book (a book of prime entry) there may be a list of sales invoices totalling $1,487. This total will then be posted to the ledger accounts as follows:

Debit receivables account $1,487
Credit sales account $1,487

The invoices will also be posted to individual customer accounts in the sales ledger. In a similar way, purchase invoices are posted first to the purchases day book, the totals from which are then posted to the ledger account (debiting the purchases account and crediting the payables account) .

For cost accounting purposes there are two possible methods of structuring the ledger accounts – an **integrated system** and an **interlocking system**.

6.1 Integrated system

An integrated system combines the cost accounting and financial accounting functions into one system of ledger accounts. This gives a saving in terms of time and cost. However it has the disadvantage of trying to fulfil two purposes with one set of ledger accounts despite the differences between financial accounting and management accounting requirements (see Chapter 2 Section 6 for a comparison).

6.2 Interlocking system

An interlocking system is one where separate ledgers are kept for the cost accounting function (the cost ledger) and the financial function (the financial ledger). The cost ledger and financial ledgers will each include a control account. Many organisations will have the usual debit and credit entries made to the financial accounting system, which also contains a memorandum cost ledger account which will have posted all items which are transferred to the cost accounting system.

Within the cost ledger there is a control account to provide a place to record items that are of a financial accounting nature.

For example when an invoice is received for materials, the materials control account will be debited but instead of crediting the payables account, as the cost ledger does not record payables, the credit is to the cost ledger control account. This means that the cost ledger does not keep a separate record of payables. This would also be the case with trade receivables: rather than debiting a receivables account when a sale is made, the cost ledger control account is debited instead.

The use of the control accounts as described above means that double entries can be made for all transactions. This preserves the integrity of the double entry system.

Although an interlocking system allows easier access to cost accounting information, it is more time consuming to prepare two sets of ledger accounts and the two ledgers will need reconciling on a regular basis to ensure that they are in agreement.

EXAM FOCUS POINT

One of the four sample questions discussed in the December 2011 examiner's reports was in this area, as it was one that candidates found particularly difficult.

QUESTION   Integrated and interlocking systems

Which of the following statements is correct?

A   An interlocking system is a single system for cost and financial accounting
B   In an integrated system there will be a financial ledger control account
C   In an interlocking system there will be a cost ledger control account
D   In an integrated system there are separate ledgers for cost and financial accounting

ANSWER

C

---

7   Computerised accounting systems

A **computerised accounting system** will allow much quicker and more accurate entries to the accounting system.

Almost all businesses now use some form of computerised accounting system.

In a full ledger computerised system the computer system will normally maintain the following ledgers:

*   General or main ledger (for all asset, liability, income and expense accounts)
*   Receivables ledger – accounts for each customer
*   Payables ledger – accounts for each supplier
*   Cash books – including the main cash book and the petty cash book

The system may also contain detailed inventory records and a programme for dealing with payroll.

Accounting using a computerised system involves inputting data, processing it according to accounting rules contained in the software, and producing output ('the accounts' or other management reports). Computerised accounting therefore follows a data processing **cycle** of **input**, **process**, and **output**.

(a)   Data is **collected**. There has to be a system or procedure for ensuring that all the data required is collected and made available for processing. The quality, accuracy and completeness of the data will affect the quality of information produced.

(b)   Data is **processed** into information, perhaps by summarising it, classifying it and/or analysing it. For example, a receivables ledger system may process data relating to customer orders so as to:

*   Produce a report of the total sales for the day/week

*   Record the total value of invoices issued in the receivables control account in the general ledger

(c) Files are **updated** to incorporate the processed data. Updating files means bringing them up to date to record current transactions. Updating the personal ledgers and the receivables control account are file updating activities to keep the receivables ledger records up to date.

(d) Data is **communicated**. Continuing the example of the receivables ledger system, output may consist of **customer statements** and **management reports**.

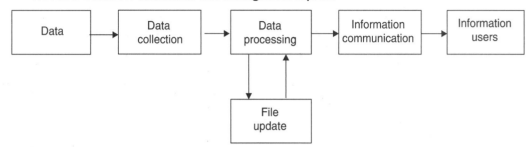

In terms of **accounting** systems and databases, a data **file** is a collection of **records** with similar characteristics. Examples of data files include the receivables ledger, the payables ledger and the general ledger.

A **record** in a file consists of data relating to one logically definable unit of business information. A collection of similar records makes up a file. For example, one record in the receivables ledger file would be one customer account.

A record is made up of several **fields**. A field is an item of data relating to a record. For example, a customer record would include a field for the customers account number, another for the customer name, another for their credit limit, and so on.

Records on a file should contain at least one key field. This is an item of data within the record by which it can be **uniquely identified**. An example would be a unique **code** for each customer.

In older systems, files may be conventionally classified into **transaction** files, and **master** files. These distinctions are particularly relevant in **batch** processing applications, described in a moment.

A transaction file is a file containing records that relate to **individual transactions.** For example, when a company sells goods, the sales for each day may be recorded in the **sales day book**. The sales day book entries are examples of **transaction records** in a **transactions file**.

A master file in such a system is a file containing **reference data**, such as customer names and addresses, and also **cumulative transaction data** such as 'year to date' sales.

For example, in a payables ledger system, master file data would include:

(a) **'Standing' reference data** for each supplier (supplier name and address, reference number, amount currently owed etc), and

(b) **Transaction totals for each supplier** showing purchases, purchase returns and payments.

The terms transaction file and master file are not used much in modern processing, which prefers to talk in terms of **'databases'**.

Files are used to **store** data and information. The main types of data processing operations involving files are file **updating**, file **maintenance** and **file enquiry.**

Both manual and computer data processing can be divided into two broad types: **batch** processing and **real-time** processing.

7.1 Batch processing

Batch processing involves transactions being **grouped** and **stored** before being processed at regular intervals, such as daily, weekly or monthly. Because data is not input as soon as it is received the system will not always be up-to-date.

For example, **payroll** processing for salaried staff is usually done in one operation once a month. To help with organising the work, the payroll office might deal with **each department separately**, and do the

salaries for department 1, then the salaries for department 2, and then department 3, and so on. If this is the case, then the batch processing would be carried out by dividing the transaction records into smaller batches eg **one batch per department**.

Transactions will be collected up over a period of time, and will then be dealt with together in a batch. Some **delay** in processing the transactions must therefore be acceptable.

Batch input allows for good **control** over the input data, because data can be grouped into **numbered batches**. The batches are dispatched for processing and processed in these batches, and printed output **listings** of the processed transactions are usually organised in **batch order**.

If any records 'go missing' it is possible to locate the batch in which the missing record should belong. Errors in transaction records can be located more quickly by identifying its **batch number**. A check can be made to ensure that every batch of data sent off for processing is eventually received back from processing, so that entire batches of records do not go missing.

The lack of up-to-date information means batch processing is usually not suitable for systems involving customer contact. Batch processing is suitable for internal, regular tasks such as payroll.

Example: batch processing of receivables ledger application

A company operates a computerised receivables ledger using batch processing based on paper records. The main stages of processing are as follows.

Step 1	Sales invoices are hand-written in a numbered invoice book (in triplicate ie three copies per invoice). At the end of the day all invoices are clipped together and a batch control slip is attached. The sales clerk allocates the next unused batch number from the batch control book. He or she enters the batch number on the control slip, together with the total number of documents and the total value of the invoices. These details are also entered in the control book.
Step 2	The batch of invoices is then passed to the accounts department for processing. An accounts clerk records the batch as having been received.
Step 3	The relevant account codes are written on the invoices and control slip. Codes are checked, and the batch is keyed into the computerised receivables ledger system.
Step 4	The clerk reconciles the totals on the batch control slip with the totals for valid and rejected data.
Step 5	The ledger update program is run to post data to the relevant accounts.
Step 6	A report is printed showing the total of invoices posted to the ledger and the clerk reconciles this to the batch totals.
Step 7	All rejected transaction records are carefully investigated and followed up, usually to be amended and then re-input with the next processing run.

7.2 Real-time, on-line processing

Real time, on-line processing involves transactions being input and processed immediately, in 'real time'.

On-line refers to a machine which is under the **direct control** of the main **central processor** for that system. A terminal is said to be on-line when it communicates with the central processor. PCs have their own processor, so are on-line by definition. (However, the term 'on-line' is increasingly being used to describe an active Internet connection.)

On-line, real time processing is appropriate when immediate processing is required, and the delay implicit in batch processing would not be acceptable.

On-line systems are the **norm** in modern business. **Examples** include the following.

(a) As a sale is made in a department store or a supermarket, the item barcode is scanned on the **point of sale terminal** and the inventory records are updated immediately.

(b) In **banking and credit card** systems whereby customer details are often maintained in a real-time environment. There can be immediate access to customer balances, credit position etc and authorisation for withdrawals (or use of a credit card).

(c) **Travel agents**, **airlines** and **theatre ticket** agencies all use real-time systems. Once a hotel room, plane seat or theatre seat is booked up everybody on the system must know about it immediately so that they do not sell the same holiday or seat to two (or more) different customers.

The workings of both batch and on-line processing methods are shown in the following diagram.

Batch processing and on-line processing

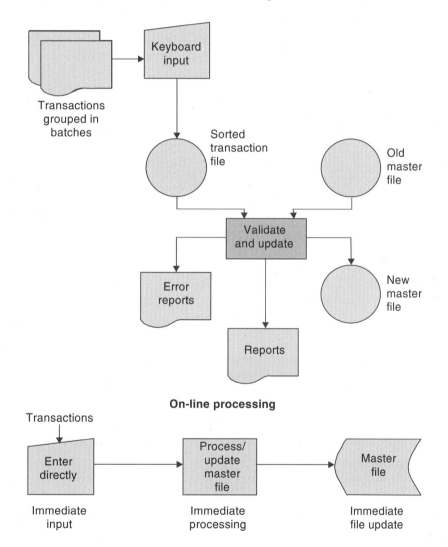

Most modern accounting software packages use real-time processing.

Most computerised ledger systems are fully integrated which means that when one transaction is input on the computer it is recorded in all the relevant accounts and records. For example if a purchase invoice for materials is entered into the computer system an integrated system will automatically make the following entries:

• Record the purchase in the general ledger accounts

- Record the invoice in the individual supplier's account in the payables ledger
- Increase the inventory balance for that type of material in the inventory records

A computerised system can also produce a variety of reports for management including:

- Inventory records
- Aged receivables listings
- Trial balances, income statements and statements of financial position
- Inventory valuations
- Payroll analysis

The main advantages of computerised accounting systems are that they are:

- Quicker than manual systems

- Generally more accurate, as large numbers of transactions can be processed according to programmed rules

- Able to provide management with a variety of reports and analyses

CHAPTER ROUNDUP

↳ The **office** in an organisation is a centre for information and administration.

↳ The most common functions in an office are **purchasing**, personnel (**human resources**), **general administration**, **finance** and **sales** and **marketing**.

↳ A **policy manual** should help to ensure that all personnel follow procedures and best practices.

↳ The main types of transactions that most businesses enter into are **sales, purchases, paying expenses, paying employees** and **purchasing non-current assets**.

↳ In order for management to control the transactions of the business there must be a system of **authorisation** of transactions in place.

↳ The basic principle of **double entry bookkeeping** is that for every debit entry there must be a corresponding credit entry.

↳ **Debit entries** in ledger accounts are increases in assets or expenses and decreases in liabilities and income.

↳ **Credit entries** in ledger accounts are increases in liabilities and income and decreases in assets and expenses.

↳ Transactions are initially recorded in **books of prime entry** which are totalled and the totals posted to the ledger accounts.

↳ An **integrated system** is one which combines the cost accounting and financial accounting functions in one system of ledger accounts.

↳ An **interlocking system** has a cost ledger for the cost accounting function and a financial ledger for the financial accounting function.

↳ A **computerised accounting system** will allow much quicker and more accurate entries to the accounting system.

QUICK QUIZ

1   Which one of the following is a potential advantage of decentralisation?

    A   Less control by senior management
    B   Duplication of services can be avoided
    C   Local offices are more self sufficient
    D   Consistency of decision-making across the organisation

2   Which one of the following is a potential disadvantage of a policy manual?

    A   It may lead to inflexibility
    B   Personnel follow best practices
    C   Procedures are formalised
    D   It acts as a form of control over activities of employees

3   Which of the following personnel in an organisation would **not** be involved in the sale of goods on credit?

    A   Credit controller
    B   Payables ledger clerk
    C   Sales person
    D   Warehouse operative

4   What document should normally be completed if a purchase of a non-current asset is required?

    A   A purchase requisition
    B   A despatch note
    C   A goods received note
    D   An invoice

5 What is the correct accounting equation?

A Assets + Liabilities = Capital + profit – drawings
B Assets + Liabilities = Capital - profit – drawings
C Assets – Liabilities = Capital + profit + drawings
D Assets – Liabilities = Capital + profit – drawings

6 What is the double entry for the purchase of materials on credit?

A	Dr	Materials control	Cr	Payables
B	Dr	Payables	Cr	Materials control
C	Dr	Materials control	Cr	Receivables
D	Dr	Receivables	Cr	Materials control

7 An integrated system combines the cost accounting and financial accounting functions into one system of ledger accounts. Is that true or false?

8 What is the double entry for the following in an integrated accounts system?

(a) Production overhead absorbed in the cost of production
(b) Completed work transferred from the production process to inventory

ANSWERS TO QUICK QUIZ

1 C Local offices have to rely on head office so are less self-sufficient.

2 A Although a policy manual is to be recommended, care must be taken that strict adherence to the rules does not create inflexibility and in cases of doubt, a more senior member of staff should be consulted.

3 B A payables ledger clerk would deal with amounts due to suppliers for purchases and would not usually have any dealings with sales.

4 A A purchase requisition will need to be completed and as non-current assets are relatively expensive, it will usually have to be authorised by senior management

5 D Assets – liabilities = Capital + profit – drawings

6 A Dr Materials control Cr Payables

7 True This is the definition of an integrated system

8 (a) Dr Work in progress control account
Cr Production overhead account

(b) Dr Finished goods control account
Cr Work in progress control account

Now try ...

Attempt the questions below from the **Exam Question Bank**

Number

Q1-4

02

The main aim of this chapter is to introduce you to the subject of **management information** and, in particular, explain what management information is and why it is needed.

Introduction to management information

TOPIC LIST	SYLLABUS REFERENCE
1 Data and information	A2(c)
2 The purpose of management information	A2(a)
3 Reports for management	A2(d)
4 Sources and categories of information	A2(e)
5 Management accounting and financial reporting	A2(b)
6 The limitations of cost and management accounting information	A2(f)
7 The trainee accountant's role in a cost and management accounting system	A2(g)

Study Guide	Intellectual level
A The nature and purpose of cost and management accounting	
2 Management information	
(a) State the purpose of management information	K
(b) Compare cost and management accounting with external financial reporting	K
(c) Distinguish between data and information	K
(d) Describe the features of useful management information	K
(e) Describe and identify sources and categories of information	K
(f) Explain the limitations of cost and management accounting information	K
(g) Describe the role of a trainee accountant in a cost and management accounting system	K

1 Data and information

Raw **data** may be processed to produce meaningful **information**.

1.1 What is data?

Data is a 'scientific' term for facts, figures, and measurements. Data are the raw materials for data processing..

Examples of data include the following.

- The number of tourists who visit Hong Kong each year
- The sales revenues of all restaurants in Zambia
- The number of people who pass their driving test each year

Note that these examples are just collections of numbers which may not be particularly useful to the person who wants to use them. In order to be useful the data may have to be processed in some way. For example a French travel agent may be interested in the number of French tourists who visit Hong Kong each year. The data which contains all tourists would have to be analysed to obtain the number of French tourists. The analysed data is known as information because it is now meaningful to the person who wants to use it.

1.2 What is information?

Information is data that has been processed in such a way as to be meaningful to the person who receives it. Information is anything that is communicated.

Information is sometimes referred to as processed data. The terms 'information' and 'data' are often used interchangeably. Let us consider the following situation in which data is **collected** and then **processed** in order to produce meaningful information.

Many companies providing a product or service research consumer opinion to ensure they provide what customers and potential customers want and will buy. A typical market research survey employs a number of researchers who request a sample of the public to answer questions relating to the product.

Several hundred questionnaires may be completed. The questionnaires are usually input into a computer system for analysis.

Individually, a completed questionnaire would not tell the company very much, only the views of one consumer. In this case, the individual questionnaires are **data**. Once they have been processed, and analysed, the resulting report is **information**. The people who run the business can consider the report and use the information to make decisions regarding the product, such as whether to improve it or scrap it.

Management is the term used for the people in charge of running a business (managers) or other organisation.

Management information can therefore be described as information that is given to the people who are in charge of running an organisation. The report described above is one example of management information.

To run a business successfully depends upon making the right decisions. Information is vital to enable good decisions to be made. Examples of the some of the questions that management might wish to have answers to include:

* How much does it cost to produce the product(s) or service(s) they supply.
* How many product(s)/service(s) they sold last month.
* How much was spent on wages last year.
* How many staff the company currently employs.

Management information is often classified into two types:

* Financial information (measured in terms of money)
* Non-financial information (not measured in terms of money)

2 The purpose of management information

The purpose of **management information** is to help managers to manage resources efficiently and effectively, by planning and controlling operations and by allowing informed **decision-making**.

One of the essential competences you require for FPER is to provide support and information which will enable the organisation to operate effectively. You can apply the knowledge you obtain from this chapter of the text to help demonstrate this competence.

In order to manage their resources, managers in any organisation need to know on a regular basis how their particular department or section is performing. They will also wish to know whether activities are going as planned and whether any problems have arisen.

Management information has the following purposes.

* **Planning**
* **Control**
* **Decision making**

Planning. Management information is used to help management **plan** the resources that a business will require and how they will be used.

Control. Once management puts a plan of action into operation, there needs to be some **control** over the business's activities to make sure that they are carrying out the original plans.

Decision making. Management at all levels within an organisation take decisions. Decision making always involves a **choice between alternatives.** Information is required that enables management to reach an informed decision.

The information required by a manager will vary according to the nature of the organisation and their individual responsibilities. Look at the following examples.

(a) Senior management will usually be interested in the financial statements (statement of financial position and income statement), on a monthly basis.

(b) A supervisor in a large factory may want a daily output report for every production shift.

(c) A sales manager may want a weekly report of orders achieved by the sales team.

Management information is used for a wide variety of purposes. In a management accounting context, **planning**, **control** and **decision making** activities include:

- Pricing
- Valuing inventory
- Assessing profitability
- Deciding on the purchase of capital assets

In the present business environment where the rate of change is increasing, good management information systems are seen by many as the key to success. Although such systems give a basis for improved management decisions they do not guarantee good management. Poor information, however, is likely to reduce a manager's chances of success.

Management information is information supplied to managers for the purposes of planning, control and decision making.

QUESTION

Helping management

The management accountant compares the profitability of two products, P and Q, and concludes that P is the best product to make. He writes a report of his findings for the board of directors. This report will primarily aid management in

A   Decision-making
B   Planning
C   Controlling
D   Implementing

ANSWER

Answer A. A decision can be made as to which product should be made using this information.

EXAM FOCUS POINT

You need to make sure that you understand the role of management and the purpose of management information.

3 Reports for management

Producing **useful management information** such as a report depends on understanding the **needs** of the end **user** and of the organisation.

Reports to managers should enable them to manage the resources for which they are responsible, and give the required level of detail.

If management information does not contain enough detail, it may fail to highlight problems within the organisation. On the other hand, too much detail may mean that the most important information is not seen.

Numbers are often rounded to make reports easier to read, eg money may be expressed to the nearest $100, $1,000 or $10,000 depending on the size of the organisation.

The **time periods** covered by reports will also vary for different organisations and for different managers within them. Some computer systems allow managers access to information on a **real time basis** and/or to construct their own reports as necessary.

It is more common for reports to be provided by the accounting department of an organisation every week or month (or any specified period).

Reporting information requires the active **co-operation** of the following groups.

- **End users**: managers and supervisors

- **The accounts department**: which usually processes the information

- **The information technology department**: which usually sets up and makes changes to the computer system

Difficulties may arise when these groups **fail to communicate effectively** or when the system itself is **not flexible** enough to respond to changing needs. Information requirements must be clearly specified.

3.1 Example: management report

SUMMARY MONTHLY REPORT TO TRUSTEES OF A CHARITY FOR THE HOMELESS

	Fund raising activities $'000	Donations $'000	Interest on investments $'000	Total $'000
Income	15.1	9.8	5.4	30.3
Associated costs	2.1	1.0	0.0	3.1
	13.0	8.8	5.4	27.2
Expenditure				
Mobile catering project				6.2
Medical services				2.1
Warm clothing				3.7
Hostel costs				16.0
				28.0
Shortfall for the month				0.8

This type of report is often backed up with appendices. An appendix would give more details of costs and income to help the trustees decide what to do about the shortfall for the month. The charity has spent $800 more than it received in the month under consideration. Individual managers (for fund raising, the catering project, the hostel etc) will need to receive more detailed reports for their own activities.

3.2 Management information

Management information reports might also show the following.

- Comparisons between planned results (budgets) and actual results
- Year-to-date (cumulative information)
- Comparison of company results and competitor results
- Comparison between current year and previous year's results
- The profitability of a product or service or the whole organisation
- The value of inventories that are still held in store at the end of a period

3.3 The qualities of good information

Good management information should be:

Accurate
Complete
Cost-beneficial
User-targeted
Relevant
Authoritative
Timely
Easy to use

Good management information helps managers makes informed decisions. The **qualities of good information** are outlined below - in the form of a mnemonic 'accurate'.

Quality		Example
A	ccurate	Figures should **add up**, the degree of **rounding** should be appropriate, there should be **no mistakes**.
C	omplete	Information should include all relevant information – information that is correct but excludes something important is likely to be of little value. For example external data or comparative information may be required.
C	ost-beneficial	It should not **cost more** to obtain the information than the **benefit** derived from having it.
U	ser-targeted	The **needs of the user** should be borne in mind, for instance senior managers may require summaries.
R	elevant	Information that is **not relevant** should be omitted.
A	uthoritative	The **source** of the information should be reputable and reliable.
T	imely	The information should be available **when it is needed**.
E	asy to use	Information should be **clearly presented**, **not excessively long**, and sent using the **right communication channel** (e-mail, telephone, intranet, hard-copy report etc).

QUESTION

Good information

Good information should be which of the following:

(i)   Complete
(ii)   Extensive
(iii)   Relevant
(iv)   Accurate

A   (i), (ii) and (iii) only
B   (i), (ii) and (iv) only
C   (ii), (iii) and (iv) only
D   (i), (iii) and (iv) only

ANSWER

Answer D. Good information is not necessarily extensive. Too much information may hide the most important points.

4 Sources and categories of information

There are many **sources** of information (both internal and external) including accounting records, websites, staff, the staff of competitors, the government, the media and many others.

Data and information come from sources both inside and outside an organisation. An information system should be designed so as to obtain - or **capture** - relevant information from whatever source.

4.1 Internal information

Capturing data/information from **inside** the organisation involves the following.

(a)   A **system** for collecting and/or measuring **transaction** data - for example sales, purchases, inventory turnover etc.

(b)   **Informal communication** of information between **managers and staff** (for example, by word-of-mouth or at meetings).

(c)   **Communication** between staff at all levels.

4.2 Internal data sources

The accounting records include receivables ledgers, payables ledgers, general ledgers, cash books etc. These hold information that may be of great value outside the accounts department, for example, sales information for the **marketing** function.

To maintain the integrity of its accounting records, an organisation requires **controls** over transactions. These also give rise to valuable information. An inventory control system for example will include details of purchase orders, goods received notes, goods returned notes and so on, which can be analysed to provide management information about speed of delivery, say, or the quality of supplies.

Other internal sources

Organisations record information to enable them to carry out operations and administrative functions.

(a)   Information about **personnel** will be held, possibly linked to the **payroll** system. Additional information may be obtained from this source if, say, a project is being costed and it is necessary to ascertain the availability and rate of pay of different levels of staff, or the need for and cost of recruiting staff from outside the organisation.

(b)   Much information will be produced by a **production** department about machine capacity, fuel consumption, movement of people, materials, and work in progress, set up times, maintenance requirements and so on.

(c)   Many **service** businesses, notably accountants and solicitors, need to keep detailed records of the **time spent** on various activities, both to justify fees to clients and to assess the efficiency and profitability of operations.

Staff themselves are one of the primary sources of internal information. Information may be obtained either informally in the course of day-to-day business or through meetings, interviews or questionnaires.

4.3 External information

Capturing information from **outside** the organisation might be a **routine** task entrusted to particular individuals, or might be collected on an 'informal' **non-routine** basis.

Routine formal collection of data from outside sources includes the following.

(a)   A company's **tax specialists** will be expected to gather information about changes in tax law and how this will affect the company.

(b)   Obtaining information about any new legislation on health and safety at work, or employment regulations, must be obtained - for example by the company's **legal expert** or **company secretary** - who must then pass on the information to other managers affected by it.

(c) Research and development (R & D) work often relies on information about other R & D work being done by another organisation.

(d) **Marketing managers** need to know the attitudes and opinions of current and potential customers. To obtain this information, they might carry out market research exercises.

Non-routine, informal gathering of information from the environment **goes on all the time, both consciously and unconsciously.** For example, employees are exposed to newspapers, television reports, websites, meetings with business associates and trade publications.

4.4 External data sources

An organisation's files (paper and/or computerised) include information from external sources - such as invoices, e-mails, letters, advertisements and so on **received from customers and suppliers.** Sometimes additional external information is required – meaning an active search outside the organisation is necessary. The following sources may be identified.

(a) The government.

(b) Advice or information bureaux.

(c) Consultancies of all sorts.

(d) Newspaper and magazine publishers.

(e) There may be specific reference works which are used in a particular line of work.

(f) Libraries and information services.

(g) Increasingly businesses can use each other's systems as sources of information, for instance via electronic data interchange (EDI).

(h) Electronic sources of information are becoming ever more important, for example companies like **Reuters** offer access to a range of business related information.

(i) Many information provision services are now provided via the **Internet**. As the rate of Internet use increases, greater numbers of people and organisations are using it to source information on a vast range of topics.

EXAM FOCUS POINT

Internal and external sources of information could easily be examined in the exam.

QUESTION   Good management information

Good management information is

A   Relevant, regular and reliable
B   Timely, regular and sufficient
C   Reliable, timely and relevant
D   Relevant, convenient and material

ANSWER

C provides the most appropriate description

5 Management accounting and financial reporting

Computer systems and coding structures help to sort the information into the categories and formats required for both financial and management accounting.

Basic (prime) sources of management information include sales invoices and purchase invoices. These will also provide information for the financial accounts of a company.

Other **sources of information** may include reports from various departments of the organisation.

- Timesheets, employee and wage information from the personnel department
- Goods received notes and material requisition notes from the warehouse
- Price lists (in-house and suppliers)
- The organisation's policy manual (to ensure that consistent procedures are followed)

Information will be sorted and amalgamated through the **coding structure** so that the reports required by management can be produced.

5.1 Computer systems and coding structures

In most organisations, this accounting information will be keyed into a **computer system** and the **coding structure** (also called the **chart of accounts**) for this system should be set up to provide information in the categories required.

For example, if the organisation is divided into different business units, costs and income must be coded to the correct unit. In a factory which makes different products, raw materials must be coded to the product which uses them. Errors in coding will lead to inaccurate information.

An example of the outline for an 8 digit code is shown as follows.

01	172	301
Originating department	Type of cost or income	End product/service
Cost centre or location		Eg project, contract, job, service, product

Therefore the code 01172301 will tell us where the cost came from, what type of cost (or income) it was and which end product or service it should be charged to. For example, it could be from factory department 1, wages, chargeable to product 301. We will be looking at coding in more detail in Chapter 5.

5.2 Cost and management accounts

There are no **external rules** governing the format or content of **management information**, unlike the financial accounts.

Cost accounting is the accumulation of costs for inventory valuation in order to meet both the requirements of external reporting and also for internal profit measurement. In other words cost accounting produces information for both financial accounting and management accounting.

The purpose of **management accounting** is to provide managers with whatever information they need to help them manage their resources efficiently and take sensible decisions. There are **no externally imposed rules** about how this is done: it depends on the needs of the organisation.

- They are distributed **internally** for use within a business only
- There is no legal requirement to prepare them and they are recorded and presented in a way that is decided by management
- They look at **past** data and also **future** data (for planning purposes)
- They include both **financial** and **non-financial** information
- They are used to help management in **planning**, **control** and **decision making**

5.3 Financial accounts

The purpose of financial accounting is to provide **accurate financial information** for the company accounts, which will be used by both senior management and external parties (for example investors).

- They are used for **external** reporting
- There is a **legal requirement** for limited companies to prepare them and presentation is dictated by accounting standards
- They are concerned with **past data** only
- They usually include only **financial information**
- They detail the results of an organisation over a **defined period** (usually a year)

6   The limitations of cost and management accounting information

We have already seen that for cost and management accounting information to be useful it must have certain characteristics. If these characteristics are not present then this will limit the usefulness of such information.

Cost and management information does not necessarily need to be accurate to the cent but the information itself will only be useful if the underlying figures that make it up are **reliable**. For example if costs have been coded to the wrong products then any management information on product profitability will be of little use.

It is not normally possible to provide management with all of the information they need every minute of the day and therefore decisions will be taken as to how frequently cost and management information is produced. Suppose that a report comparing actual production costs to budgeted production costs is prepared every month although any problems that this report highlights can be addressed for the next month it has not been helpful in addressing the problems in the current month.

It is often the case that managers **do not necessarily communicate** with the cost and management accountant and therefore the information that is provided to the manager is not **of the type or in the format** that he/she requires.

Many types of cost and management accounting information take the form of comparison of figures over time. Care must be taken here as if prices are changing then the **comparison may not be valid** and will therefore limit the use of the information.

The information that the cost and management accountant provides for management may be reliable and timely but if it is not **complete** then it will be of limited use. For example if management are taking a decision about the future of a product they will require **information on its profitability**. However if the sales manager has provided sales forecast figures but omitted to mention that these are dependent upon $50,000 being spent on advertising then the information will not be complete and will be of limited use for management decisions.

Management accounting will often require **estimates of future periods,** in order to plan and make decisions, which may be difficult to establish with a high level of accuracy.

Many managers are not accountants and therefore the form in which cost and management information is provided, normally in accountant's terms, **will limit its use**. Care should be taken, as an accountant, when providing information to **avoid accountancy jargon** and to explain matters in non-accountant terms whenever possible.

By its very nature, cost and management accounting information comes from the cost and income records. However in many cases there will be **non-financial** matters that are relevant to planning, decision-making and control and these may not be included in the cost and management information that is provided. For example the future sales of a product may be extremely dependent upon the level of customer satisfaction with the product or the service that is provided and the cost and **management information may well not include such non-financial factors as customer satisfaction**.

Other limitations include the difficulty in establishing the relevance of different costs in particular decisions and also calculating the cumulative effect that a number of decisions may have.

7 The trainee accountant's role in a cost and management accounting system

In a cost and management accounting system, the **role** of the **trainee accountant** is to provide answers to questions on costs and revenues. The organisation must have a cost accounting system capable of analysing cost information **quickly** and **easily**.

You have now had a brief introduction to cost accounting and cost information. Let us now consider the role of the trainee accountant in a cost accounting system.

Remember that the trainee accountant will have access to a **large amount of information** which is all recorded in the **cost accounting records**. With so much information at his/her fingertips, it is inevitable that **many people** are going to want to ask him/her **lots of questions**!

So, what sort of questions is the trainee accountant going to provide answers for? Well, here are a few examples.

(a)   What has the **cost of goods produced** or services provided been?

(b)   What has the **cost of operating a department** been?

(c)   What have **revenues** been?

All of these questions may relate to **different periods**. For example, if someone wants to know what revenues have been for the past ten years, the trainee accountant will need to extract this information from the cost accounting records. It is important therefore that the cost accounting system is capable of analysing such information.

If the trainee accountant knows all about the costs incurred or revenues earned, he may also be asked to do the following types of task.

(a)   To assess **how profitable** certain products or departments are.

(b)   To **review the costs** of products, and to use this information to enable him/her to **evaluate the impact of a range of selling prices**.

(c)   To put **a value to inventories** of goods (such as raw materials) which are unsold at the end of a period. As you will learn later on in your studies, the **valuation of inventory** is a **very important part of cost accounting**.

The trainee accountant may also need to provide information on **future costs** of goods and services. This is an integral part of the planning or budgeting process.

By comparing current costs with budgeted costs, the trainee accountant should be able to highlight areas which show **significant variances**. These variances should then be **investigated**.

Most cost accounting systems should be capable of producing regular performance statements, though the trainee accountant is likely to be the person producing them, and distributing them to the relevant personnel.

The role of an trainee accountant in a cost accounting system is therefore fairly **varied**. The role is likely to include spending much time providing answers to the many questions which may be directed at the trainee accountant (such as those that we have considered here).

CHAPTER ROUNDUP

- Raw **data** may be processed to produce meaningful **information**.

- The purpose of **management information** is to help managers to manage resources efficiently and effectively, by planning and controlling operations and by allowing informed **decision-making**.

- Producing **useful management information** such as a report depends on understanding the **needs** of the end **user** and of the organisation.

- Good management information should be:

  Accurate
  Complete
  Cost-beneficial
  User-targeted
  Relevant
  Authoritative
  Timely
  Easy to use

- There are many **sources** of information (both internal and external) including accounting records, websites, staff, the staff of competitors, the government, the media and many others.

- **Computer systems** and **coding structures** help to sort the information into the categories and formats required for both financial and management accounting.

- There are no **external rules** governing the format or content of **management information**, unlike the financial accounts.

- In a cost and management accounting system, the **role** of the **trainee accountant** is to provide answers to questions on costs and revenues. The organisation must have a cost accounting system capable of analysing cost information **quickly** and **easily**.

QUICK QUIZ

1   Two statements follow about information:

1.   Information is the scientific term for facts, figures and processing.

2.   Management information is information that is given to the people who are in charge of running an organisation.

Are the above statements true or false?

A   Both statements are true
B   Both statements are false
C   Statement 1 is false but statement 2 is true
D   Statement 1 is true but statement 2 is false

2   Which one of the following is not usually considered to be one of the purposes of management information?

A   Implementing
B   Planning
C   Control
D   Decision making

3   What is the main factor to consider when designing a management report?

A   The needs of the user
B   The length of the report
C   Confidentiality
D   Neat handwriting

4 Which one of the following does not appear in the mnemonic 'accurate'?

    A   Accurate
    B   Communication
    C   Complete
    D   User-targeted

5 Which one of the following sources of information would you expect to be an internal source of information for a business?

    A   The government
    B   Tax consultants
    C   The internet
    D   The receivables ledger

6 Two statements follow about the format and content of information.

    1.   There are no external rules governing the format and content of management information
    2.   There are no external rules governing the format and content of financial information

Are the above statement true or false?

    A   Both statements are true
    B   Both statements are false
    C   Statement 1 is false but statement 2 is true
    D   Statement 1 is true but statement 2 is false

7 Which one of the following questions would you not expect to be answered by the trainee accountant?

    A   What has the cost of goods produced been?
    B   What have revenues been?
    C   What should our business strategy be for the next five years?
    D   What has the cost of operating department A been?

ANSWERS TO QUICK QUIZ

1   C   Statement 1 is false. It is **data** which is the term for facts, figures and processing. Statement 2 is true.

2   A   Implementing. The purpose of management information is to help managers to manage resources efficiently and effectively by planning and controlling operations and by allowing informed decision making.

3   A   The needs of the user. When considering the needs of the user you may also want to consider the length of the report and confidentiality but the first consideration should be the user's needs.

4   B   Communication. Communication is not a 'quality of information'. It is worth memorising the mnemonic for the exam.

5   D   The receivables ledger. The question says 'usually' because a tax specialist company would probably not need to use external tax consultants so their source of tax information would be internal.

6   D   Statement 1 is true, management information has no external rules. Statement 2 is false as financial information is subject to external rules and regulations

7   C   The trainee accountant is likely to provide answers to questions on costs and revenues. Questions on business strategy would normally be discussed at board level. The trainee accountant may well be told what the business strategy is, but would not be expected to decide on the strategy himself/herself.

Now try ...

Attempt the questions below from the **Exam Question Bank**

Number

Q5-9

part

B

Cost classification and measurement

CHAPTER

03

In this chapter we will look in more detail at the type of costs that are incurred in the manufacture of goods including different ways of classifying those costs.

Cost units, cost classification and profit reporting

TOPIC LIST	SYLLABUS REFERENCE
1 Introduction to costs	N/A
2 Cost units	C2(a)
3 Production costs	C1(a), (c)
4 Direct and indirect costs	C1(a)
5 Cost behaviour	C1(b)
6 Functional costs	C1(a)
7 Calculating the cost of a product or service	C1(e)
8 Profit reporting	C1(d)

Study Guide	Intellectual level
C **Cost classification and measurement**	
1 **Cost classification**	
(a) Define cost classification and describe the variety of cost classifications used for different purposes in a cost accounting system, including by responsibility, function, behaviour, direct/indirect.	S
(b) Describe and illustrate the nature of variable, fixed and mixed (semi-variable, stepped-fixed) costs.	S
(c) Describe and illustrate the classification of material and labour costs.	S
(d) Prepare and explain the nature and purpose of profit statements in absorption and marginal costing formats.	S
(e) Calculate the cost of a product or service.	S
2 **Cost units, cost centres, profit centres and investment centres**	
(a) Explain and illustrate the concept of cost units.	K

1   Introduction to costs

Let us suppose that in your hand you have a red biro which you bought in the newsagent's down the road for 50c. Why does the newsagent charge 50c for it? In other words what does that 50c represent?

From the newsagent's point of view the cost can be split into two.

Price paid by newsagent to wholesaler	Z
Newsagent's 'mark-up'	Y
	50 c

If the newsagent did not charge more for the biro than he paid for it (Y) there would be no point in him selling it. The mark-up itself can be split into further categories.

Pure profit	X
Amount paid to shop assistants	X
Expenses of owning and operating a shop (rent, electricity, cleaning and so on)	X
	Y

The newsagent's **profit** is the amount he personally needs to live: it is like your salary. Different newsagents have different ideas about this: this is why you might pay 60c for an identical biro if you went into another newsagent's. The shop expenses are amounts that have to be paid, whether or not the newsagent sells you a biro, simply to keep the shop going. Again, if other newsagents have to pay higher rent than our newsagent, this might be reflected in the price of biros.

The amount paid to the wholesaler can be split in a similar way: there will be a profit element and amounts to cover the costs of running a wholesaling business. There might also be a cost for getting the biro from the wholesaler's premises to the shop and, of course, there will be the amount paid to the manufacturer.

2 Cost units

> A **cost unit** is a unit of product or service to which costs can be related.

2.1 Cost units

A **cost unit** is a unit of product or service to which costs can be related.

One factor that may cause things to become slightly more complicated is that a cost unit is not always a single item. It might be a batch of 1,000 if that is how the individual items are made. In fact, a cost per 1,000 (or whatever) is often more meaningful information.

Examples of cost units include the following.

- Room (in a hotel)
- Batch of 1,000 shoes
- Patient night (the cost of a patient staying in a hospital for a night)

A possible cost unit for a hospital might be 'cost per patient'. This however, is not particularly useful for control purposes as different patients will spend different amounts of time in hospital. The patient per night cost unit is much more useful. Notice that this is made up of **two parts**, the patient and the night. These two-part cost units are known as **composite cost units** and they are used most often in service organisations.

> Cost information is needed to aid price setting, decision making, planning and budgeting, control and reporting.

Managers need to know what resources are used and what costs are incurred in the production of a cost unit. This information may be used in a number of ways – such as the situations described below.

(a) **Setting a selling price** that covers the cost of manufacture and makes a profit.

(b) **Decision-making**. For example, whether to sell product A or B, which will depend upon how much profit each product makes, for which we need to know the cost.

(c) **Planning and budgeting** future activities relies on knowing production quantities and costs so that we know what resources we will need, how much this will cost and whether we can afford it.

(d) **Control** of resources and costs of production is possible if we know what the quantities and costs ought to be. If costs are higher, or if more time is needed to make the cost units than was expected, then this would need investigation so that any problems can be ironed out.

(e) **Reporting** the results of the business relies on knowing the costs incurred and the value of inventory of the manufactured goods.

Cost classification is the grouping of costs under common characteristics. Examples include direct or indirect costs, fixed or variable costs.

3 Production costs

Look at your biro (pen) and consider what it consists of. There is probably a red plastic cap and a little red thing that fits into the end, and perhaps a yellow plastic sheath. There is an opaque plastic ink holder with red ink inside it. At the tip there is a gold plastic part holding a metal nib with a roller ball.

Let us suppose that the manufacturer sells biros to wholesalers for 20c each. How much does the little ball cost? What share of the 20c is taken up by the little red thing in the end of the biro? How much did somebody earn for putting it there?

To elaborate still further, the manufacturer probably has machines to mould the plastic and do some of the assembly. How much does it cost, per biro, to run the machines: to set them up so that they produce the right shape of moulded plastic? How much are the production line workers' wages per biro?

Any of these separate production costs could be calculated and recorded on a unit cost card which records how the total cost of a unit (in this instance, a biro) is arrived at.

A unit cost card is shown below.

BIRO – UNIT COST CARD		
Direct materials	$	$
Yellow plastic	X	
Red plastic	X	
Opaque plastic	X	
Gold plastic	X	
Ink	X	
Metal	X̲	
		X
Direct labour		
Machine operators' wages	X	
Manual assembly staff wages	X̲	
		X̲
		X
Direct expenses		X
Total direct cost (or prime cost)		X
Overheads (production)		X̲
Production cost (or factory cost)		X
Overheads (administration, distribution and selling)		X̲
Total cost		X̲

4 Direct and indirect costs

Costs can be divided into three elements, **materials, labour** and **expenses.**

The cost card above separates out the three main elements of the cost unit.

- Materials
- Labour
- Expenses

For manufacturers it is useful to further subdivide costs into direct and indirect costs.

Costs can be classified as **direct** or **indirect**.

Direct costs can be traced specifically to a cost unit.

- **Direct materials** – which form part of the end product
- **Direct labour** – involved directly in making the product
- **Direct expenses** – it is rare for expenses to be directly traceable to the product

The sum of the direct costs is known as the **prime cost**.

The factory will also have **indirect costs** or **factory overheads** which are not directly traceable to the product but are still part of the cost of making it.

- **Indirect materials** – such as lubricants for machinery
- **Indirect labour** – such as supervisors and maintenance workers
- **Indirect expenses** – such as heating and lighting for the factory

There are also **non-manufacturing overheads** in a manufacturing business. These are not included in the production cost of goods or for inventory valuation purposes. An appropriate portion of these overheads is sometimes included on the cost card so that an appropriate price can be set.

Examples include

- The accountant's salary (a non-manufacturing labour cost)
- The office rates (non-manufacturing expenses)

QUESTION

Indirect labour

Canine Ltd makes dog leads. It buys in leather, thread and metal clips to make them, employs people to operate stitching machines and assemble the finished leads and has various running costs (overheads) for the rented factory space it uses.

Which of the following costs would be classified as indirect labour?

A   Dog lead clip
B   Factory rent
C   Wages for machine operator
D   Wages for factory manager

ANSWER

D   The factory manager's wages are a production cost, but are not directly traceable to each cost unit. The wages are therefore classified as indirect labour. A is direct materials, B is an indirect expense and C is direct labour.

EXAM FOCUS POINT

An exam question might well ask you to classify a cost as direct or indirect or determine which costs are direct or indirect.

5   Cost behaviour

Cost behaviour patterns demonstrate the way in which costs are affected by changes in the level of activity.

Instead of categorising materials, labour and expenses costs into direct and indirect costs, it can sometimes be very useful to use a different system, one that is based on cost behaviour.

Cost behaviour is the way that costs change as the level of activity changes.

5.1 Level of activity

The level of activity refers to the amount of work done, or the volume of production.

The basic principle of cost behaviour is that **as the level of activity rises, costs will usually rise**. It will cost more to produce 2,000 units of output than it will cost to produce 1,000 units; it will usually cost more to make five telephone calls than to make one call and so on. However, this system identifies several types of cost which respond differently to a change in activity level.

5.2 Variable costs

A variable cost is a cost which tends to vary in total directly with the volume of output. The variable cost per unit is the same amount for each unit produced whereas *total* variable cost increases as volume of output increases. A sketch graph of total variable costs would look like this.

Graph of total variable cost

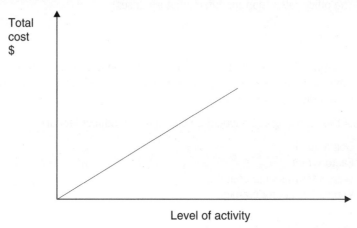

The cost will be the same for each unit produced giving the following graph for variable cost per unit.

Graph of variable cost per unit

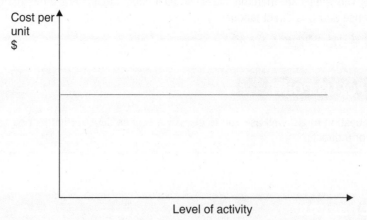

A constant variable cost per unit implies that the purchase price per unit of material purchased or cost per labour hour worked and so on is constant, and that the rate of material usage/labour productivity is also constant. In other words, **constant rate and efficiency levels are implied in variable costs.**

The following are variable costs.

(a)   The cost of raw materials, because the volume of raw materials purchased relates to the volume used in production.

(b)   Direct labour costs. This is due to the ability to increase or decrease the number of workers and therefore the total cost.

(c)   Sales commission is variable in relation to the volume or value of sales.

At this point it is important to stress that variable cost is *not* just another name for a direct cost. The distinctions that can be made are as follows.

(a)   **Costs are either variable or fixed, depending upon whether they change in total when the volume of production changes.**

(b)   **Costs are either direct or indirect, depending upon how easily they can be traced to a specific unit of production.**

It is therefore quite possible for a direct cost to be fixed. For example, if bulk discounts are available for purchases of materials, then the cost of each unit will not be the same before and after the application of the discount. In this case the cost is direct but not variable. Another example of this type of cost is direct labour that is paid overtime: in this case the cost per unit of labour depends on whether it is worked as normal time or as overtime. Since the cost is not the same for each unit, labour overtime is not a true variable cost.

5.3 Fixed costs

A fixed cost is a cost which tends to be unaffected in total by increases or decreases in the volume of output. Fixed costs are a period charge, in that they relate to a span of time; as the time span increases, so too will the fixed costs (which are sometimes referred to as period costs for this reason).

A sketch graph of a total fixed cost would look like this.

Graph of total fixed cost

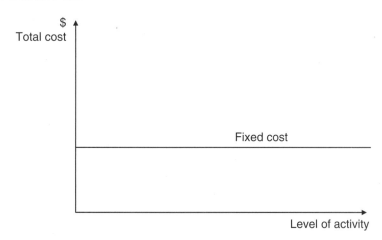

The following are fixed costs.

(a)   The salary of the managing director (per month or per annum)
(b)   The rent of a single factory building (per month or per annum)
(c)   Straight line depreciation of a single machine (per month or per annum)

Because the total fixed costs remain the same for all levels of activity, if you calculate the fixed cost per unit, this will decrease as more units are produced.

Graph of fixed cost per unit

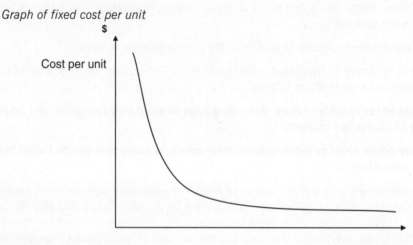

5.4 Stepped-fixed costs

Stepped-fixed costs are costs which are fixed in nature within certain levels of activity.

Many items of cost are a fixed cost in nature within certain levels of activity. For example the depreciation of a machine may be fixed if production remains below 1,000 units per month, but if production exceeds 1,000 units, a second machine may be required, and the cost of depreciation (on two machines) would go up a step. A sketch graph of a total stepped-fixed cost would look like this.

Graph of total stepped-fixed cost

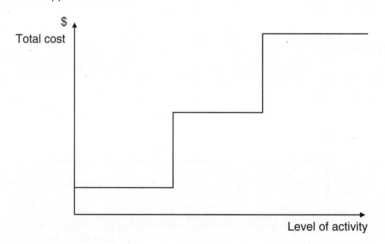

Graph of stepped-fixed cost per unit

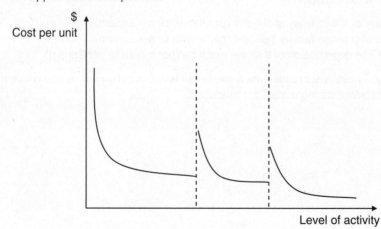

Other examples of stepped-fixed costs are as follows.

(a) **Rent**, where accommodation requirements increase as output levels get higher.

(b) **Supervisor salaries**. One supervisor may be able to supervise a maximum of 10 employees. When the number of employees increases above a multiple of 10 an extra supervisor will be required.

5.5 Mixed costs (or semi-variable costs or semi-fixed costs)

Mixed costs (semi-variable/semi-fixed costs) are partly fixed and partly variable, and therefore only partly affected by changes in activity levels.

These are cost items which are **part fixed** and **part variable**, and are therefore partly affected by changes in the level of activity.

Graph of total semi-variable cost

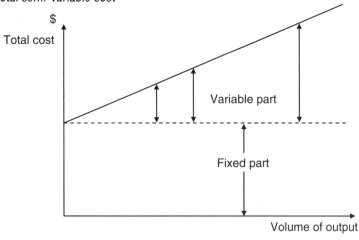

Graph of semi-variable cost per unit

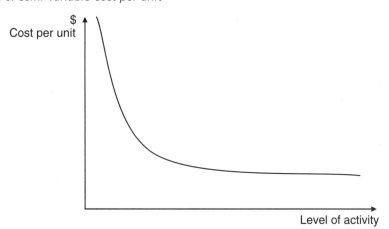

Examples of these costs can include utility bills, if there is a standing basic charge plus a variable charge per unit of consumption. A example of this is a telephone bill with a fixed charge for line rental and a variable charge for calls made.

QUESTION

Variable and fixed costs

Are each of the following likely to be variable or fixed costs?

(a) Charges for telephone calls made
(b) Charges for rental of telephone
(c) Annual salary of the chief accountant
(d) Managing director's subscription to the Institute of Directors
(e) Cost of materials used to pack 20 units of product X into a box

ANSWER

(a) Variable
(b) Fixed
(c) Fixed
(d) Fixed
(e) Variable

EXAM FOCUS POINT

The graphs of these cost behaviours are important as a question might give you a graph and ask you to decide which cost behaviour is depicted.

6 Functional costs

Costs can also be analysed according to their **function**. For example, production, distribution and selling, administration and financing costs.

When we talk about functional costs we are not talking about a different **type** of cost from those we have met already, but about a way of grouping costs together according to what aspects of an organisation's operations (what **function**) cause them to be incurred.

A convenient set of functions is the following.

(a) **Production costs**. Materials and labour used and expenses incurred to make things and get them ready for sale.

(b) **Distribution and selling costs**. Costs incurred both to get the finished items to the point where people can buy them and to persuade people to buy them.

(c) **Administration costs**. This is a vague term. You might like to think of these costs as the materials and labour used and the expenses incurred in co-ordinating the activities of the production function and the distribution and selling function.

(d) **Financing costs**. The expenses incurred when a business has to borrow to purchase non-current assets, say, or simply to operate on a day to day basis.

These divisions are not the only ones that could be made, nor are there rigid definitions of what is a production cost, what is an administration cost and so on.

7 Calculating the cost of a product or service

The cost of a product or service can be built up on a **cost card**, which identifies

–   Direct costs
–   Prime cost (sum of direct costs)
–   Production overheads
–   Production costs
–   Non-production overheads
–   Total cost

Returning to the cost card at the start of the chapter, you should now be in a position to understand all the different types of cost referred to. Our next step is to build a cost card up for ourselves.

In practice, this means measuring the amount of materials used and the time taken to perform the tasks. These quantities can then be costed from the cost bookkeeping records.

For overheads, or indirect costs, it is more difficult to ascertain the exact amount that relates to each cost unit, so a method has to be found of sharing out the cost over the cost units made.

In later chapters we will cover how these costs are recorded and calculated in more detail, but for now we will concentrate on producing a cost card and understanding the types of costs involved.

7.1 Example: calculating the cost of a product

Skeggy Limited makes 20,000 Braces per year. Each Brace requires ½ hour of labour at $5 per hour and 3 bought-in components, costing $1.25, $2 and 40c each respectively. The packaging for the Brace costs $16 for 100 boxes. The business incurs fixed production costs of $4,000 per annum, and the cost of selling, administration and distribution works out at 50c per item sold. Calculate the production cost and the total cost of a Brace and record this information on a cost card.

Firstly, it is necessary to decide which costs fall into the different categories that you would use on a cost card.

- Direct materials – components
- Direct labour – labour
- Production overheads – fixed production costs
- Non-production overheads – selling, administration and distribution costs

Then, the amount of each cost per unit of product can be calculated and slotted in to the cost card.

Brace – Unit cost card	$
Direct materials – components (1.25 +2.00+0.40)	3.65
– box ($16/100)	0.16
Direct labour (1/2 h @ $5 per h)	2.50
Prime cost	6.31
Production overheads ($4,000 / 20,000 units)	0.20
Production cost	6.51
Non-manufacturing overheads	0.50
Total cost	7.01

Service organisations are those which offer services, for example

- Professional services: accountants and solicitors
- Personal services: hairdressers
- Repairs and maintenance: plumbers and garages.

They will need to cost their cost units in a similar way. A garage will need to cost a standard vehicle service, a hairdresser will cost a cut and blow dry and an accountant will cost an audit and tax service for a particular type of client. In service organisations, the major cost tends to be labour.

QUESTION
Prime cost

A service for a sports car requires 3 hours of a skilled mechanic's time followed by ½ hour of unskilled labour. Rates of pay are

(a)   Skilled: $9 per hour
(b)   Unskilled: $5 per hour

Oil, oil filter, screen wash and spark plugs cost $6.90 in total. Rent and rates for the industrial unit from which the service centre operates, work out at $4 per hour. Administration costs are $2 per service.

The prime cost of the service is

A $29.50
B $36.40
C $50.40
D $52.40

ANSWER

Answer B. Prime cost is the total direct cost. A is the labour cost only, C is the service cost and D is the total cost, as shown in the cost card below.

Sports car service cost card

		$
Direct materials		6.90
Direct labour – skilled	(3h @ $9 per h)	27.00
– unskilled	(½h @ $5 per h)	2.50
Prime cost		36.40
Production overheads	(3½h @ $4)	14.00
Service cost		50.40
Non-manufacturing overheads		2.00
Total cost		52.40

(Note that the production overheads were shared amongst service jobs on the basis of time taken)

---

8 Profit reporting

Absorption costing and **marginal costing** are different ways of accounting for costs. If there are changes in inventory levels during a period, marginal costing and absorption costing give different profit figures.

Earlier on, we mentioned that an important reason for finding the cost of cost units produced was so that we could report the profit made and value any closing inventory. For management accounting purposes there are two ways of doing this, which differ in their treatment of fixed costs.

- **Absorption costing**: the cost of the product for inventory valuation is the variable production cost plus the fixed production cost.

- **Marginal costing**: the cost of the product for inventory valuation is the variable production cost only. Fixed production costs are treated as a period cost rather than a product cost, and are charged to the income statement in full in the period in which they are incurred.

This will lead to different inventory values, and to a different reported profit if inventory quantities rise or fall over the period in question.

QUESTION

Production costs

Which of the following costs is not included as a product cost for inventory valuation in marginal costing?

A   Direct labour
B   Direct materials
C   Variable production overheads
D   Fixed production overheads

ANSWER

Answer D

Direct labour, direct materials and variable production overheads are all variable costs and are included as a product cost in marginal costing, so A, B and C are incorrect. Fixed production overheads are not a product cost in marginal costing; they are treated as a period cost.

8.1 Example: absorption costing and marginal costing

Robbers Limited makes one product, the Cop. At 1 June, there are 40 Cops in inventories held. Each Cop requires 2 hours of labour and 1kg of raw material. Labour is paid $8 per hour, and raw material costs $12 per kg. Robbers Limited incurs fixed production overheads of $2,000 per month and the factory produces 1,000 Cops each month.

A Cop sells for $35. Sales in June were 1,000 Cops, but in July, sales fell to 900 Cops.

8.2 Absorption costing

The absorption cost of a Cop can be found by drawing-up a unit cost card. The variable costs are found by multiplying the quantity used by the cost. The fixed production cost is spread over the units produced.

Cop – unit cost card (absorption costing)	$
Variable production costs	
Direct material 1kg @ $12 per kg	12.00
Direct labour 2h @ $8 per hour	16.00
Total variable cost	28.00
Fixed production overheads $2,000/1,000	2.00
Total production cost	30.00

A profit statement can now be produced for June and July, using these costs.

	June		July	
	$	$	$	$
Sales		35,000		31,500
Opening inventory (40 × $30)	1,200		1,200	
Production (1,000 × $30)	30,000		30,000	
	31,200		31,200	
Less: closing inventory (40 × $30)	1,200	(140 × $30)	4,200	
Cost of sales		30,000		27,000
Gross Profit		5,000		4,500

Let's now compare these figures with those generated by marginal costing.

8.3 Marginal costing

Cop – unit cost card (marginal costing)	$
Variable production costs	
Direct material 1kg @ $12 per kg	12.00
Direct labour 2h @ $8 per hour	16.00
Total variable cost or marginal cost	28.00

The marginal costing profit statement is a little different. Firstly, the fixed overheads are not included in the product cost, but are brought in to the income statement in full. Secondly, a new sub-heading is needed in marginal costing: **contribution**.

Contribution is sales less variable, or marginal, costs.

This term can also be used in relation to an individual unit; in this case contribution is the selling price less the variable cost per unit. The term contribution is short for 'contribution towards covering fixed costs and making a profit'.

	June		July	
	$	$	$	$
Sales		35,000		31,500
Opening inventory (40 × $28)	1,120		1,120	
Production (1,000 × $28)	28,000		28,000	
	29,120		29,120	
Less: closing inventory (June 40 × $28; July 140 × $28)	1,120		3,920	
Variable cost of sales		28,000		25,200
Contribution		7,000		6,300
Less: fixed overheads		2,000		2,000
Profit		5,000		4,300

Note: In this example there are no variable non-production costs such as sales and distribution but be aware that contribution is sales less all variable costs (production and non-production).

8.4 Marginal costing and absorption costing compared

Marginal costing and absorption costing are different.

(a)   In marginal costing

    (i)   Closing inventory is valued at marginal production cost.

    (ii)   Fixed costs are charged in full against the profit of the period in which they are incurred.

(b)   **In absorption costing** (sometimes referred to as **full costing**):

    (i)   Closing inventory is valued at full production cost including a share of fixed production costs.

    (ii)   The effect of this is that under absorption costing the cost of sales in a period will include some fixed overhead incurred in a previous period (in opening inventory values). The cost of sales will also exclude some fixed overhead incurred in the current period as this is carried forward in closing inventory values to be charged to a subsequent accounting period.

Refer back to the examples in sections 8.2 and 8.3. In June, the absorption costing profit was the same as the marginal costing profit: $5,000. This is because the production quantity was 1,000 units, and the quantity sold was the same, 1,000 units. Therefore, both absorption costing and marginal costing will have charged $2,000 of fixed production overheads against profit.

In July, however, production was 1,000 units but only 900 units were sold; inventory increased by the 100 unsold units, rising from 40 to 140 units. In marginal costing this made no difference to the fixed overheads charged: the full $2,000 was still charged in this period. But under absorption costing, each unit of inventory produced in the period that was still held at the end of the period will include $2 of the fixed overheads incurred in the period. This part of the fixed overheads will be carried forward in the value of closing inventory and charged against profit in a future period.

So, under absorption costing 100 units of inventory will carry $200 of fixed overheads out of this profit statement, which accounts for the $200 additional absorption costing profit compared with the marginal costing profit. Of course, when the inventory is sold, this will 'release' the fixed overheads to be charged against the absorption costing profit. So, in a future period the profit related to these 100 units of inventory will be $200 less under absorption costing than under marginal costing.

QUESTION

Marginal profit vs absorption profit

Which of the following statements is true?

A   In the long term, there will be no difference between marginal costing profits and absorption costing profits

B   Marginal costing profits are always greater than absorption costing profits

C   Absorption costing profits are always greater than marginal costing profits

D   Differences between marginal costing profits and absorption costing profits always reverse in the following period

ANSWER

Answer A

In general, as inventory levels rise and fall, any differences will tend to reverse. This does not necessarily happen in the following period, so D is incorrect. B and C are incorrect as any differences depend on whether inventory levels are rising or falling.

EXAM FOCUS POINT

Contribution is an important concept which could be tested in the exam.

8.5 Absorption costing or marginal costing?

Both methods are widely used for costing purposes, but marginal costing has the advantage of being better for decision-making purposes.

CHAPTER ROUNDUP

↪ A **cost unit** is a unit of product which has costs attached to it.

↪ Cost information is needed to aid price setting, decision making, planning and budgeting, control and reporting.

↪ Costs can be divided into three elements, **materials, labour** and **expenses.**

↪ Costs can be classified as **direct** or **indirect**.

↪ **Cost behaviour patterns** demonstrate the way in which costs are affected by changes in the level of activity.

↪ **Stepped-fixed costs** are costs which are fixed in nature within certain levels of activity.

↪ **Mixed costs** (semi-variable/semi-fixed costs) are partly fixed and partly variable, and therefore only partly affected by changes in activity levels.

↪ Costs can also be analysed according to their **function**. For example, production, distribution and selling, administration and financing costs.

↪ The cost of a product or service can be built up on a **cost card**, which identifies

- Direct costs
- Prime cost (sum of direct costs)
- Production overheads
- Production costs
- Non-production overheads
- Total cost

↪ **Absorption costing** and **marginal costing** are different ways of accounting for costs. If there are changes in inventory levels during a period, marginal costing and absorption costing give different profit figures.

QUICK QUIZ

1   A unit of product or service to which costs can be related is known as?

    A   A cost centre
    B   A cost unit
    C   A product unit
    D   A service unit

2   Which one of the following cost elements does not form part of the overheads?

    A   Indirect expenses
    B   Indirect labour
    C   Indirect materials
    D   Direct labour

3   The basic principle of cost behaviour is that as the level of activity rises, total costs will usually _____ . Which is/are the missing word/words?

    A   Fall
    B   Rise
    C   Stay consistent
    D   Fall then rise again

4   A cost which is unaffected in total by increases and decreases in the volume of output is called?

    A   Stepped-fixed
    B   Variable
    C   Constant
    D   Fixed

5 Which one of the following is an example of a mixed cost?

 A Factory rent
 B Salaries
 C Telephone bill
 D Straight line depreciation

6 Costs can be analysed according to their function. Which one of the following is not an example of a functional cost heading?

 A Production costs
 B Administration costs
 C Financing costs
 D Carriage out costs

7 XYZ Co produces a component W. The standard cost card for component W is as follows:

		$
Production costs	Fixed	255.70
	Variable	483.50
Selling costs	Fixed	124.80
	Variable	75.60
	Profit	60.40
	Selling price	1,000.00

 (a) Under an absorption costing system, what would be the value of inventory?

  • $255.70 • $739.20 • $483.20 • $227.80

 (b) Under a marginal costing system, what would be the value of inventory?

  • $483.50 • $75.60 • $136.00 • $124.80

ANSWERS TO QUICK QUIZ

1 B This is the definition of a cost unit.

2 D Direct labour is a direct cost and therefore not part of overheads.

3 B The basic principle of cost behaviour is that as the level of activity rises, costs will usually rise.

4 D The name given to cost unaffected by increases and decreases in the volume of output is fixed costs.

5 C Telephone bills usually have a fixed element (the line rental) and a variable element (the charge per call made). Options A, B and D are all usually fixed costs.

6 D Carriage out costs. These costs would normally come under the functional heading of 'distribution and selling costs'.

7 (a) $255.70 + $483.50 = $739.20

   Selling costs are never included in inventory valuations. The valuation under absorption costing is the full production cost so it is the sum of the fixed production cost and the variable production cost.

  (b) $483.50

   Selling costs are never included in inventory valuations. The valuation under a marginal costing system is the variable production cost.

Now try ...

Attempt the questions below from the **Exam Question Bank**

Number

Q10-13

So far we have taken a general look at what management information is, how it is presented and how an accounting system can collect relevant pieces of data and information. We are now going to look at one particular type of management information: measures of management performance.

The managers of a business need to monitor how their particular section of the business is performing; this an important aspect of controlling the activities of the business, but it might also have some bearing on their remuneration.

The performance measures used will depend upon the way in which the business is organised and the type of business, as explained in this chapter.

Management responsibility and performance measurement

TOPIC LIST	SYLLABUS REFERENCE
1 Responsibility centres	C2 (b), (c), (d)
2 Performance measures	C2 (e), (f)

Study Guide	Intellectual level
C Cost classification and measurement	
2 Cost units, cost centres, profit centres and investment centres	
(b) Explain and illustrate the concept of cost centres	K
(c) Explain and illustrate the concept of profit centres	K
(d) Explain and illustrate the concept of investment centres	K
(e) Describe performance measures appropriate to cost, profit and investment centres (cost/profit per unit / % of sales: efficiency, capacity utilisation and production volume ratios; ROCE/RI, asset turnover)	S
(f) Apply performance measures appropriate to cost, profit and investment centres	S

1 Responsibility centres

A **responsibility centre** is a function or department of an organisation that is headed by a manager who has direct responsibility for its performance.

Responsibility accounting is a system of accounting that segregates revenue and costs into areas of personal responsibility in order to monitor and assess the performance of each part of an organisation.

What are the manager's resources?	Finance, inventory of raw materials, spare machine capacity, labour availability, the balance of expenditure remaining for a certain budget, target date for completion of a job.
At what rate are the manager's resources being consumed?	How fast is the labour force working, how quickly are the raw materials being used up, how quickly are other expenses being incurred, how quickly is available finance being consumed?
How well are the resources being used?	How well are his objectives being met?

Responsibility centres are usually divided into different categories. Here we shall describe cost centres, profit centres and investment centres.

1.1 Cost centres

A **cost centre** is any section of an organisation to which costs can be separately attributed.

A **cost centre** is a production or service location, function, activity or item of equipment for which costs are accumulated.

To collect costs to a cost centre, each cost centre will have a **cost code**. Items of expenditure will be recorded with the appropriate cost code. For example, the equipment maintenance department in a printing factory would be one example of a cost centre. When costs are eventually analysed, there may well be some apportionment of the costs of one cost centre to other cost centres. If this happens:

(a)   The costs of those cost centres which receive an apportionment of shared costs should be divided into directly attributable costs (for which the cost centre manager is responsible) and shared costs (for which another cost centre is directly accountable).

(b)   The control system should trace shared costs back to the cost centres from which the costs have been apportioned, so that their managers can be made accountable for the costs incurred.

Information about cost centres might be collected in terms of **total actual costs, total budgeted costs** and **total cost variances** (the differences between actual and budgeted costs). In addition, the information might be analysed in terms of **ratios.**

In general, for cost accounting purposes, departments are termed **cost centres** and the product produced by an organisation is termed the **cost unit**. In an example of a bakery, the cost centres of the production function could be the mixing department, the baking department and the stores department and the organisation's cost unit could be one chocolate cake.

1.1.1 Examples of cost centres

Cost centres may include the following.

*   A **department** (as in our example above)

*   A **machine** or group of machines

*   A **project** (eg the installation of a new computer system)

*   A **new product** (to enable the costs of development and production to be identified)

*   A **person** (eg a marketing director. Costs might include salary, company car and other expenses incurred by the director)

1.2 Profit centres

A **profit centre** is any section of an organisation to which both revenues and costs are assigned, so that the profitability of the section may be measured.

A profit centre is part of a business accountable for both costs and revenues.

Profit centre information is needed by managers who are responsible for both revenue and costs. For example, an individual branch of a hairdressing chain would incur costs and generate revenue.

The manager of the profit centre has some influence over both revenues and costs, that is, a say in both sales and production policies.

A profit centre manager is likely to be a fairly senior person within an organisation, and a profit centre is likely to cover quite a large area of operations. A profit centre might be an entire division within the organisation, or there might be a separate profit centre for each product, product range, brand or service that the organisation sells.

In the hierarchy of responsibility centres within an organisation, there are likely to be several cost centres within a profit centre.

1.2.1 Examples of profit centres

*   A sales division selling products to customers
*   A service division providing after sales service
*   Individual shops in a retail chain
*   Local branches in a regional or nationwide distribution business
*   A geographical region eg a country or group of countries
*   A team or individual eg a sales team, a team of equipment installers

1.3 Investment centres

An **investment centre** is a profit centre which has additional responsibilities for capital investment.

Investment centres refer to profit centres with additional responsibility for capital investment and possibly for financing, and whose performance is measured by its return on capital employed.

Managers may or may not have the power to make decisions about capital investment – senior management quite often retains control over decisions on high value investments.

Many public sector organisations are required to make a particular level of profit related to their non-current assets (**return on capital**). Some commercial organisations also use investment centres.

Several profit centres might share the same capital items, for example the same buildings, stores or transport fleet, and so investment centres are likely to include several profit centres, and provide a basis for control at a very senior management level.

1.4 Summary

- **Cost centres** collect information on costs

- **Profit centres** collect information on costs, revenues and profits

- **Investment centres** collect information on costs, revenues and profits in relation to the value of non-current assets and working capital

QUESTION   Investment centres

An information system would use investment centres to provide useful information for which of the following.

A   The supervisor of the accounts payable section of the finance department of a large charity.
B   One of three divisional managers for a trading company.
C   The personnel manager of a manufacturing company.
D   A swimming pool manager with authority to buy non-current assets up to $50,000.

ANSWER

D is the correct answer.

A is a cost centre. This person will have no control over revenue.

B is a profit centre. This person will be responsible for revenue as well as costs for the division.

C is a cost centre. The personnel department does not earn revenue.

D is the only investment centre. Responsibility will be for costs, revenues and capital expenditure.

2 Performance measures

Performance measurement aims to establish how well something or somebody is doing in relation to a planned activity.

2.1 Performance measures for cost centres

2.1.1 Productivity

This is the quantity of the product or service produced **(output) in relation to** the resources put in (**input**). For example so many units produced per hour, or per employee, or per tonne of material. It measures **how efficiently resources are being used**.

2.1.2 Cost per unit

Cost per unit is total costs ÷ number of units produced.

For the manager of a cost centre which is also a production centre one of the most important performance measures will be cost per unit. This is simply the total costs of production divided by the number of units produced in the period.

Example: cost per unit

The total costs and number of units produced for a production cost centre for the last two months are as follows:

	May	June
Production costs	$128,600	$143,200
Units produced	12,000	13,500
Cost per unit	$128,600	$143,200
	12,000	13,500
	= $10.72	$10.61

2.1.3 Measures of performance using the standard hour

Performance measures for **materials** and **labour** include differences between actual and expected (budgeted) performance. Performance can also be measured using the **standard hour**.

Sam Ltd manufactures plates, mugs and eggcups. Production during the first two quarters of 20X5 was as follows.

	Quarter 1	Quarter 2
Plates	1,000	800
Mugs	1,200	1,500
Eggcups	800	900

The fact that 3,000 products were produced in quarter 1 and 3,200 in quarter 2 does not tell us anything about Sam Ltd's performance over the two periods because plates, mugs and eggcups are so different. The fact that the production mix has changed is not revealed by considering the total number of units produced. We also need to consider the number of hours in which these units are produced. Once we have this information, then we can measure the rate of production. This then allows us to **measure output when a number of dissimilar products are manufactured**. The rate is measured using the concept of the **standard hour**.

The standard hour (or standard minute) is the **quantity of work achievable at standard performance, expressed in terms of a standard unit of work done in a standard period of time.**

Using the example of Sam Ltd above, if we also know the number of hours taken to product those numbers of goods, then we can work out the standard hour, ie the rate of production.

Product	Quarter 1		Standard hours	Quarter 2		Standard hours
Plate	1,000	500	2 units	800	400	2 units
Mug	1,200	400	3 units	1,500	500	3 units
Eggcup	800	200	4 units	900	225	4 units
		1,100			1,125	

The output level in the two quarters was therefore identical, as measured by the standard hour.

The standard hour can also be expressed in terms of the standard time allowed to produce one unit of each of products: In the case of Sam Ltd:

	Standard hour	Standard time
Plate	2 units	$1/2$ hour (1hr ÷ 2 units)
Mug	3 units	$1/3$ hour (1hr ÷ 3 units)
Eggcup	4 units	$1/4$ hour (1hr ÷ 4 units)

2.1.4 Efficiency, capacity utilisation and production volume

Standard hours are useful in computing levels of **efficiency, capacity utilisation and production volume (or activity)**. Any management accounting reports involving budgets and variance analysis should incorporate control ratios. The three main control ratios are the **efficiency**, **capacity utilisation** and **production volume** ratios.

(a) The efficiency ratio measures the efficiency of the labour force by comparing equivalent standard hours for work produced and actual hours worked.

(b) The capacity utilisation ratio compares actual hours worked and budgeted hours, and measures the extent to which planned utilisation has been achieved.

(c) The production volume ratio compares the number of standard hours equivalent to the actual work produced and budgeted hours.

2.1.5 Example: ratios and standard hours

Given the following information about Sam Ltd for quarter 1 of 20X5, calculate an efficiency ratio, capacity utilisation ratio and a production volume ratio and explain their meaning.

Budgeted hours	1,100 standard hours
Standard hours produced	1,125 standard hours
Actual hours worked	1,200

Solution

$$\text{Efficiency ratio} = \frac{\text{Standard hours produced}}{\text{Actual hours worked}} \times 100\% = \frac{1,125}{1,200} \times 100\% = 93.8\%$$

The labour force worked 6.2% below standard levels of efficiency (as 93.8 is 100-6.2)

$$\text{Capacity utilisation ratio} = \frac{\text{Actual hours worked}}{\text{Budgeted hours}} \times 100\% = \frac{1,200}{1,100} \times 100\% = 109.1\%$$

$$\text{Production volume ratio} = \frac{\text{Standard hours produced}}{\text{Budgeted hours}} \times 100\% = \frac{1,125}{1,100} \times 100\% = 102.3\%$$

These ratios show that a 9.1% increase in capacity resulted in a 2.3% increase in production.

The capacity utilisation ratio multiplied by the efficiency ratio gives us the activity or production volume ratio: 109.1% × 93.8% = 102.3%

QUESTION

Ratios

If   X = Actual hours worked
        Y = Budgeted hours
        Z = Standard hours produced

What is $\dfrac{Z}{Y}$?

A   Capacity utilisation ratio
B   Production volume ratio
C   Efficiency ratio
D   Standard hours produced ratio

ANSWER

B

2.2 Productivity

If the cost centre is not a production centre, then relevant performance measures would include variances, which are covered in Chapter 11 of this Interactive Text.

2.3 Performance measures for profit centres

Ratios and **percentages** are useful performance measurement techniques.

The **profit margin** (profit to sales ratio) is calculated as (profit ÷ sales) × 100%.

2.3.1 Profit margin

The **profit margin** (profit to sales ratio) is calculated as (profit ÷ sales) × 100%.

The profit margin provides a simple measure of performance for profit centres. Investigation of unsatisfactory profit margins enables control action to be taken, either by reducing excessive costs or by raising selling prices.

Profit margin is usually calculated using operating profit.

The **operating profit** is the difference between the value of sales (excluding sales tax) and the costs incurred during operations (total operating expenses).

2.3.2 Example: the profit to sales ratio

A company compares its year 2 results with year 1 results as follows.

	Year 2 $	Year 1 $
Sales	160,000	120,000
Cost of sales		
Direct materials	40,000	20,000
Direct labour	40,000	30,000
Production overhead	22,000	20,000
Marketing overhead	42,000	35,000
	144,000	105,000
Operating profit	16,000	15,000
Profit to sales ratio	$\left(\dfrac{16{,}000}{160{,}000}\right) \times 100\%$	10%
	$\left(\dfrac{15{,}000}{120{,}000}\right) \times 100\%$	12½%

The above information shows that there is a decline in profitability in spite of the $1,000 increase in profit, because the profit margin is less in year 2 than year 1.

2.3.3 Gross profit margin

The **gross profit margin** is calculated as gross profit ÷ sales × 100%

Gross profit is the difference between the value of sales (excluding sales tax) and the cost of the goods sold.

The profit to sales ratio above was based on a profit figure which included non-production overheads. The gross profit margin calculates how efficiently a business is using its materials, labour and production overhead in the production process. It is calculated as (gross profit = turnover) ×100%.

For the company in Paragraph 2.2.2 the gross profit margin would be:

Year 2: $\left(\frac{(16,000+42,000)}{160,000}\right) \times 100\% = 36.25\%$

Year 1: $\left(\frac{(15,000+35,000)}{120,000}\right) \times 100\% = 41.67\%$

2.3.4 Cost/sales ratios

When target profits are not met, further ratios may be used to shed some light on the problem.

- Production cost of sales ÷ sales
- Distribution and marketing costs ÷ sales
- Administrative costs ÷ sales

Subsidiary ratios can be used to examine problem areas in greater depth. For example, for production costs the following ratios might be used.

- Material costs ÷ sales value of production
- Works labour costs ÷ sales value of production
- Production overheads ÷ sales value of production

2.3.5 Example: cost/sales ratios

Look back to the example in Paragraph 2.2.2. A more detailed analysis would show that higher direct materials are the probable cause of the decline in profitability.

	Year 2	Year 1
Material costs/sales	$\left(\frac{40,000}{160,000}\right) \times 100\%$	25%
	$\left(\frac{20,000}{120,000}\right) \times 100\%$	16.7%

Other cost/sales ratios have remained the same or improved.

QUESTION

Profit margins

Use the following summary income statement to answer the questions below

	$
Sales	3,000
Cost of sales	1,800
	1,200
Manufacturing expenses	300
Administrative expenses	200
Operating profit	700

1   The profit margin is

    A   60%
    B   40%
    C   30%
    D   23%

2   The gross profit margin is

    A   60%
    B   40%
    C   30%
    D   23%

ANSWER

1   D $\dfrac{700}{3,000} \times 100\% = 23\%$

The profit margin usually refers to operating profit / sales.

2   B $\dfrac{1,200}{3,000} \times 100\% = 40\%$

The gross profit margin takes the gross profit/sales.

2.4 Performance measures for investment centres

> **Return on capital employed (ROCE)** or **return on investment (ROI))** shows how much profit has been made in relation to the amount of resources invested.

2.4.1 Return on capital employed (ROCE)

Return on capital employed (ROCE) (also called **Return on investment (ROI)**) is calculated as (profit/capital employed) $\times$ 100% and shows how much profit has been made in relation to the amount of resources invested.

ROCE is generally used for measuring the performance of investment centres; profits alone do not show whether the return is sufficient when different values of assets are used. Thus if company A and company B have the following results, company B would have the better performance.

	A	B
	$	$
Profit	5,000	5,000
Sales	100,000	100,000
Capital employed	50,000	25,000
ROCE	10%	20%

The profit of each company is the same but company B only invested $25,000 to achieve that profit whereas company A invested $50,000.

ROCE may be calculated in a number of ways, but **profit before interest and tax** (that is, net profit) is usually used.

Similarly **all assets of a non-operational nature** (for example trade investments and intangible assets such as goodwill) **should be excluded** from capital employed.

Profits should be related to average capital employed. In practice many companies calculate the ratio **using year-end assets**. This can be misleading. If a new investment is undertaken near to the year end, the capital employed will rise but profits will only have a month or two of the new investment's contribution.

What does the ROCE tell us? What should we be looking for? There are **two principal comparisons** that can be made.

- The change in ROCE from one year to the next
- The ROCE being earned by other entities

2.4.2 Residual income (RI)

Residual income (RI) is an alternative way of measuring the performance of an investment centre. It is a measure of the centre's profits after deducting a notional or imputed interest cost.

An alternative way of measuring the performance of an investment centre, instead of using ROCE, is residual income (RI). **Residual income is a measure of the centre's profits after deducting a notional or imputed interest cost** (calculated on the whole of the capital employed - **not** just on borrowed funds).

Residual income (RI) is pretax profits less a notional interest charge for invested capital.

QUESTION

Residual income

A division achieved the following results:

	$
Profit before interest and tax	41,000
Capital employed	555,000

Assuming a notional interest charge of 11%, what is the division's residual income?

A $20,050
B $102,050
C   ($20,050)
D   ($102,050)

ANSWER

C

	$
Divisional profit	41,000
Notional interest (555,000 × 0.11)	(61,050)
Residual income	(20,050)

2.4.3 Asset turnover

Asset turnover measures how efficiently the assets of the business are being used.

Asset turnover is a measure of how well the assets of a business are being used to generate sales. It is calculated as (sales ÷ capital employed).

Suppose that two companies both have capital employed of $100,000. However Company A has sales revenue for the year of $150,000 and Company B has sales revenue for the year of $250,000. The asset turnover figure shows how much revenue is being earned for every $1 of capital employed:

$$\text{Company A} = \frac{\$150,000}{\$100,000} = 1.5$$

$$\text{Company B} = \frac{\$250,000}{\$100,000} = 2.5$$

This shows that Company B is earning $2.50 of sales revenue for every $1 invested compared to only $1.50 of sales revenue for Company A.

Note that the asset turnover figure is an absolute figure and not a percentage.

Asset turnover is an important figure in its own right as it shows how efficiently the assets or capital of the business is being used to create sales revenue. However, it is also important as it is one of the elements that make up return on capital employed.

Return on capital employed = Asset turnover × Net profit margin

$$\frac{\text{Net profit}}{\text{Capital employed}} = \frac{\text{Sales revenue}}{\text{Capital employed}} \times \frac{\text{Net profit}}{\text{Sales revenue}}$$

2.5 Example: return on capital employed, asset turnover and net profit margin

A company has the following figures:

	$
Sales revenue	540,000
Net profit	50,000
Capital employed	300,000

$$\text{Return on capital employed} = \frac{\$50,000}{\$300,000} \times 100 = 16.67\%$$

$$\text{Asset turnover} = \frac{\$540,000}{\$300,000} = 1.8$$

$$\text{Net profit margin} = \frac{\$50,000}{\$540,000} \times 100 = 9.26\%$$

Return on capital employed	= Asset turnover	×	Net profit margin
16.67%	= 1.8	×	9.26%

This is an important relationship as it means that any changes in return on capital employed can be accounted for by changes in the profitability measured by net profit margin and in the efficiency of the use of the net assets measured by asset turnover.

EXAM FOCUS POINT

One or more questions on any of these performance measures is likely in this exam.

CHAPTER ROUNDUP

- A **responsibility centre** is a function or department of an organisation that is headed by a manager who has direct responsibility for its performance.

- A **cost centre** is any section of an organisation to which costs can be separately attributed.

- A **profit centre** is any section of an organisation to which both revenues and costs are assigned, so that the profitability of the section may be measured.

- An **investment centre** is a profit centre whose performance is measured by its return on capital employed.

- **Performance measurement** aims to establish how well something or somebody is doing in relation to a planned activity.

- **Cost per unit** is total costs ÷ number of units produced.

- Performance measures for **materials** and **labour** include differences between actual and expected (budgeted) performance. Performance can also be measured using the **standard hour**.

- **Ratios** and **percentages** are useful performance measurement techniques.

- The **profit margin** (profit to sales ratio) is calculated as (profit ÷ sales) × 100%.

- The **gross profit margin** is calculated as gross profit ÷ sales × 100%

- **Return on capital employed (ROCE)** or **return on investment (ROI)** shows how much profit has been made in relation to the amount of resources invested.

- **Residual income (RI)** is an alternative way of measuring the performance of an investment centre. It is a measure of the centre's profits after deducting a notional or imputed interest cost.

- Asset turnover measures how efficiently the assets of the business are being used.

QUICK QUIZ

1   A function or department of an organisation that is headed by a manager who has direct responsibility for its performance is called:

A   A profit centre
B   An investment centre
C   A cost centre
D   A responsibility centre

2   What is the main aim of performance measurement?

A   To obtain evidence in order to dismiss someone
B   To establish how well something or somebody is doing in relation to a planned activity
C   To collect information on costs
D   To award bonuses

3   Quantitative measures are expressed in numbers whereas qualitative measure are not. Is this true or false?

4   Place the correct letters in the boxes.

ROCE = $\boxed{} \over \boxed{}$ × 100%   Profit margin = $\boxed{} \over \boxed{}$ × 100%

A   Profit
B   Capital employed
C   Sales

BPP
LEARNING MEDIA

5   Which one of the following is the correct formula for asset turnover?

   A   Sales ÷ capital employed
   B   Net profit ÷ sales
   C   Capital employed ÷ sales
   D   Sales ÷ net profit

1   D   This is the definition of a responsibility centre.

2   B   Note that the question said 'the **main** aim'. Performance measurement may well be used to decide on bonus levels but this is not the main aim.

3   True   This is how quantitative and qualitative performance measures differ.

4 $\text{ROCE} = \dfrac{A}{B} \times 100\%$ $\text{Profit margin} = \dfrac{A}{C} \times 100\%$

5   A   Asset turnover = sales ÷ capital employed. Net profit margin = net profit ÷ sales revenue

---

Now try ...

Attempt the questions below from the **Exam Question Bank**

Number

Q14-17

part

C

Source documents and coding

Source documents and coding

This chapter is concerned with procedures and authorisation within an organisation. One important procedure, as part of the recording and accounting for all costs in a business, is that of coding. Only if the costs are correctly coded will they be accounted for correctly so we start the chapter with a section on coding in general. We will then look at the source documents required to record and code material and labour costs. We will also briefly consider the coding of sales income.

Study Guide	Intellectual level
B **Source documents and coding**	
1 **Source documents**	
(a) Describe the material control cycle (including the concept of 'free' inventory, but excluding control levels and EOQ) and the documentation necessary to order, receive, store and issue materials	K
(b) Describe the procedures required to ensure the correct authorisation, analysis and recording of direct and indirect material costs.	K
(c) Describe the procedures required to ensure the correct authorisation, coding, analysis and recording of direct and indirect labour and expenses	K
(d) Describe the procedures required to ensure the correct analysis and recording of sales	K
2 **Coding system**	
(a) Explain and illustrate the use of codes in categorising and processing transactions	S
(b) Explain and illustrate different methods of coding data (including sequential, hierarchical, block, faceted and mnemonic)	K
(c) Identify and correct errors in coding of revenue and expenses	S

Two of the technical competences for FPER that relate to paper MA1 are to verify and record purchases and payments from originating documents and also to verify and record income and receipts from originating documents. You can apply the knowledge you obtain from this chapter of the text to help to demonstrate these competences.

1 Coding

For elements of **cost** and **income** to be correctly analysed, classified and recorded they must initially be correctly coded for entry into the accounting records.

We have discussed the various types of income and expenditure, and the importance of ensuring that these items are recorded accurately so as to ensure accurate management information. We will now look at the practical aspects of ensuring this.

In many organisations, income and expenditure items are **coded** before they are included in the accounting records. Coded means giving something a **code**. What exactly is a code?

A code is a system of words, letters, figures or symbols used to represent others.

Most organisations use computers to record their accounting transactions because they have the following advantages.

- They record and retrieve information quickly and easily
- They are automatically accurate and have built in checking facilities
- They can file a large amount of information in a small space
- They are capable of sorting information in many different ways

Management information is only one part of the organisation's information system, which will be based on **transaction processing** (data processing). Other applications can be built on top of the basic information system, and spreadsheets can be used in conjunction with it for reporting purposes.

The information system will also support the needs of the **financial accounts** which, as we have explained, are subject to **external regulations.** Under UK company law, directors are responsible for ensuring that accounting records do the following.

- Show an analysis of all income and expenditure
- Show the financial position of the company at any particular moment in time
- Record all assets and liabilities of the company (including inventory where applicable)

Accounting records must be retained for future reference.

Some information must be separately identifiable in order to meet other regulatory requirements (for example **sales tax**) or specific accounting requirements (for example **donations** to political causes or charities).

Some computer systems are able to sort information from transaction processing into the correct categories for both financial and management accounting purposes. This avoids the need to enter data more than once.

When data is entered into an accounting system, each item is coded with a specific **code** from a list of accounts.

Codes can be **alphabetical** and/or **numerical**. The length and complexity of a coding system will depend upon the needs and complexity of the organisation.

For financial accounting purposes it is common to use **general ledger codes** which correspond to the different areas of the statement of financial position and income statement.

1.1 Features of a good coding system

A good coding system will possess the both of the following features:

- Items each have a unique code
- Codes are uniform in structure and length

1.2 Types of code

Here are some examples of codes.

(a) **Sequential (or progressive) codes**

Numbers are given to items in ordinary numerical sequence, so that there is no obvious connection between an item and its code. For example:

000042	4cm nails
000043	Office stapler
000044	Hand wrench

(b) **Block (or group classification) codes**

These are an improvement on simple sequences codes, in that a digit (often the first one) indicates the classification of an item. For example:

4NNNNN	Nails
5NNNNN	Screws
6NNNNN	Bolts

(Note. 'N' stands for another digit; 'NNNNN' indicates there are five further digits in the code.)

(c) **Faceted codes**

These are a refinement of block codes, in that each digit of the code gives information about an item. For example:

(i)	The first digit:	1	Nails
		2	Screws
		3	Bolts
			etc...
(ii)	The second digit:	1	Steel
		2	Brass
		3	Copper
			etc...
(iii)	The third digit:	1	50mm
		2	60mm
		3	75mm
			etc...

A 60mm steel screw would have a code of 212.

(d) **Mnemonic codes**

Meaning of mnemonic is a learning technique to aid the memory. Under this type of coding the code means something, it may be an abbreviation of the object being coded. A well-known example of this type of code is the three letter coding used for airports. For example:

LAX	Los Angeles	SIN	Singapore
CAI	Cairo	LHR	London Heathrow

(e) **Hierarchical codes**

This is a type of faceted code where each digit represents a classification, and each digit further to the right represents a smaller subset than those to the left. For example:

3	=	Screws	32	=	Round headed screws
31	=	Flat headed screws	322	=	Steel (round headed) screws and so on

A coding system does not have to be structured entirely on any one of the above systems. It can mix the various features according to the items which need to be coded.

1.3 Example: numeric codes

Type of account	Code range
Non-current asset	1000 – 1999
Current asset	2000 – 2999
Current liability	3000 – 3999
Revenue	4000 – 4999
Long-term liability	5000 – 5999
Capital	6000 – 6999
Within each section, the codes can be broken down into smaller sections:	
Fixtures and fittings	1000 – 1099
Land and buildings	1100 – 1199
Plant and machinery	1200 – 1299
Motor vehicles	1300 – 1399
and so on. Gaps between the numbers used give scope for breaking the categories down further (for example there could be a separate account for each building) and for adding new categories if necessary.	

This is an example of a block coding system.

Some types of account require **more detail**. For example, each customer needs a separate account, although in the statement of financial position the total 'receivables' will be shown. Suppliers (payables) also need an account each and a total for the statement of financial position.

Alphabetical codes, using part of the company or person's name, are common but, because names can be duplicated, an additional code may be necessary.

1.4 Example: alphabetical codes

Customer	Code
J Miller Ltd	MIL 010
M Miller	MIL 015
A Milton	MIL 025

Some computer systems save time for operators by offering a **'menu'** of accounts when part of the name is typed in.

Some codes can help users to **recognise the items** they describe. For example, a shoe shop could code their inventory by type of shoe, colour, size, style and male or female. A pair of red women's sandals, size 5, style 19 could then become:

Shoe type	Colour	Size	Style	Male/Female
SA	R	5	19	F
BO	B	8	11	M

and the second item would be men's brown boots, size 8, style 11.

We have already stressed the importance of coding costs and revenues correctly for management information (and financial accounting) purposes. The key to achieving this in any organisation is an **understanding** of the coding list and any related guidance in the policy manual.

We have already explained that correct coding requires you to have a good understanding of the **organisation** as well as the **coding list**. You need to know the following.

- The main activities of the organisation
- The main sources of income
- The main items of expenditure
- Details of the organisational structure

In some cases, you may need to ask for **help from other people** in order to code transactions correctly.

An **organisation chart** can help to make sense of the coding structure. Here is a simple one for an accounting firm divided into departments.

Partners

Audit   Taxation   Corporate finance   General administration

Coding errors can happen in a variety of ways, such as errors in keying in the original data and applying the wrong code (because either the transaction or the coding structure have not been understood).

When management information is produced, large errors are often obvious. For example a doubling of sales revenue in one month is rather unlikely unless there has been a sales campaign in that month. It is more likely that a decimal point has been misplaced in a figure or another form of income has been incorrectly coded to sales revenue.

1.5 The advantages of a coding system

(a)   A code is usually **briefer** than a description, thereby saving clerical time in a manual system and storage space in a computerised system.

(b)   A code is **more precise** than a description and therefore **reduces ambiguity**.

(c)   Coding **facilitates data processing**.

1.6 Example: coding problems

Motor expenses for the three cars belonging to J Miller & Son are all coded to a single expense account and are usually around $1,200 a month. In June the total is almost $15,000. Mr Miller (the firm's owner) asks you to look into the reasons why. You decide to get a print-out of the motor expenses account for June. It looks like this.

Code M057	Motor expenses	$
3.6.X1	Petrol	22.70
5.6.X1	Petrol	18.50
7.6.X1	Repairs to S 657 PNO	235.70
8.6.X1	Petrol	22.00
10.6.X1	Petrol	18.00
12.6.X1	Tyres for R 393 FGH	140.00
15.6.X1	Petrol	24.50
18.6.X1	Petrol	230.00
22.6.X1	Purchase of T 191 PJF	12,950.00
25.6.X1	Petrol	21.50
29.6.X1	Road tax R 393 FGH	155.00
30.6.X1	Depreciation charge S 657 PNO	290.00
30.6.X1	Depreciation charge R 393 FGH	250.00
30.6.X1	Depreciation charge T 191 PJF	310.00

Total for the month of June $14,711.55

(a)   There are two problems which should be fairly obvious:

18/6 $230 seems an unlikely petrol bill
22/6 The purchase of a car has been coded to expenses instead of non-current assets

There are also bills for repairs, tyres and road tax all in one month which is probably not typical. Having spotted these anomalies, you should now act by investigating them, correcting any errors.

(b)   (i)   The petrol receipt should be checked and the entry corrected.

(ii)   The entry for the purchase of the car should be corrected, ie removed from the expense account and re-entered under the appropriate non-current asset code. Any items of expenditure on long-term non-current assets which a company intends to retain for its own use are capital items, not expense items.

(iii)   No action is needed for the other motor expenses which are correctly coded.

2 Documents for buying and selling

 When goods are required by a business the person requiring the goods must normally complete a **purchase requisition** which must be authorised by an appropriate manager.

The documents involved in buying and selling are prime sources of cost and revenue information. Their number and complexity will depend on the type and size of both the organisation and the purchase. In this section we will look at the typical administrative procedure for the purchase of 25 desks by Abacus Ltd, a retailer of office furniture.

2.1 Purchase requisition

A **purchase requisition** is prepared by the person who identifies a need for the goods to be bought, such as the storekeeper, and then it must be countersigned (**authorised**) by the supervisor or departmental head who is responsible for the department's budget.

The purchase requisition is then passed to the **purchasing department** who will decide on the most appropriate supplier.

The requisition is passed to the buyer (purchasing department) who will find out about suppliers, prices and other details relating to the items that have been requisitioned. If Abacus Ltd has a regular supplier for the goods, then the purchase requisition may show their catalogue number at this stage. Otherwise, it will be filled in later, along with the order number and supplier's name.

PURCHASE REQUISITION				
			Number: 62	
			Date: 21.02.20X1	
Quantity	Description	Suppliers Catalogue No	Purchase Order No	Supplier
25	Executive desks	BX 320	489	Desks'n'us

Signed: .....John Marshall......   Approved: .....*Jim Davey*.....

Authorised: ....*Mary Great*.......

If an appropriate supplier is not already used by the buying department then they may send out a **letter of enquiry** to several suppliers in order to find out a price, delivery date, delivery charges, discounts available, and terms of payment, for twenty five desks.

2.2 Quotation / estimate

The **supplier** may then provide a **quotation** or an **estimate** which may include either trade or cash discounts.

The different suppliers might respond with a catalogue and a price list (for standard goods), a **quotation** (for non-standard goods) or a letter of reply. For services such as building work or repairs, an **estimate** will usually be provided.

The buyer must select an appropriate supplier based on the information received. If **discounts** are offered they may be of two types.

(a) A **trade discount** is given for large orders or special customers and will be shown as a deduction on the invoice.

(b) A **cash discount** is usually given for prompt payment within a stated period (for example payment within 7 days gives a 3% discount). It cannot be shown as a deduction until payment has been made.

If **sales tax** is payable, discounts are deducted from the cost of the goods before the **sales tax** is calculated and added to the invoice.

2.3 Purchase order

The purchasing department will then send a **purchase order** to the supplier.

Once a supplier has been selected, the buyer will prepare a **purchase order** to ask for the goods to be supplied. Copies of the order are sent to the following.

- The **supplier** – to ask for the goods.
- The **accounts department** – for checking against the invoice when it arrives.
- The **stores section** – for updating the inventory records.
- The **goods received** section – so that they expect the goods.

The buyer should also retain a copy on file.

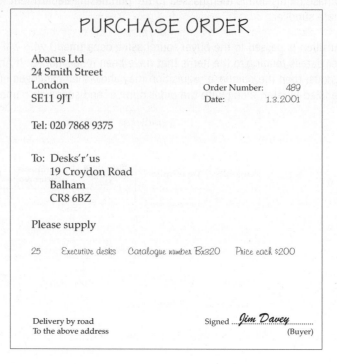

2.4 Delivery note

> The goods will be sent, normally accompanied by a **delivery note**, and when received by the business a **goods received note** will be completed.

The supplier will usually send an **advice note** to say when the goods will be delivered and, if delivering the goods with its own transport, a **delivery note** will be sent with the driver for the customer to sign.

The customer's copy of the delivery note confirms that the goods have been delivered. Another copy of the delivery note is taken by the driver and given to the supplier to confirm that the customer has received the goods. If the supplier does not use its own transport, a **consignment note** will provide the same evidence as the advice note.

2.5 Goods received note

When the desks arrive at the goods received section at Abacus Ltd, a **goods received note** is prepared and sent to other departments so that they know that the goods have arrived. An example of a goods received note is shown here.

GOODS RECEIVED NOTE WAREHOUSE COPY

NO 5565

DATE: _____ TIME: _____

OUR ORDER NO: --- WAREHOUSE A

SUPPLIER AND SUPPLIER'S ADVICE NOTE NO: ----------------------------------

QUANTITY	CAT NO	DESCRIPTION

RECEIVED IN GOOD CONDITION: (INITIALS)

Copies of the goods received note are sent to the following.

- The **accounts department** – to check against the invoice
- The **stores section** – for updating inventory records
- The **buyer** – to confirm that the goods ordered have arrived
- The **goods received section** will keep a record on file

2.6 Purchase invoice

Finally, a **purchase invoice** will be received by the business from the supplier detailing the amount that is due to be paid – the net of sales tax amount of the invoice must be coded to ensure that it is correctly recorded in the accounting records as must the sales tax.

The **supplier's sales department** will send the customer an **invoice** detailing the amount that they need to pay for the desks.

INVOICE

From: Desks'r'us
     19 Croydon Road
     Balham
     CR8 6BZ

Number:	1340
Date/tax point:	10.3.20X1
Sales tax reg number	774 5513 23

Tel: **020 8775 0679**

To: **Abacus Ltd**
      24 Smith Street
      London
      SE11 9JT

Your order number: 489

Quantity	Description	Price	$
25	Executive desks Catalogue number BX 320	$200 each	5,000.00
		VAT AT 17.5%	875.00
		Total due	5,875.00

Terms: Payment in 30 days

Delivered on 9.3.20X1

The customer (Abacus Ltd) should check the sales invoice carefully. In particular, they should check the following.

(a) That the goods have been delivered and are in satisfactory condition (check goods received note).
(b) That the price and terms are as agreed (look at the purchase order).
(c) That the calculations on the invoice are correct (including **sales tax**).

If the sales invoice is correct, it is passed for entry to the payables ledger. Once it is entered into the payables ledger it is recorded as a purchase and the invoice is authorised for payment according to agreed settlement terms. If the sales invoice is thought to be incorrect, the supplier is notified of the discrepancies.

If the supplier has made any errors on the sales invoice, he will usually issue a credit note (which is effectively the reverse of an invoice). A credit note may be issued for the whole of the invoice, in order to enable both companies to remove it from their books and replace it with a correct invoice.

If a customer has been overcharged, a **credit note** may be issued to reduce the original sales invoice to its correct value.

Not all organisations will go through these steps in their buying and selling procedures but they must all check that goods and services purchased are properly ordered, received and paid for and that sales revenue is properly recorded. Many **computerised accounting systems** will carry out some of these checks automatically.

The procedures we have described in this section can be summarised as follows.

		CUSTOMER	**SUPPLIER**
Step 1		Purchase requisition to tell buyer what is required	
Step 2		Enquiry to suppliers	⟶
Step 3		⟵	Catalogue, quotation, letter of reply
Step 4		Select supplier and send purchase order	⟶
Step 5		⟵	Advice note of delivery date
Step 6		⟵	Delivery or consignment note to detail goods delivered and signature on delivery
Step 7		**Goods received note (to other departments)**	
Step 8		⟵	Invoice to tell the customer what to pay
Step 9		Check invoice and make payment	

EXAM FOCUS POINT

The documents involved in the purchasing/selling cycle are important and an exam question could ask you to identify a particular document.

2.7 Coding purchases

Imagine that you work for a firm of gardeners and are sitting at your computer looking at a **purchase invoice** for fertiliser. Firstly you must check this invoice, secondly, you must enter it into the accounting system, using the principles of double entry. The purchase invoice will create an **account payable** so you need to know how suppliers are coded. It will also be a cost to the firm, but under which category should it be analysed?

Don't forget that the cost to the company will be the **net** cost and **sales tax** will be coded to the **sales tax account** to be set off against **tax on sales**. Coding the net cost will depend on the firm's **policy** for dealing with this type of supply. If the jobs undertaken are mostly large and fertiliser is ordered for particular customers then it will probably be coded so that it can be charged to that **particular job** (ie treated as a direct cost). If, on the other hand it is delivered to the firm in bulk and used as needed it may well be treated as an **overhead** or indirect cost.

Telephone bills are obviously an overhead cost to the business. Depending on the coding structure and the organisational structure, different telephone lines may be charged to different parts of the business. The individual codes give information for different departments, while the code range for telephone expenses will give a total telephone cost for the organisation.

In the same way, details of **motor expenses** may be dealt with in one expense account with different accounts for different types of cost.

- Insurance
- Road fund licence
- Petrol
- Repairs and maintenance

Alternatively details of motor expenses may be analysed by individual vehicles (perhaps using the registration number in the code). In companies with many vehicles, the fleet manager may well want information on costs per vehicle (or type of vehicle) but in small organisations with few vehicles, this may not be necessary.

QUESTION

Coding

Extract from code list
Telephone expenses 5500-5599
5510 General administration
5530 Sales and marketing
5570 Manufacturing

Telephone numbers and locations
020 7668 9923 Managing director
020 7668 9871 Marketing manager
020 7668 9398 Factory floor
020 7668 9879 Accounts office
0879 6534 Salesperson's mobile

Which telephone lines would you charge to code 5510?

A Sales persons mobile and the marketing manager
B Managing director and accounts office
C Factory floor and accounts office
D Managing director and marketing manager

ANSWER

Answer B

The marketing manager's line and the salesperson's mobile would be classed as sales and marketing. The factory floor line would be given a manufacturing code.

QUESTION

Sales coding

Here is a summary of the net value of sales invoices for the month of September and an extract from the coding list of a company that sells cosmetics worldwide. What is the net sales value analysed to code R140 (Europe)?

Invoice No	Net sales value $	Country
8730	10,360.00	Canada
8731	12,750.73	England
8732	5,640.39	Spain
8733	15,530.10	Northern Ireland
8734	3,765.75	South Africa
8735	8,970.22	Kenya
8736	11,820.45	Italy
8737	7,640.00	France
8738	9,560.60	Australia
8739	16,750.85	Germany

Sales revenue codes: R100 – R199

R110	Area 1	UK
R120	Area 2	North America
R130	Area 3	South America
R140	Area 4	Europe
R150	Area 5	Africa
R160	Area 6	Australia

Helping hand. If you are not sure whether the countries listed are in a particular area of the world – find yourself an atlas and look them up.

A $25,100.84
B $41,851.69
C $54,602.42
D $70,132.52

ANSWER

Answer B

The invoices would be coded as shown below.

Invoice no	Net sales value $	Country	Code
8730	10,360.00	Canada	R120
8731	12,750.73	England	R110
8732	5,640.39	Spain	R140
8733	15,530.10	Northern Ireland	R110
8734	3,765.75	South Africa	R150
8735	8,970.22	Kenya	R150
8736	11,820.45	Italy	R140
8737	7,640.00	France	R140
8738	9,560.60	Australia	R160
8739	16,750.85	Germany	R140

QUESTION   Accounting documents

You work for the accounts department of Abacus Ltd and have received invoice number 1340 from Desks'r'us (see previous paragraphs) for checking. Which documents will you need to check the details of the invoice to?

A   Purchase order and goods received note
B   Goods received note and purchase requisition
C   Delivery note and purchase requisition
D   Advice note and despatch note

ANSWER

Answer A

QUESTION   Goods received notes

The goods received note relating to invoice 1340 is shown below.

GOODS RECEIVED NOTE

NUMBER 547

SUPPLIER: Desks'r'us
19 Croydon Road
Balham
CR8 6BZ

Date received: 9.3.2001

Quantity	Description	Order number
25	Executive desks	489

Carrier	Received by	Checked by	Location
Desks'r'us	M Smith	B Martin	Bay 5

Condition of goods: 1 desktop badly scratched

Distribution:
accounts   ✓
stock control
buyer

Abacus Ltd should now

A   Pay the invoice in full on the due date and request a refund
B   Pay the invoice in full on the due date and request a credit note
C   Wait for a replacement desk before any payment is made
D   Pay the net amount of the invoice and credit note, when received

ANSWER

Answer D

This is the best course of action. A replacement desk may not be available immediately, so C is incorrect. A is inappropriate as businesses tend to cancel errors on invoices by means of a credit note rather than a refund. B would be pointless as a refund would be required.

3 Documents for recording materials

> The physical quantity of each line of inventory will often be recorded on a **bin card** in the stores department and a similar document known as the **stores ledger account** will be kept by the accounts department which also includes inventory values.

An important item purchased by a manufacturing business is materials. These are generally kept in a warehouse or inventory room, which is usually referred to as the stores department. The storekeeper will keep an eye on the inventory of raw materials, and raise a purchase requisition when the stores run low.

Most businesses will keep track of the quantities of materials that they have in inventories held by maintaining an inventory record for each type of material held. This will be updated each time material is received into, or issued from, stores, and a new balance of inventories held can be calculated. This is known as a **perpetual inventory system**, and it can be manual or computerised. There are two types of inventory record which may be kept, and sometimes they will both be used. These are **bin cards** and **stores ledger accounts**.

3.1 Bin cards

These are manual records that are written up and kept in the stores department. An example is shown here.

BIN CARD
Description: reels (30 cm diameter)   Bin No. 232
Code No: R4089
Stock units: units

Receipts			Issues			Balance
Date	Reference	Quantity	Date	Reference	Quantity	Quantity
20X3						
1 May						40
5 May	GRN 0067	200				240
			7 May	MR 296	30	210
			10 May	MR 304	20	190
			11 May	MR 309	50	140
13 May	MRN 127	10				150

The information on the bin card gives all the details the storekeeper needs to know.

(a)   Description: of the inventory item for which this is a record.

(b)   Inventory code: for unambiguous identification and for ease of updating computerised inventory records, a code is essential.

(c)   Inventory units: the units in which the material is measured e.g. metres, kilograms, boxes etc.

(d)   Bin number: the location of the items in the store.

(e)   Issues to production: date, quantity and a reference to the materials requisition (MR), the document which the production department use to request material from stores.

(f)   Receipts: date, quantity and details of the GRN for goods delivered to the business or materials returned note (MRN) for goods returned to inventory when they have not been used in production.

(g)   Balance: the quantity of inventory on hand after each inventory movement.

3.2 Stores ledger accounts

The stores ledger accounts are very similar to bin cards. They carry all the information that a bin card does, and they are updated from the same sources: GRNs, MRs and MRNs. But there are two important differences.

1. Cost details are recorded in the stores ledger account, so that the unit cost and total cost of each issue and receipt is shown. The balance of inventory after each inventory movement is also valued. The value is recorded as these accounts form part of the costing bookkeeping records.

2. The stores ledger accounts are written up and kept in the costing department, or in a stores office separate from the stores by a clerk experienced in costing bookkeeping.

Stores ledger accounts are very often computerised, and this would enable the amount of **free inventory** to be monitored.

At any point in time the amount of **free inventory** can be calculated as inventory on hand plus inventory on order less any inventory that has been scheduled for use.

Free inventory is inventory on hand + inventory on order − inventory that has been scheduled for use.

3.2.1 Example: Free inventory

Suppose that a company currently has a stock of 10,000 kgs of material X. It has ordered another 2,500 kgs and 5,000 kgs have been committed for future use. The free inventory of material X is

$10,000 + 2,500 - 5,000 = 7,500$ kgs

Sometimes, inventory that is physically present in the stores, or even inventory that has not been received into stores yet, will already be allocated to a job or a department. Of course, it is helpful to take this into account when monitoring inventory levels, as only free inventory is free to be issued to other departments or jobs.

Because bin cards and stores ledger accounts are independent, they can be used as a control to check the accuracy of the records. Theoretically, the quantities of inventory recorded should be the same; if they are not, this would have to be investigated and the appropriate adjustment made.

3.3 Materials requisitions

A materials requisition will be completed when materials are needed from stores by the production department. An official from production will sign the form to authorise it, and stores will issue the materials when the form is given to them. It is then used as a source document for:

(a) Updating the bin card in stores;
(b) Updating the stores ledger account in the costing department; and
(c) Charging the job, overhead or department that is using the materials.

The originating department will fill in the requisition as shown below.

MATERIALS REQUISITION				
Material required for: **Job 1478** (job)				No 309
Department: **Assembly**				Date **11 May 20X4**
Quantity	Description	Code No	Price per unit	$
50	30 cm diam reels	R4089		
Foreman: **D Jameson**				

The price details and value will be filled in by the cost department prior to updating the stores ledger accounts and charging the relevant job/overhead/department.

A materials returned note will accompany any unused material back to stores. This will contain the same details as the materials requisition, and will be used as the source document to update the same records. This time, though, the material will be a receipt into inventory and a deduction from the job originally charged with the material issued.

EXAM FOCUS POINT

You could be given numerical information about inventory and asked to calculate free inventory.

The documents considered in the sections 3 and 4 of this chapter can be combined into a flowchart showing the material control cycle as follows:

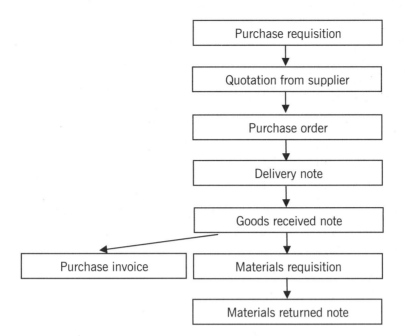

4 Documents for labour costs

Hourly paid workers are generally paid a **flat rate per hour** with a premium for overtime hours.

The hours worked are often recorded on **clock cards**, **job cards** or **timesheets**.

Labour costs are an important element of **total costs**. Labour costs include **wages** (usually weekly) and salaries (usually monthly) paid to employees, and other payments such as agency workers or contractors who supply labour.

Records showing how each individual's pay has been calculated are known as **payslips**. Records of total labour costs paid to employees are known as the **payroll.**

4.1 Recording of employee time and time sheets

The bare minimum record of employees' time is a simple **attendance record** showing days absent because of holiday, sickness or other reason.

Some workers earn a **flat rate** per hour or week or month, while others may have a 'normal' **hourly rate** and special **overtime rates**. Workers who are paid hourly often record their hours by using a **clock card** to show the times at which they arrived and left work each day. An example is shown below.

No				Ending	
Name					
	HOURS	RATE	AMOUNT	DEDUCTIONS	
Basic				Income Tax	
O/T				Benefits	
Others				Other	
Total				Total	
Less: deductions					
Net due					

		Time	Day	Basic time	Overtime
		0910	M		
		1700	M		
		0803	T		
		1700	T		
		0840	W		
		1740	W		
		0902	Th		
		1648	Th		
		0848	F		
		1622	F		

Signature . . . .

Where **routine, repetitive** work is carried out it might not be practical to record the precise details. There are several possible ways in which employee time can be recorded.

(a) **Daily timesheets**. A timesheet is filled in by the employee as a record of how their time has been spent. The total time on the timesheet should correspond with time shown on the attendance record.

(b) **Weekly timesheets**. These are similar to daily timesheets but are passed to the cost office at the end of the week. An example of a weekly timesheet is shown below.

Time Sheet No. _____							
Employee Name _____			Clock Code _____			Dept _____	
Date _____			Week No. _____				
Job No.	Start Time	Finish Time	Qty	Checker	Hrs	Rate	Extension

Timesheets may be used for hourly paid and salaried staff. The purposes of timesheets are as follows.

(a)   Timesheets provide management with information (eg product costs) for further analysis.

(b)   Timesheet information may provide a basis for billing for services provided (eg service firms where clients are billed based on the number of hours work done).

(c)   Timesheets are used to record hours spent and so support claims for or authorise overtime payments.

An example of a timesheet (as used in the service sector) is shown as follows.

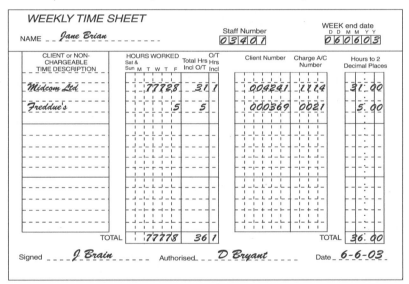

As can be seen from the above timesheet, it is signed by the employee and has been authorised by a manager or supervisor. The authorisation is a form of control to ensure that the time charged is accurate and then this forms a basis for the coding of labour costs. Although this is an example of a paper timesheet, signatures and authorisations can be incorporated into a computer timesheet system.

4.2 Job cards

Job cards can be prepared for each job or batch. When an employee works on a job he or she records on the job card the time spent on that job. Job cards are therefore likely to contain entries relating to numerous employees. On completion of the job it will contain a full record of the times and quantities involved in the job or batch. A typical job card is shown as follows.

JOB CARD

Department _ _ _ _ _ _ _ _ _ _ _ _ _ _ _	Job no _ _ _ _ _ _ _ _ _ _ _ _ _ _ _ _ _ _ _
Date _ _ _ _ _ _ _ _ _ _ _ _ _ _ _	Operation no _ _ _ _ _ _ _ _ _ _ _ _ _ _ _ _

Time allowance _ _ _ _ _ _ _ _ _ _ _ _ _ _	Time started _ _ _ _ _ _ _ _ _ _ _ _ _ _ _
	Time finished _ _ _ _ _ _ _ _ _ _ _ _ _ _
	Hours on the job _ _ _ _ _ _ _ _ _ _ _ _

Description of job	Hours	Rate	Cost

Employee no_ _ _ _ _ _ _ _ _ _ _ _ _ _ _	Certified by _ _ _ _ _ _ _ _ _ _ _ _ _ _
Signature _ _ _ _ _ _ _ _ _ _ _ _ _ _ _	

A job card will be given to the employee, showing the work to be done and the expected time it should take. The employee will record the time started and time finished for each job. Breaks for tea and lunch may be noted on the card, as standard times, by the production planning department. The hours actually taken and the cost of those hours will be calculated by the accounting department.

Management will be most interested to know how much individual cost and profit centres spent on wages in a particular period. It is important therefore that the total wages for individual employees are collected to the correct cost centres.

If employees work on different jobs or products that span more than one cost centre, they will need to keep a record of the time spent on each job or product. This can be done by recording wages information on a jobcard such as the one shown below.

JOB CARD

Department	*Machining hours*	Job No	*M 431*
		Operation no	*6*

Time allowance	*2 hours*	Time started	*9.30*
		Time finished	*11.15*
		Hours on job	*1³/₄*

Description of job	Hours	Rate	Cost
File raw edges	*1³/₄*	*$4*	*$7*

Employee no	*129*	Authorised by	*J Dowson*
Signature	*P Potter*		

BPP LEARNING MEDIA

As with the timesheet, the jobcard is signed by the employee and authorised by a manager. Jobcards have the same purposes and uses as timesheets.

- Ensuring that time recorded is accurate
- Authorisation of overtime payments
- Allow analysis of labour hours
- Assist coding of labour costs

4.3 Coding labour

A production foreman running two production departments of equal size may have his labour cost shared 50 : 50 between them.

A computer programmer serving various departments within the organisation as required may have his labour cost shared by reference to the time spent in each department.

In many **service organisations**, where labour is a very important part of total costs, **charges** to clients will be based upon the hours worked for them. For example, lawyers, accountants and garage mechanics will keep timesheets to show the hours of work done for individual clients and the charge made to the client will have to cover this, plus an amount for overheads.

Therefore it is important to code labour correctly, so that labour time is charged to the correct cost object.

4.3.1 Example: Coding of labour costs

A company has a production department which produces two products the Morgan and the Smith. The direct labour costs of the manufacturing staff for the last week were as follows.

Product	Direct labour hours worked	Labour rate per hour $	Total direct labour cost $
Morgan	185	6.5	1,202.50
Smith	175	6.5	1,137.50

The company has the following coding structure

5510 General administration
5530 Sales and marketing
5570 Manufacturing
10 Morgan
20 Smith

The company codes by department first, then by product.

Therefore $1,202.50 should be charged to code 557010.

$1,137.50 should be charged to code 557020.

5 Sales income

The sales income of the business may be analysed in a number of different ways depending upon the needs of management – whatever analysis is required each sales invoice must be carefully coded.

In the next two chapters we will see how the cost accountant will analyse, code and record the three elements of cost – materials, labour and overheads. The cost accountant will also need to ensure that sales income is also correctly analysed, coded and accounted for.

The sales of a business may be analysed in a number of different ways for management accounting purposes depending upon the needs of management. The possible ways of analysing sales income include by:

- Product
- Geographical region
- Department
- Division

Whatever analysis is required by management each sales invoice must be coded to ensure that the sales income is correctly recorded. As with expenses it is the net amount of the invoice that must be coded as the sales tax will be recorded separately in the sales tax control account. The sales figure used should also be net of any trade discount.

When the sales invoices have been coded the double entry will be:

DEBIT   Receivables or bank
CREDIT   Sales

There may be a number of different sales accounts according to the analysis required for example a sales account for each product or for each geographical region.

CHAPTER ROUNDUP

⤷ For elements of **cost** and **income** to be correctly analysed, classified and recorded they must initially be correctly coded for entry into the accounting records.

⤷ When goods are required by a business the person requiring the goods must normally complete a **purchase requisition** which must be authorised by an appropriate manager.

⤷ The purchase requisition is then passed to the **purchasing department** who will decide on the most appropriate supplier.

⤷ The **supplier** may then provide a **quotation** or an **estimate** which may include either trade or cash discounts.

⤷ The purchasing department will then send a **purchase order** to the supplier.

⤷ The goods will be sent, normally accompanied by a **delivery note**, and when received by the business a **goods received note** will be completed.

⤷ Finally, a **purchase invoice** will be received by the business from the supplier detailing the amount that is due to be paid – the net of sales tax amount of the invoice must be coded to ensure that it is correctly recorded in the accounting records as must the sales tax.

⤷ The physical quantity of each line of inventory will often be recorded on a **bin card** in the stores department and a similar document known as the **stores ledger account** will be kept by the accounts department which also includes inventory values.

⤷ At any point in time the amount of **free inventory** can be calculated as inventory on hand plus inventory on order less any inventory that has been scheduled for use.

⤷ Hourly paid workers are generally paid a **flat rate per hour** with a premium for overtime hours.

⤷ The hours worked are often recorded on **clock cards, job cards** or **timesheets**.

⤷ The sales income of the business may be analysed in a number of different ways depending upon the needs of management – whatever analysis is required each sales invoice must be carefully coded.

QUICK QUIZ

1   When materials are received by a business what is the internal document completed by the receiving department?

   A   Purchase requisition
   B   Goods received note
   C   Invoice
   D   Despatch note

2   Statement 1. A cash discount is given for large orders or special customers and will be shown as a deduction on the invoice.

   Statement 2. A trade discount is usually given for prompt payment within a stated period. It cannot be shown as a deduction until payment has been made.

   A   Both statements are false
   B   Both statements are true
   C   Statement 1 is true and statement 2 is false
   D   Statement 1 is false and statement 2 is true

3   The sales tax inclusive amount (rather than the net amount) should be coded on a purchase invoice. Is this true or false?

4   Which type of coding system uses an aid to memory in its code?

5   Which document is filled in by a company when goods have been delivered to them?

ANSWERS TO QUICK QUIZ

1   B   Goods received note. This is prepared when the goods arrive and it is sent to other departments so that they know that the goods have arrived.

2   A   They are both false because statement 1 describes a trade discount not a cash discount. Statement 2 describes a cash discount, not a trade discount.

3   False   It is the net amount which should be coded on a purchase invoice.

4   Mnemonic

5   A goods received note is filled in by a company when goods have been received into inventory. A delivery note will be supplied by the delivery company.

Now try ...

Attempt the questions below from the **Exam Question Bank**

Number

Q18-21

part

D

Cost accounting

CHAPTER

06

In this chapter we cover the two elements of business costs, material and labour.

Accounting for material and labour costs

1 Types of materials

Materials can be **classified** according to the substances that make them up, how they are measured, or their physical properties.

1.1 Classifying materials

There are a number of different ways in which materials can be classified. The three main ways of classifying materials are as follows.

- They can be classified according to the **substances that make them up**
- They can be classified according to **how they are measured**
- They can be classified according to their **physical properties**

Materials may be made of one or more substances. For example, when classifying materials according to the substances that make them up, they may be classified as either **wood, plastic, metal, wool** and so on. Many items may be made up of a **combination of substances.**

You may also classify materials according to how they are measured. Accounting text books could make it easy for you to believe that all materials come by the **litre, metre** or **kilogram.** In practice however, you will find that materials really come in **bags, packets** or **by the thousand.**

Finally, materials may also be classified by one or more of their physical properties. The same basic piece of material may be distinguished by one or more of the following features.

- Colour
- Shape
- Fire resistance
- Water resistance
- Abrasiveness
- Flexibility
- Quality

1.2 Raw materials

Raw materials are goods purchased for incorporation into products for sale.

Raw materials is a term which you are likely to come across often, both in your studies and your workplace. But what are raw materials?

Examples of raw materials are as follows.

- Clay for making terracotta garden pots
- Timber for making dining room tables
- Paper for making books

QUESTION

Raw materials

Without getting too technical, what are the main raw materials used in the manufacture of the following items?

(a) A car
(b) A box of breakfast cereal
(c) A house (just the basic structure)
(d) Your own organisation's products

ANSWER

(a) Metal, rubber, plastic, glass, fabric, oil, paint, glue

(b) Cereals, plastic, cardboard, glue. You might have included sugar and preservatives and so on, depending upon what you eat for breakfast

(c) Sand, gravel, cement, bricks, plaster, wood, metal, plastic, glass, slate

(d) You will have to mark your own answer. If you work for a service organisation like a firm of accountants, you could view the paper (and binding) of sets of accounts sent out to clients as raw materials, although in practice such materials are likely to be regarded as indirect costs

1.3 Work in progress

Work in progress is a term used to represent an intermediate stage between the manufacturer purchasing the materials that go to make up the finished product and the finished product.

Work in progress is another term which you are likely to come across often, and valuing work in progress is one of the most difficult tasks in costing.

Work in progress means that some work has been done on the materials purchased as part of the process of producing the finished product, but **the production process is not complete.** Examples of work in progress are as follows.

(a) Terracotta pots which have been shaped, but which have not been fired, and are therefore unfinished.

(b) Dining room tables which have been assembled, but have not been polished, and are therefore not ready for sale.

(c) Paper which has been used to print books, but which has not yet been bound. The books are therefore not yet assembled, and not yet ready for sale.

1.4 Finished goods

A **finished good** is a product ready for sale or despatch.

Did you notice how all of the examples of work in progress were items which were not ready for sale? It therefore follows that examples of finished goods are as follows.

- Terracotta pots ready for sale or despatch
- Dining room tables ready for sale or despatch
- Books ready for sale or despatch

The examples in the previous paragraph show terracotta pots which have now been fired, dining room tables which have now been polished, and books which have now been bound. These final processes have transformed our **work in progress** into **finished goods.**

QUESTION
Materials

(a) Distinguish between raw materials, work in progress and finished goods.
(b) Give three examples of indirect materials costs.

ANSWER

(a) Raw materials are goods purchased for incorporation into products for sale, but not yet issued to production. Work in progress is the name given to the materials while they are in the course of being converted to the final product. Finished goods are the end products when they are ready to be sold.

(b) Some examples of indirect materials costs are as follows.

   (i) Oil for machine maintenance

   (ii) Cleaning fluids and substances

   (iii) Rags, dusters and the like

   (iv) Glue if used in small quantities

   (v) Secondary packaging, for example the sort of boxes you can pick up at the check-out in supermarkets

2 Ordering inventory

When the store keeper places an order for materials the **amount** that will be **ordered** will be dependent upon the sales and / or manufacturing plans for the immediate future.

As we have seen, from time to time the stores manager will decide that a requisition needs to be placed. The manager will also have to determine how many units of the item of inventory are needed. In some organisations a set amount will be required each time a requisition is placed. In other organisations the amount will be determined by the future plans for sales and production.

Make sure that you learn this formula.

Units produced = units sold + units in closing inventory – units in opening inventory.

The business must produce enough to cover its sales volume and to leave enough in closing inventory, but it gets a 'head start' from opening inventory. This is why opening inventory is deducted.

You can apply this principle to other areas. For example

Materials purchases = materials usage + closing inventory material – opening inventory material

2.1 Example: order amounts – finished goods

A business buys Deltas, puts them through a finishing process and then sells them. At the beginning of June the stores manager realises that there are only 35 Deltas in inventory and wants to know how many he will need to order in each of the next three months. He ascertains that planned sales for the next three months and planned closing inventories of Deltas in units are as follows:

	June	*July*	*August*
Planned sales	120	150	130
Closing inventories	60	70	50

How many Deltas must he order in each month?

Solution

Processing

	June Units	*July* Units	*August* Units
Sales quantity	120	150	130
Closing inventories	60	70	50
	180	220	180
Less opening inventories	35	60	70
Number of Deltas to order	**145**	**160**	**110**

The opening inventory units are deducted as we already have these in inventory and therefore do not need to buy them. The closing inventory however is added as we want to have these left over at the end of each period.

If raw materials that are used in production are being replenished then similar calculations are required but this will be based upon the production plans for the period under consideration.

2.2 Example: order amounts – raw materials

XYZ company produces three products X, Y and Z. For the coming accounting period the following sales, usage and inventories are planned.

Sales

Product X	2,000 at $100 each
Product Y	4,000 at $130 each
Product Z	3,000 at $150 each

Usage of raw material (units of material per unit of product)

	RM11	*RM22*	*RM33*
Product X	5	2	–
Product Y	3	2	2
Product Z	2	1	3
Cost per unit of material	$5	$3	$4

Finished inventories

	Product X	*Product Y*	*Product Z*
Opening	500	800	700
Closing	600	1,000	800

Raw materials inventory

	RM11	*RM22*	*RM33*
Opening	21,000	10,000	16,000
Closing	18,000	9,000	12,000

Required

Calculate the raw materials to be purchased for each of the products

Production

	Product X Units	Product Y Units	Product Z Units
Sales quantity	2,000	4,000	3,000
Closing inventories	600	1,000	800
	2,600	5,000	3,800
Less opening inventories	500	800	700
Production	**2,100**	**4,200**	**3,100**

Raw material usage

	Production Units	RM11 Units	RM22 Units	RM33 Units
Product X	2,100	10,500	4,200	–
Product Y	4,200	12,600	8,400	8,400
Product Z	3,100	6,200	3,100	9,300
Material usage		**29,300**	**15,700**	**17,700**

Raw material purchases

	RM11 Units	RM22 Units	RM33 Units
Budgeted material usage	29,300	15,700	17,700
Closing inventories	18,000	9,000	12,000
	47,300	24,700	29,700
Less opening inventories	21,000	10,000	16,000
Material purchases (units)	26,300	14,700	13,700
Cost per unit	$5	$3	$4
Material purchases	$ **131,500**	$ **44,100**	$ **54,800**

QUESTION

A business sells a product called the Inka and each unit of Inka requires 5.5kg of material K. Inventories of material K are 1,600 kg at the start of August 20X4 and the following production is planned for the next three months.

	August	September	October
Production in units of Inkas	1,000	1,100	1,200

The stores manager is about to place an order for material K and he requires there to be enough closing inventory of material K in order to produce 200 Inkas. What is the size of the order he must place in order to ensure that there is enough material K for the three months of the production and for the closing inventory requirements?

A   16,750 kg
B   17,650 kg
C   18,150 kg
D   18,650 kg

ANSWER

Answer B

	kg
Material required for production (3,300 × 5.5kg)	18,150
Less: opening inventory	(1,600)
Add: closing inventory(200 × 5.5kg)	1,100
	17,650 kg

3 Accounting for materials

> The materials purchased are recorded as a debit in the **materials control account**.

In Chapter 1 we revised the basics of double entry bookkeeping. In this section we will look at the detailed accounting for materials purchased by a business and then issued to production.

> Materials issued to production must be classified as either **direct** or **indirect** materials. Direct materials are credited to the materials control account and debited to the work in progress account. Indirect materials are credited to the materials control account and debited to the production overhead account.

A distinction was made in Chapter 3 between direct costs and indirect costs. Direct costs are those which can be directly associated to the production of a cost unit whereas indirect costs are those which cannot. This is the case with materials.

Direct materials are those which are part of the cost of making the product. **Indirect materials** are other materials that are part of the production process. Either they are materials such as machine lubricant which cannot be allocated to a specific cost unit or alternatively they are small components in the cost unit which due to their immaterial value are treated as indirect materials such as screws and bolts.

The accounting treatment will vary depending on whether the materials are being accounted for as direct or indirect costs.

When direct materials are issued to production the accounting entry is to debit a work in progress account. This is the account which gathers together the costs of production for a period. However when indirect materials are issued to production they are debited instead to the production overhead control account. The treatment of these overheads will be dealt with in Chapter 7.

3.1 Example: accounting for materials costs

A manufacturing business has purchased materials costing $102,000 on credit during the month of July 20X3. At the start of July there were inventories of raw materials of $13,000. During the month $88,000 of direct materials were issued to production and $15,000 of indirect materials.

We will now prepare the accounting entries for the materials for the month of July.

Solution

We must start with entering the opening inventory and the purchases into the materials control account.

MATERIALS CONTROL ACCOUNT

	$		$
Opening inventory	13,000		
Payables	102,000		

The other side of the entry for the purchases will be to the payables account in an integrated system but to the cost ledger control account in an interlocking system.

Now we will deal with the issues of materials to the production process. For both the direct and indirect materials the materials control account will be credited but the debit entries will be different – for the direct materials the debit entry is to the work in progress control account whereas the debit entry for the indirect materials is to the production overhead control account.

MATERIALS CONTROL ACCOUNT

	$		$
Opening inventory	13,000	Work in progress control	88,000
Payables	102,000	Production overhead control	15,000

WORK IN PROGRESS CONTROL

	$		$
Materials control	88,000		

PRODUCTION OVERHEAD CONTROL

	$		$
Materials control	15,000		

Finally the materials control account can be balanced to find the closing balance of materials at the end of July.

MATERIALS CONTROL ACCOUNT

	$		$
Opening inventory	13,000	Work in progress control	88,000
Payables	102,000	Production overhead control	15,000
		Closing inventory	12,000
	115,000		115,000

As you can see the accounting treatment of direct and indirect materials is very different therefore it is important that they are correctly classified. This is done by ensuring that each materials requisition is correctly coded as to whether the materials are direct materials or indirect materials.

We saw earlier in the chapter that sometimes materials are returned from production unused and this is recorded on a materials returns note. Again any return must be correctly coded to ensure that the materials movement is correctly classified as either a movement of direct materials or a movement of indirect materials.

The double entry for any such returns would be as follows:

Direct materials

DEBIT   Materials control
CREDIT   Work in progress control

Indirect materials

DEBIT   Materials control
CREDIT   Production overhead control

QUESTION

Double entry for materials

A manufacturing business has issued $67,400 of direct materials to the production department during the month and $12,600 of indirect materials.

What is the double entry for these issues?

A	DEBIT	Materials control account	$80,000	
	CREDIT	Work in progress control		$67,400
	CREDIT	Production overhead control		$12,600

B	DEBIT	Materials control account	$80,000	
	CREDIT	Work in progress control		$12,600
	CREDIT	Production overhead control		$67,400

C	DEBIT	Work in progress control	$67,400	
	DEBIT	Production overhead control	$12,600	
	CREDIT	Materials control		$80,000

D	DEBIT	Work in progress control	$12,600	
	DEBIT	Production overhead control	$67,400	
	CREDIT	Materials control		$80,000

ANSWER

Answer C

3.2 Inventory valuation methods

There are a number of different methods of valuing inventory.

(a) **FIFO – First in, first out**

This method values issues at the prices of the oldest items in inventory at the time the issues were made. The remaining inventory will thus be valued at the price of the most recent purchases. Say, for example, ABC Co's inventory consisted of four deliveries of raw material in the last month:

	Units		
1 September	1,000	at	$2.00
8 September	500	at	$2.50
15 September	500	at	$3.00
22 September	1,000	at	$3.50

If on 23 September 1,500 units were issued to production, 1,000 of these units would be priced at $2 (the cost of the 1,000 oldest units in inventory), and 500 at $2.50 (the cost of the next oldest 500). 1,000 units of closing inventory would be valued at $3.50 (the cost of the 1,000 most recent units received) and 500 units at $3.00 (the cost of the next most recent 500).

(b) **LIFO – Last in, first out**

This method is the opposite of FIFO. Issues will be valued at the prices of the most recent purchases; hence inventory remaining will be valued at the cost of the oldest items. In the example above it will be 1,000 units of issues which will be valued at $3.50, and the other 500 units issued will be valued at $3.00. 1,000 units of closing inventory will be valued at $2.00, and 500 at $2.50.

(c) **Weighted average pricing methods**

There are two main weighted average pricing methods: **cumulative** and **periodic**.

(i) **Cumulative weighted average pricing**

With this method we calculate an **average cost** of all the units in inventory whenever a new delivery is received.

(ii) **Periodic weighted average pricing**

The periodic weighted average pricing method involves calculating an average cost per unit at the end of a given period (rather than whenever new inventory is purchased, as with the cumulative weighted average pricing method). The periodic weighted average pricing method is easier to calculate than the cumulative weighted average method, and therefore requires less effort, but it must be applied retrospectively since the costs of materials used cannot be calculated until the end of the period.

3.2.1 Example: FIFO, LIFO and weighted average pricing methods

The following transactions should be considered in order to demonstrate FIFO, LIFO and weighted average pricing methods.

EXAM FOCUS POINT

Getting to grips with these inventory valuation methods is a very important part of your studies at this stage. This area featured in the December 2011 examiner's report as a specific example of somewhere that candidates scored especially poorly in their exam.

TRANSACTIONS DURING MAY 20X3

	Quantity Units	Unit cost $	Total cost $	Market value per unit on date of transaction $
Opening balance, 1 May	100	2.00	200	
Receipts, 3 May	400	2.10	840	2.11
Issues, 4 May	200			2.11
Receipts, 9 May	300	2.12	636	2.15
Issues, 11 May	400			2.20
Receipts, 18 May	100	2.40	240	2.35
Issues, 20 May	100			2.35
Closing balance, 31 May	200			2.38
			1,916	

(a) **FIFO**

FIFO assumes that materials are issued out of inventory in the order in which they were delivered into inventory: issues are priced at the cost of the earliest delivery remaining in inventory.

Using FIFO, the cost of issues and the closing inventory value in the example would be as follows.

Date of issue	Quantity issued Units	Value	$	$
4 May	200	100 o/s at $2	200	
		100 at $2.10	210	
				410
11 May	400	300 at $2.10	630	
		100 at $2.12	212	
				842
20 May	100	100 at $2.12		212
Cost of issues				1,464
Closing inventory value	200	100 at $2.12	212	
		100 at $2.40	240	
				452
				1,916

Notes

(i) The cost of materials issued plus the value of closing inventory equals the cost of purchases plus the value of opening inventory ($1,916).

(ii) In a period of inflation, there is a tendency with FIFO for:

- materials to be issued at a cost lower than the current market value
- closing inventories to be valued at a cost approximating to current market value.

(b) **LIFO**

LIFO assumes that materials are issued out of inventory in the reverse order to which they were delivered, with the most recent deliveries being issued before earlier ones. Issues are priced at the cost of the latest delivery remaining in inventory.

Using LIFO, the cost of issues and the closing inventory value in the example above would be as follows.

Date of issue	Quantity issued Units	Valuation	$	$
4 May	200	200 at $2.10		420
11 May	400	300 at $2.12	636	
		100 at $2.10	210	
				846
20 May	100	100 at $2.40		240
Cost of issues				1,506
Closing inventory value	200	100 at $2.10	210	
		100 at $2.00	200	
				410
				1,916

Notes

(i)   The cost of materials issued plus the value of closing inventory equals the cost of purchases plus the value of opening inventory ($1,916).

(ii)   In a period of inflation there is a tendency with LIFO for the following to occur.

- Materials are issued at a price which approximates to current market value.
- Closing inventories become undervalued when compared to market value.

(c)   **Cumulative weighted average pricing**

The cumulative weighted average pricing method calculates a **weighted average price** for all units in inventory. Issues are priced at this average cost, and the balance of inventory remaining would have the same unit valuation. The average price is determined by dividing the total cost by the total number of units.

A new weighted average price is calculated whenever a new delivery of materials into store is received. This is the key feature of cumulative weighted average pricing.

In our example, issue costs and closing inventory values would be as follows.

Date	Received Units	Issued Units	Balance Units	Total inventory value $	Unit cost $	$
Opening inventory			100	200	2.00	
3 May	400			840	2.10	
			* 500	1,040	2.08	
4 May		200		(416)	2.08	416
			300	624	2.08	
9 May	300			636	2.12	
			* 600	1,260	2.10	
11 May		400		(840)	2.10	840
			200	420	2.10	
18 May	100			240	2.40	
			* 300	660	2.20	
20 May		100		(220)	2.20	220
						1,476
Closing inventory value			200	440	2.20	440
						1,916

* A new inventory value per unit is calculated whenever a new receipt of materials occurs.

Notes

(a)   The cost of materials issued plus the value of closing inventory equals the cost of purchases plus the value of opening inventory ($1,916).

(b)   In a period of inflation, using the cumulative weighted average pricing system, the value of material issues will rise gradually, but will tend to lag a little behind the current market value at the date of issue. Closing inventory values will also be a little below current market value.

BPP
LEARNING MEDIA

(d)   **Periodic weighted average pricing**

Under the periodic weighted average pricing method, a retrospective average price is calculated for *all* materials issued during the period. The average issue price is calculated for our example as follows.

$$\frac{\text{Cost of all receipts in the period} + \text{Cost of opening inventory}}{\text{Number of units received in the period} + \text{Number of units of opening inventory}}$$

$$= \frac{\$1,716 + \$200}{800 + 100}$$

Issue price = $2.129 per unit

Closing inventory values are a balancing figure.

The issue costs and closing inventory values are calculated as follows.

Date of issue	Quantity issued Units	Valuation $
4 May	200 × $2.129	426
11 May	400 × $2.129	852
20 May	100 × $2.129	213
Cost of issues		1,491
Value of opening inventory plus purchases		1,916
Value of 200 units of closing inventory (at $2.129)		425

3.2.2 Which method is correct?

This is a trick question, because there is no one correct method. Each method has **advantages** and **disadvantages.**

The advantages and disadvantages of the **FIFO** method are as follows.

(a)   **Advantages**

(i)   It is a logical pricing method which probably represents what is physically happening: in practice the oldest inventory is likely to be used first.

(ii)   It is easy to understand and explain to managers.

(iii)   The closing inventory value can be near to a valuation based on the cost of replacing the inventory.

(b)   **Disadvantages**

(i)   FIFO can be cumbersome to operate because of the need to identify each batch of material separately.

(ii)   Managers may find it difficult to compare costs and make decisions when they are charged with varying prices for the same materials.

(iii)   Prices may diverge widely from market price when there is a high rate of inflation, thereby understating the cost of sales.

The advantages and disadvantages of the **LIFO** method are as follows.

(a)   **Advantages**

(i)   Inventories are issued at a price which is close to current market value.

(ii)   Managers are continually aware of recent costs when making decisions, because the costs being charged to their department or products will be current costs.

(b)   **Disadvantages**

(i)   The method can be cumbersome to operate because it sometimes results in several batches being only part-used in the inventory records before another batch is received.

(ii)   LIFO is often the opposite to what is physically happening and can therefore be difficult to explain to managers.

(iii)   As with FIFO, decision making can be difficult because of the variations in prices.

The advantages and disadvantages of weighted **average pricing** are as follows.

(a)   **Advantages**

(i)   Fluctuations in prices are smoothed out, making it easier to use the data for decision making.

(ii)   It is easier to administer than FIFO and LIFO, because there is no need to identify each batch separately.

(b)   **Disadvantages**

(i)   The resulting issue price is rarely an actual price that has been paid, and can run to several decimal places.

(ii)   Prices tend to lag a little behind current market values when there is gradual inflation.

3.2.3 Points to remember for the exam

In a period of **rising raw material prices** the following points are true:

(a)   Closing inventory values will be **higher** using cumulative weighted average pricing rather than periodic weighted average.

(b)   Closing inventory values will be **higher** using FIFO rather than LIFO.

(c)   Under FIFO, production costs would be lower than under LIFO.

In a period of **falling raw material prices**, the opposite will occur.

4   Remuneration methods

Employees who agree to work shifts, in particular different shifts over a period of time, receive extra wage payments. These extra payments are known as **shift allowances.**

Sometimes, employees may receive wages that are directly related to the output that they produce. This is known as **output related pay.** For example, workers in a widget factory might receive a basic wage rate plus:

*   An extra $100 if they produce more than 1,000 widgets per week
*   An extra $150 if they produce more than 1,200 widgets per week

Some employees are paid according to the number of units of a product that they produce in a week or month. This is known as **piecework**. In these cases the employees are paid a set amount for each good unit that they produce.

However there are two variations to the system. In some cases there may be a guaranteed weekly minimum payment in case there is not enough work available for the employee. In other cases there may be a differential piecework system whereby a higher unit amount is paid the more the employee produces.

4.1 Example: piecework

An alternative to hourly pay is a **piecework system** where employees are paid according to the number of good units of production.

A business has a piecework system for remuneration of its employees. The system works as follows:

$3.20 per unit for up to 40 units per week
$3.50 per unit for each unit between 41 and 50 units per week
$3.80 per unit for each unit over 51 units per week

There is a guaranteed weekly wage of $120 per week.

One employee has produced the following amounts for the last two weeks:

Week 1   35 units
Week 2   44 units

What is the employee's gross wage for week 1 and week 2?

Solution

	Week 1 $	Week 2 $
35 units × $3.20	112	
40 units × $3.20		128
4 units × $3.50		14
	112	142

In week 1 as the piecework rate is less than the guaranteed weekly minimum the amount to be paid will be the guaranteed amount of $120. In week 2 the employee's earnings are $142.

In other remuneration systems employees are paid a flat hourly rate but are then rewarded for higher productivity by a bonus scheme. Such schemes can be for an individual or on a group basis.

An individual bonus scheme only works where the employee has full control over his own productivity or speed of his work which means that the speed of his work is not dependent upon either the production of other employees or the speed of machinery. Bonus schemes can be set up in many ways but typically under an individual scheme a standard will be set for productivity such as production of 20 units per hour. If the employee exceeds this standard then the value of the time saved or extra production is split between the employer and employee according to some formula so that the employee benefits from a bonus.

In other types of work environment a group bonus scheme may be set up. Under this type of scheme if a group of employees or even the whole factory exceed a certain target then a bonus is payable to all members of the group.

4.2 Example: Premium bonus scheme

The following data relate to work at a certain factory.

Normal working day	8 hours
Basic rate of pay per hour	$6
Standard time allowed to produce 1 unit	2 minutes
Premium bonus	75% of time saved at basic rate

What will be the labour cost in a day when 340 units are made?

   A $48   B $51   C $63   D $68

Solution

The correct answer is C.

	Minutes
Standard time for 340 units (× 2 minutes)	680
Actual time (8 hours per day)	480
Time saved	200

	$
Bonus = 75% × 200 minutes × $6 per hour	15
Basic pay = 8 hours × $6	48
Total labour cost	63

Using basic MCQ technique you can eliminate option A because this is simply the basic pay without consideration of any bonus. You can also eliminate option D, which is based on the standard time allowance without considering the basic pay for the eight-hour day. Hopefully you were not forced to

guess, but had you been you would have had a 50% chance of selecting the correct answer (B or C) instead of a 25% chance because you were able to eliminate two of the options straightaway.

5 Unit labour costs

The labour cost is often a large element of the cost of a product and the remuneration method and productivity of the workforce can significantly affect the unit cost of the product.

5.1 Example: change of remuneration method

The **labour cost** can often be a significant element of unit cost and it can change if different remuneration methods are introduced or if there is a change in productivity.

A business makes one product which is made individually by each employee. In the past the 10 employees have been paid at an hourly rate of $5 per hour for 38 hours each week and any overtime hours are paid at the rate of time and a half. In a typical week the employees would each work for 6 overtime hours and on average produced 1,000 units of the product each week.

In an attempt to improve productivity the management have decided to change the remuneration package to a piecework system where each employee will be paid at the rate of $2.10 per unit for the first 80 units produced and $2.50 per unit for any units produced over and above 80. It is anticipated that each employee will produce 110 units per week.

What is the unit labour cost under the hourly rate system and under the piecework system?

Solution

Unit labour cost – hourly rate

	$
Labour cost (10 × 38 hours × $5)	1,900
Overtime (10 × 6 × $7.50)	450
Total labour cost	2,350
Cost per unit ($2,350/1,000)	$2.35 per unit

Unit labour cost – piecework

	$
10 × 80 × $2.10	1,680
10 × 30 × $2.50	750
Total labour cost	2,430
Unit labour cost ($2,340/1,100)	$2.21 per unit

5.2 Example: increase in productivity

A business has a factory in which the 40 employees are paid at an hourly rate of $6.80 per hour for a 35 hour week. Any overtime hours are paid at a rate of $9.00 per hour. Each unit of the product takes an average of 2 hours to produce and in an average week each of the employees works 3 hours of overtime.

In an attempt to improve productivity the management are considering investing some new machinery which it is anticipated will reduce the time required for each unit by 15 minutes. It is hoped that there will now be no overtime worked.

What is the effect on the total labour cost and the labour cost per unit of the increase in productivity.

Solution

	$
Labour cost (40 × 35 × $6.80)	9,520
Overtime (40 × 3 × $9.00)	1,080
Total labour cost	10,600

Current number of units (40 × 38 hours/2)   760 units
Current cost per unit (10,600/760) $13.95 per unit
New labour cost (40 × 35 × $6.80)   9,520
New number of units (40 × 35 hours/1.75)   800 units
New cost per unit (9,520/800) $11.90 per unit

6 Gross pay and deductions

> The employer must **deduct** income tax and employee's benefit contributions from the gross pay before paying the net pay to the employees.
>
> The **total labour cost** for an employer is the gross pay plus the employer's benefit contributions.

Whatever method of remuneration a business chooses the amount due to the employees is known as the **gross pay.** However this is not the amount that the employee will receive as the employer has a statutory duty to deduct income tax (in the form of PAYE in the UK) and also the Employee's benefit contributions. The resulting figure after these deductions is the **net pay** that the employee will receive.

6.1 Example: gross pay to net pay

An employee is paid at an hourly rate of $7.00 for a 35 hour week with any overtime hours paid at time and a half. During week 22 the employee worked for 41 hours.

The income tax to be deducted was $55 and the Employee's benefit contributions for the week were $28.

What is the employee's net pay?

Solution

	$
Gross pay – 41 hours x $7.00	287
6 hours x $3.50	21
Total gross pay	308
Less: Income tax	(55)
benefit contributions	(28)
Net pay	225

It is also possible that there may be other deductions from an employee's gross pay as well as income tax and benefit contributions. For example if the company runs a contributory pension scheme there may be a further deduction for pension contributions that the employee makes (and which are taken out of the employee's pay).

As far as the employer is concerned the cost of employment is the gross pay of the employee. Although the employee is only paid the net amount, the employer must pay the deductions from gross pay (for income tax and the employee's benefit contributions) over to the relevant authorities.

There is also a further cost to the employer as he must also pay Employer's benefit contributions on behalf of each employee, together with any additional employer's pension contributions that may be made into the pension scheme for the employee.

6.2 Example: labour cost

Returning to the employee from the previous example the Employer's benefit contribution for the week is $31. What is the labour cost to the employer for this employee for the week?

Solution

	$
Gross pay	308
Employer's benefit contribution	31
Total labour cost	339

In some business's there may be an additional cost to the employer for example if the employer's agreement is that he will contribute to the pension scheme on the employee's behalf.

QUESTION

Labour costs

Two payslips for the month of April for advisers working for a financial services firm, and a corresponding extract from the firm's payroll, follow. Examine the two slips and the extract, then answer this question:

What is the total labour cost to the firm of employing these two advisers for the month?

A $2,275.20
B $2,925.00
C $3,025.00
D $3,383.11

PAY ADVICE

Name: *Carol Hathaway*   Employee number: *173*

Month number: I   Date: **28.4.20X1**   Tax Code: 453L

	$	$
Basic pay		*1,000.00*
Commission		*575.00*
Total gross pay		*1,575.00*
Less pension		*50.00*
Gross taxable pay		*1,525.00*
Deductions:		
Income tax	*233.50*	
Benefits contribution	*114.70*	
		348.20
Net pay		*1,176.80*

PAY ADVICE

Name: **Mark Greene**   Employee number: **174**

Month number: **1**   Date: **28.4.20X1**   Tax Code: **490L**

	$	$
Basic pay		1,000.00
Commission		450.00
Total gross pay		1,450.00
Less pension		50.00
Gross taxable pay		1,400.00
Deductions:		
Income tax	199.40	
Benefits contribution	102.20	
		301.60
Net pay		1,098.40

EXTRACT FROM PAYROLL

Employee no	Gross pay	Employee pension	Tax	Employee benefits	Net pay	Employer pension	Employer benefits
173	1,575.00	50.00	233.50	114.70	1,176.80	50.00	136.49
174	1,450.00	50.00	199.40	102.20	1,098.40	50.00	121.62

ANSWER

Answer D

The total labour cost for the two employees is made up of gross pay plus employer's contributions to pension and benefits. This comes to $3,383.11.

QUESTION

Wage payment schedule

You are the Accounts Assistant at Mark Balding's clothes factory (Mark Balding's Ltd).

It is your first day back in the office after a week's holiday. One of the items on your desk is a memo from a cost centre manager and is shown below.

MEMO

To: Accounts Assistant

From: Cost Centre Manager (Denim range)

Date: 9 May 20X1

Subject: Missed wage payment

We missed a wage payment for Sandra Bloggs, a sewing machinist (denim range) for the last week of April 20X1. Sandra works four days a week and worked 28 hours at the rate of $6 per hour and then worked on her day off (7 hours at time and a half) so that the order for Alma's Ltd was finished by the end of April.

Please calculate the basic wage payments and employee costs and then pass the details on to the payroll department for the personal deductions and coding. Sandra is entitled to an employer's pension contribution of 5% of basic wage payment and Employer's benefit contributions are 12½% above $84 per week.

Many thanks

Task

Complete the wage payment schedule shown below.

PAYROLL CALCULATION SCHEDULE APRIL 20X1		
NAME:		
DEPARTMENT:		
BASIC RATE:		
HOURS WORKED:		
HOURS FOR OVERTIME PREMIUM:		
	Calculation	Amount $
BASIC PAY		
OVERTIME PREMIUM		
EMPLOYER'S PENSION CONTRIBUTION		
EMPLOYER'S BENEFIT CONTRIBUTION		

ANSWER

PAYROLL CALCULATION SCHEDULE APRIL 20X1		
NAME:	Sandra Bloggs	
DEPARTMENT:	Denim Range	
BASIC RATE:	$6.00 per hour	
HOURS WORKED:	35	
HOURS FOR OVERTIME PREMIUM:	7	
	Calculation	Amount $
BASIC PAY	35 hrs × $6	210
OVERTIME PREMIUM	7 hrs × $6 × 0.5	21
EMPLOYER'S PENSION CONTRIBUTION	5% × $210	10.50
EMPLOYER'S BENEFIT CONTRIBUTION	$210 + $21 = $231 $231 − $84 = $147 $147 × 12.5%	18.37

EXAM FOCUS POINT

You need to understand all the costs involved in the total wages cost to the business.

7 Accounting for labour costs

Direct labour costs are the costs of the hours worked by the production workers, who are involved directly in the business's productive activities, at the normal hourly rate.

Indirect labour costs normally include the overtime premium for direct workers and any idle time hours for direct workers as well as the indirect workers employment costs.

In just the same way as for materials the labour costs of a business must be classified as either direct labour costs or indirect labour costs as these will be accounted for differently.

We have already seen that the total labour cost to an employer is the gross pay plus the Employer's benefit contribution and any other further payments such as pension contributions that the employer pays on behalf of the employee. Now we must determine how the total labour cost is analysed between direct and indirect costs.

The basic distinction for classification of labour costs is that the labour costs of production workers are direct costs and the labour costs of other workers are indirect costs. However there are two specific areas where the costs of the production workers are often treated as indirect rather than direct.

When overtime is worked by employees they tend to be paid an additional premium over the general hourly rate, known as the **overtime premium** or premium piecerate. The overtime premium is generally treated as an indirect cost rather than a direct cost of production. This is because the overtime is an effect not of the production itself but of its organisation and timing, and is therefore more like an indirect overhead than a direct cost of production. However, there is an exception to this: if a customer requests that overtime is worked in order to complete a job earlier, then the entire overtime payment will normally be treated as a direct cost of that job.

EXAM FOCUS POINT

The December 2011 examiner's report used this as a specific example of somewhere that candidates did badly in their exam, with many failing to spot that an overtime premium paid to direct workers in order to meet *general* production requirements in a factory should be treated as a production overhead.

At some point during the working day it is entirely possible that production workers find that there is no work for them to do. This could be due to factors such as production scheduling problems or machine breakdowns. These hours which are paid for but during which no work is being done are known as **idle time.** The cost of idle time hours tends to be treated as an indirect labour cost.

7.1 Example: overtime and idle time

Given below are the labour costs incurred by a manufacturing business for the week commencing 23 July 20X5.

Direct production workers 1,200 hours @ $6.40 per hour
Direct production workers overtime hours 200 @ $9.40 per hour
Indirect workers 400 hours @ $5.20 per hour
Indirect workers overtime hours 50 @ $8.00 per hour
Of the hours paid to the direct production workers 40 of these were idle time hours.

What is the total for direct labour and indirect labour for the week?

Solution

Direct labour cost

	$
Direct production workers basic hours (1,200 + 200 – 40) @ $6.40	8,704

Indirect labour cost

Direct production workers – overtime premium

	$
200 hours × ($9.40 – 6.40)	600
Idle time hours 40 × $6.40	256
Indirect workers (400 × $5.20)	2,080
Indirect workers – overtime (50 × $8.00)	400
	3,336

QUESTION   Direct and indirect labour cost

During the week ending 30 June 20X3 the direct production workers in a factory worked for 840 hours in total. Of these hours 60 were idle time hours and 100 were overtime hours. The hourly rate of pay is $8.00 with overtime hours being paid at time and a half.

During the same week the indirect workers worked for 120 hours at a rate of $6.00 per hour with no overtime hours.

What is the direct labour cost and the indirect labour cost for the week?

	Direct labour cost	Indirect labour cost
A	$5,440	$2,400
B	$6,240	$1,600
C	$6,640	$1,200
D	$6,720	$1,120

ANSWER

Answer B

	$
Direct labour (840 – 60) × $8.00	6,240

	$
Indirect labour	
Indirect workers 120 × $6.00	720
Direct workers overtime premium	
100 hours × $4	
Direct workers idle time	
60 hours × $8	480
	1,600

Once the distinction between the direct labour and indirect labour costs has been made we can go on to consider the detailed ledger account entries for the labour cost. The main accounting takes place in the wages control account.

7.2 Example: ledger accounting for labour costs

The **gross pay** is **debited** to the **wages control account** and the direct cost element is then transferred to the work in progress account whilst the indirect cost element is transferred to the production overhead control account.

A business paid its employees net pay of $15,000 for week 34. This was after deductions for income tax and benefit contributions of $6,000. The direct labour element of this was $18,000 and the indirect labour cost was $3,000.

Write up the ledger accounts to reflect the labour cost.

Solution

The first step is to debit the wages control account with the gross pay which is made up of the net amount paid to the employees and the income tax and benefit contributions. The other sides of the

entries are to the bank account for the net pay and to a tax authorities creditor account for the income tax and benefit contributions as these amounts must be paid over to the tax authorities shortly.

WAGES CONTROL ACCOUNT

	$		$
Bank – net pay	15,000		
Tax authorities – deductions	6,000		

The direct labour cost is then credited to the wages control account and debited to the work in progress account, as were direct materials, as part of the direct cost of making the products.

The indirect labour cost is credited to the wages control account and debited to the production overhead control account together with any indirect materials used.

WAGES CONTROL ACCOUNT

	$		$
Bank – net pay	15,000	Work in progress	18,000
Tax authorities – deductions	6,000	Production overhead	3,000
	21,000		21,000

WORK IN PROGRESS

	$		$
Direct materials	50,000		
Wages control	18,000		

PRODUCTION OVERHEAD CONTROL

	$		$
Indirect materials	4,000		
Wages control	3,000		

QUESTION

Labour double entry

A business has incurred direct labour costs of $25,600 and indirect labour costs of $3,800. What is the double entry required to record these?

A	DEBIT	Wages control	$29,400	
	CREDIT	Work in progress		$25,600
	CREDIT	Production overhead		$3,800

B	DEBIT	Wages control	$29,400	
	CREDIT	Work in progress		$3,800
	CREDIT	Production overhead		$25,600

C	DEBIT	Work in progress	$25,600	
	DEBIT	Production overhead	$3,800	
	CREDIT	Wages control		$29,400

D	DEBIT	Work in progress	$3,800	
	DEBIT	Production overhead	$25,600	
	CREDIT	Wages control		$29,400

ANSWER

Answer C

As we have seen the labour cost is the gross wages or salaries of the employees. It is important that we distinguish between direct labour and indirect labour and this will be done by careful coding of the payroll.

The payroll will consist of a listing for each department of the net pay, deductions and overtime details. These must be coded correctly to ensure that the gross pay is correctly analysed between direct and indirect labour and is collected by the correct cost centre.

EXAM FOCUS POINT

The cost accounting double entry for labour costs is highly examinable.

CHAPTER ROUNDUP

↳ Materials can be **classified** according to the substances that make them up, how they are measured, or their physical properties.

↳ When the storekeeper places an order for materials the **amount** that will be **ordered** will be dependent upon the sales and / or manufacturing plans for the immediate future.

↳ The materials purchased are recorded as a debit in the **materials control account.**

↳ Materials issued to production must be classified as either **direct** or **indirect** materials. Direct materials are credited to the materials control account and debited to the work in progress account. Indirect materials are credited to the materials control account and debited to the production overhead account.

↳ An alternative to hourly pay is a **piecework system** where employees are paid according to the number of good units of production.

↳ The **labour cost** can often be a significant element of unit cost and it can change if different remuneration methods are introduced or if there is a change in productivity.

↳ The employer must **deduct** income tax and employee's benefit contributions from the gross pay before paying the net pay to the employees.

↳ The **total labour cost** for an employer is the gross pay plus the employer's benefit contributions.

↳ **Direct labour costs** are the costs of the hours worked by the production workers, who are involved directly in the business's productive activities, at the normal hourly rate.

↳ **Indirect labour costs** normally include the overtime premium for direct workers and any idle time hours for direct workers as well as the indirect workers employment costs.

↳ The **gross pay** is **debited** to the **wages control account** and the direct cost element is then transferred to the work in progress account whilst the indirect cost element is transferred to the production overhead control account.

QUICK QUIZ

1 What is the name of the amount paid in excess of the normal hourly rate for overtime hours?

 A   Overtime payments
 B   Overtime premium
 C   Overtime excess
 D   Overtime special payment

2 If overtime is worked at the request of the customer how is the overtime premium normally treated?

 A   As a direct labour cost
 B   As an indirect labour cost

3 How is the cost of idle time hours usually treated?

 A   As a direct labour cost
 B   As a indirect labour cost
 C   Neither of the above

4 What is the double entry for direct labour costs?

A	Dr	Wages control	Cr	WIP
B	Dr	Wages control	Cr	Payables
C	Dr	WIP	Cr	Wages control
D	Dr	Payables	Cr	WIP

5 A system where the amount paid per unit increases as the individual's production increases is known as:

- A Shiftwork
- B Idle time work
- C Bonus scheme
- D Differential piecework

6 What is the double entry for issues of materials to production?

A	Dr	Materials control account	Cr	WIP account
B	Dr	Materials control account	Cr	Payables
C	Dr	WIP account	Cr	Materials control account
D	Dr	Payables	Cr	Materials control account

7 In a period of rising prices, which one of the following will be true with a FIFO system of costing inventory when compared to LIFO?

- A Product costs are overstated and profits understated
- B Product costs are overstated and profits overstated
- C Product costs are understated and profits understated
- D Product costs are understated and profits overstated

ANSWERS TO QUICK QUIZ

1 B Overtime premium. Note that an overtime payment is the total payment made for overtime hours whereas the overtime premium is the amount paid in excess of the normal hourly rate for the overtime hours.

2 A At the request of a customer, overtime premium is usually treated as a direct cost. If it's due to general pressures of production then it will be treated as an indirect cost.

3 B Idle time hours are usually treated as an indirect labour cost

4 C Debit   Work in progress
Credit   Wages control

5 D This is the definition of differential piecework

6 C Dr WIP account Cr Materials control account. (Remember that indirect materials would be debited to the production overhead)

7 D FIFO uses the price of the oldest items in inventory for inventory issues. When prices are rising these will be the lowest priced items. Consequently costs are lower and profits are higher.

Now try ...

Attempt the questions below from the **Exam Question Bank**

Number

Q22-26

In this chapter we cover the third element of business costs, expenses. On fairly rare occasions an expense will be classified as a direct expense. For example if a piece of machinery was hired for a particular job then the hire charges are a direct cost of that job. However, in the majority of cases expenses are indirect expenses - such as rent, rates, insurance, heat and light etc.

Overhead costs

Study Guide   **Intellectual level**

D   Cost accounting

3   Accounting for other expenses

(a)   Explain the process of charging indirect costs to cost
      centres and cost units and illustrate the process of cost
      apportionment for indirect costs (excluding reciprocal
      services)   S

(b)   Explain and illustrate the process of cost absorption for
      indirect costs   S

1   Absorption costing

Overheads are made up of indirect materials, indirect labour and indirect expenses.

Under **absorption costing principles**, the production overheads of a business are absorbed into the cost
of each of the products.

Absorption costing is a costing method where direct costs are assigned to cost units along with
production overheads using an overhead absorption rate.

Overheads are made up of indirect materials, indirect labour and indirect expenses.

The overheads of the business, under absorption costing are required to be included in the cost of the
products of the business. For inventory valuation requirements only **production overheads** are included
in the valuation of the product, For product costing and profitability purposes all overheads need to be
considered. In this chapter we will mainly consider the process whereby the **production overheads** are
absorbed into the cost of the production units.

In overview, the process is to share out all of the production overheads amongst the cost centres that
incur them and then to share their overheads amongst the products made in the cost centre. However
we have to recognise that not all of these cost centres are **production cost centres**, ie cost centres that
actually produce goods. Some of the cost centres which incur overheads are **service cost centres**. These
are areas of the business that provide necessary services to the production cost centres such as stores,
maintenance or a canteen.

The overheads incurred by the service cost centres must in turn be shared amongst the production cost
centres until all of the overheads are within the production cost centres. Then finally the total overhead
can be shared amongst the units which are made in each of the production cost centres.

2   Allocation and apportionment of overheads

The first stage of the process is the allocation of specific overheads to specific **cost centres** – then joint
overheads are apportioned to each cost centre on an **appropriate basis**.

The first stage in the process is to **allocate** any specific production overheads to individual cost centres
that have incurred them. These will often be items such as indirect materials and indirect labour.

However there will be many expenses of the business such as rent and rates which are shared by a
number of different cost centres. These joint expenses must be **apportioned** between the cost centres on
some suitable basis. For example rent and rates are often apportioned or shared out between cost
centres on the basis of the amount of floor area that each cost centre occupies. The machinery
insurance costs might be apportioned on the basis of the value of the machinery in each cost centre.

There is not necessarily any right or wrong basis to use for apportionment, but the basis chosen should be fair.

2.1 Example: allocation and apportionment

A manufacturing business has two production cost centres, assembly and finishing, and two service cost centres, stores and maintenance. The following expenses are expected to be incurred in the forthcoming year.

	$
Indirect materials – assembly	13,500
finishing	8,000
maintenance	2,000
Indirect labour – assembly	14,000
finishing	9,000
stores	28,000
maintenance	36,000
Machinery depreciation	10,000
Rent and rates	60,000
Heat and light	15,000
Power	18,000
Insurance of machinery	8,000

You are also given the following information:

	Assembly	Finishing	Stores	Maintenance	Total
Floor area (sq m)	1,000	500	400	100	2,000
Power usage (%)	55%	35%	5%	5%	100%
Net book value of machinery $000	50	30	15	5	100

We will now allocate and apportion the production overheads to the four cost centres.

Solution

	Assembly $	Finishing $	Stores $	Maintenance $	Total $
Indirect materials	13,500	8,000	–	2,000	23,500
Indirect labour	14,000	9,000	28,000	36,000	87,000
Machinery depreciation (net book value)					
(10,000 × 50/100)	5,000				
(10,000 × 30/100)		3,000			
(10,000 × 15/100)			1,500		
(10,000 × 5/100)				500	10,000
Rent and rates – floor area					
(60,000 × 1,000/2,000)	30,000				
(60,000 × 500/2,000)		15,000			
(60,000 × 400/2,000)			12,000		
(60,000 × 100/2,000)				3,000	60,000
Heat and light – floor area					
(15,000 × 1,000/2,000)	7,500				
(15,000 × 500/2,000)		3,750			
(15,000 × 400/2,000)			3,000		
(15,000 x 100/2,000)				750	15,000
Power (% usage)					
(18,000 × 55%)	9,900				
(18,000 × 35%)		6,300			
(18,000 × 5%)			900		
(18,000 × 5%)				900	18,000
Insurance (net book value)					
(8,000 × 50/100)	4,000				
(8,000 × 30/100)		2,400			
(8,000 × 15/100)			1,200		
(8,000 × 5/100)				400	8,000
	83,900	47,450	46,600	43,550	221,500

QUESTION

Cost centres

A business has two production cost centres, A and B, and one service cost centre, the warehouse. The rent and rates expense for the business is anticipated to be $25,000 for the coming year. The floor space occupied by each cost centre in square metres is as follows:

Cost centre A   1,200 sq m
Cost centre B   1,800 sq m
Warehouse   2,000 sq m

How much of the rent and rates expense should be apportioned to cost centre B?

A $6,000
B $9,000
C $10,000
D $25,000

ANSWER

Answer B

$25,000 × 1,800/5,000 = $9,000

> The **overheads** of the **service cost centres** must then be reapportioned to the production cost centres on an appropriate basis.

The next stage in the apportionment process is to reapportion the service cost centre overheads to the production cost centres. The reason for this is that each production centre is likely to make different use of the service cost centres, and this should be reflected in the costs they are deemed to have incurred. In order to do this there needs to be an appropriate basis of apportionment, usually an approximation of the use that each production cost centre makes of the service cost centres.

EXAM FOCUS POINT

For exam questions you will need to be able to carry out basic apportionment of overheads.

2.2 Example: reapportionment of service cost centre costs

You now have further information about the use that assembly and finishing make of stores and maintenance:

	Assembly	Finishing
Number of stores requisitions	100	30
Maintenance call outs per annum	30	20

Reapportion the service centre costs to the production cost centres.

Solution

	Assembly $	Finishing $	Stores $	Maintenance $	Total $
	83,900	47,450	46,600	43,550	221,500
Stores (requisitions)					
(46,600 × 100/130)	35,846				
(46,600 × 30/130)		10,754	(46,600)		–
Maintenance (call outs)					
(43,550 × 30/50)	26,130				
(43,550 × 20/50)		17,420		(43,550)	–
	145,876	75,624	–	–	221,500

QUESTION

Reapportionment of service cost centre

The process of allocation and apportionment of production overheads has been carried out for a business with the following totals calculated:

	Production cost centres		Service	Cost centres
	A $	B $	canteen $	stores $
Allocated and apportioned overhead	24,600	32,400	18,500	8,200

The production cost centres have the following details:

	Production cost centres	
	A	B
Number of employees	100	150
Number of materials requisitions	60	104

What is the total overhead for production cost centre B after reapportionment of the service cost centre overheads?

A $10,400
B $16,300
C $35,000
D $48,700

ANSWER

Answer D

	$
Allocated and apportioned overhead	32,400
Canteen overhead (18,500 × 150/250)	11,100
Stores overhead (8,200 × 104/164)	5,200
Total overhead	48,700

3 Absorption of overheads

Once all of the production overheads have been apportioned to the production cost centres an **overhead absorption rate** is determined normally based upon direct labour hours or machine hours.

Overhead absorption rate is 'a means of attributing overhead to a product or service, based for example on direct labour hours, direct labour cost or machine hours'. CIMA *Official Terminology*

The final stage of the process now that all of the production overheads have been allocated and apportioned to the production cost centres is to find an absorption rate with which to absorb or include the overhead into the cost of each unit of production. This is done by finding a basis for absorption which will generally tend to be based upon the activity of the department.

3.1 Example: absorption of overheads

The assembly department is a largely machine based department whereas the finishing department is largely labour based. The management of the business have decided that the assembly department overheads should be absorbed on the basis of machine hours and that the finishing department overheads should be absorbed on the basis of labour hours.

The machine hours in the assembly department are 100,000 whereas the labour hours for the finishing department are 20,000.

The overhead absorption rate is as follows:

Assembly $\dfrac{\$145,876}{100,000}$ = $1.46 per machine hour

Finishing $\dfrac{\$75,624}{20,000}$ = $3.78 per labour hour

QUESTION   Overhead absorption rate

A business has two production cost centres, manufacturing and packaging. The overheads and other details for these cost centres are as follows:

	Manufacturing	Packaging
Overhead	$154,000	$89,000
Labour hours	110,000	68,000
Machine hours	35,000	60,000

Management have decided that the overheads are to be absorbed on the basis of labour hours in the manufacturing department and on the basis of machine hours in the packaging department.

What is the overhead absorption rate per hour in each department (to the nearest cent)?

	Manufacturing	Packaging
A	$1.40	$1.31
B	$1.40	$1.48

BPP
LEARNING MEDIA

| C | $4.40 | $1.31 |
| D | $4.40 | $1.48 |

ANSWER

Answer B

$$\text{Manufacturing} = \frac{\$154,000}{110,000} = \$1.40 \text{ per labour hour}$$

$$\text{Packaging} = \frac{\$89,000}{60,000} = \$1.48 \text{ per machine hour}$$

> The **overhead absorption rate** is then used to cost each product depending upon how many relevant hours each product takes in each production cost centre.

For each product that is produced in the two departments a certain amount of overhead will be included in the cost of the product based upon the number of hours that the product spends in each production cost centre.

3.2 Example: product costs

One of the products of the business is the Powerpuff. This product has direct material costs of $14.30 per unit and direct labour costs of $16.50 per unit. Each unit of the Powerpuff spends 6 machine hours in the assembly department and 3 labour hours in the finishing department.

What is the final unit cost of the Powerpuff?

Solution

	$
Direct materials	14.30
Direct labour	16.50
Assembly overhead (6 hours × $1.46)	8.76
Finishing overhead (3 hours × $3.78)	11.34
Total unit cost	50.90

QUESTION

Total overhead per product

A business has two production departments, assembly and polishing. One of the products made in these departments is the Stun. Details for these departments and the Stun are as follows:

	Assembly	Polishing
Overhead	$94,800	$74,800
Labour hours	20,000	40,000
Machine hours	60,000	15,000
Stun – labour hours per unit	3 hours	5 hours
Stun – machine hours per unit	4 hours	2 hours

Overheads in the assembly department are to be absorbed on the basis of machine hours and in the polishing department on the basis of labour hours.

How much overhead in total would be included in the cost of a Stun?

A	$3.45
B	$8.48
C	$10.06
D	$15.67

ANSWER

Answer D

$$\text{Assembly overhead absorption rate} = \frac{\$94,800}{60,000} = \$1.58 \text{ per machine hour}$$

$$\text{Polishing overhead absorption rate} = \frac{\$74,800}{40,000} = \$1.87 \text{ per labour hour}$$

	$
Overhead to be absorbed	
Assembly $1.58 × 4 hours	6.32
Polishing $1.87 × 5 hours	9.35
Total overhead	15.67

In order for overheads to be initially allocated and apportioned to the correct cost centres all overhead invoices must be carefully coded.

So the process of absorbing overheads into the costs of production starts with the allocation and apportionment of the indirect expenses to the each cost centre. It is therefore important that each individual expense is correctly coded to the correct cost centre.

For items of expense that are to be allocated to a specific cost centre, there will be only one code. These amounts will tend to be indirect materials which will be coded on the materials requisition and indirect labour which will be coded from the payroll. If any invoices are received for expenses for a specific cost centre then the net amount of the invoice must be coded to that cost centre.

For expenses which have to be apportioned between cost centres then the cost accountant will carry out the apportionment on the approved basis of apportionment and the amounts for each cost centre will be coded to that cost centre.

3.3 Predetermined absorption rates

In absorption costing, it is usual to add overheads into product costs by applying a **predetermined overhead absorption rate**. The predetermined rate is set annually, in the budget.

Overheads are not absorbed on the basis of the actual overheads incurred but on the basis of estimated or budgeted figures (calculated prior to the beginning of the period). The rate at which overheads are included in cost of sales (**absorption rate**) is predetermined before the accounting period actually begins for a number of reasons.

(a) Goods are produced and sold throughout the year, but many actual overheads are not known until the end of the year. It would be inconvenient to wait until the year end in order to decide what overhead costs should be.

(b) An attempt to calculate overhead costs more regularly (such as each month) is possible, although estimated costs must be added for occasional expenditures such as rent and rates (incurred once or twice a year). The difficulty with this approach would be that actual overheads from month to month would fluctuate randomly; therefore, overhead costs charged to production would depend on a certain extent on random events and changes. A unit made in one week might be charged with $4 of overhead, in a subsequent week with $5, and in a third week with $4.50. Only units made in winter would be charged with the heating overhead. Such charges are considered misleading for costing purposes and administratively and clerically inconvenient to deal with.

(c) Similarly, production output might vary each month. For example actual overhead costs might be $20,000 per month and output might vary from, say, 1,000 units to 20,000 units per month. The unit rate for overhead would be $20 and $1 per unit respectively, which would again lead to administration and control problems.

3.4 Calculating predetermined overhead absorption rates

> The **absorption rate** is calculated by dividing the budgeted overhead by the budgeted level of activity. For production overheads the level of activity is often budgeted direct labour hours or budgeted machine hours.

Overhead absorption rates are therefore predetermined as follows.

(a) The overhead **likely to be incurred** during the coming period is estimated.

(b) The total hours, units, or direct costs on which the overhead absorption rates are to be based (activity level) are estimated.

(c) The estimated overhead is divided by the budgeted activity level to arrive at an absorption rate for the forthcoming period.

3.5 Selecting the appropriate absorption base

> Management should try to establish an absorption rate that provides a **reasonably 'accurate' estimate** of overhead costs for jobs, products or services.

There are a number of different **bases of absorption** (or 'overhead **recovery** rates') which can be used. Examples are as follows.

- A percentage of direct materials cost
- A percentage of direct labour cost
- A percentage of prime cost
- A rate per machine hour
- A rate per direct labour hour
- A rate per unit

The choice of an absorption basis is a matter of judgement and common sense. There are no strict rules or formulae involved, although factors which should be taken into account are set out below. What is required is an absorption basis which realistically reflects the characteristics of a given cost centre and which avoids undue anomalies.

Many factories use a **direct labour hour rate** or **machine hour rate** in preference to a rate based on a percentage of direct materials cost, wages or prime cost.

(a) A **direct labour** hour basis is most appropriate in a **labour intensive** environment.

(b) A **machine hour** rate would be used in departments where production is controlled or dictated by **machines**. This basis is becoming more appropriate as factories become more heavily automated.

IMPORTANT

A **rate per unit** would be effective only if all units were identical.

4 Over and under absorption of overheads

The rate of overhead absorption is based on **estimates** (of both numerator and denominator) and it is quite likely that either one or both of the estimates will not agree with what *actually* occurs. Actual overheads incurred will probably be either greater than or less than overheads absorbed into the cost of production.

(a) **Over absorption** means that the overheads charged to the cost of production are greater than the overheads actually incurred.

(b) **Under absorption** means that insufficient overheads have been included in the cost of production.

4.1 Example: over and under absorption of overheads

Suppose that the budgeted overhead in a production department is $80,000 and the budgeted activity is 40,000 direct labour hours. The overhead recovery rate (using a direct labour hour basis) would be $2 per direct labour hour.

Actual overheads in the period are, say $84,000 and 45,000 direct labour hours are worked.

	$
Overhead incurred (actual)	84,000
Overhead absorbed (45,000 × $2)	90,000
Over absorption of overhead	6,000

In this example, the cost of produced units or jobs has been charged with $6,000 more than was actually spent. An adjustment to reconcile the overheads charged to the actual overhead is necessary and the over-absorbed overhead will be written as a credit to the **income statement** at the end of the accounting period.

4.2 The reasons for under-/over-absorbed overhead

The overhead absorption rate is **predetermined from budget estimates** of overhead cost and the expected volume of activity. Under or over recovery of overhead will occur in the following circumstances.

- Actual overhead costs are different from budgeted overheads.
- The actual activity level is different from the budgeted activity level.
- Both actual overhead costs and actual activity level are different from budget.

4.3 Example: under and over absorption of overheads

Rex Co is a small company which manufactures two products, A and B, in two production departments, machining and assembly. A canteen is operated as a separate production service department.

The budgeted production and sales in the year to 31 March 20X3 are as follows.

	Product A	Product B
Sales price per unit	$50	$70
Sales (units)	2,200	1,400
Production (units)	2,000	1,500
Material cost per unit	$14	$12

	Product A Hours per unit	Product B Hours per unit
Direct labour:		
Machining department ($8 per hour)	2	3
Assembly department ($6 per hour)	1	2
Machine hours per unit:		
Machining department	3	4
Assembly department	1/2	

Budgeted production overheads are as follows.

	Machining department $	Assembly department $	Canteen $	Total $
Allocated costs	10,000	25,000	12,000	47,000
Apportionment of other general production overheads	26,000	12,000	8,000	46,000
	36,000	37,000	20,000	93,000
Number of employees	30	20	1	51
Floor area (square metres)	5,000	2,000	500	7,500

Required

(a) Calculate an absorption rate for overheads in each production department for the year to 31 March 20X3 and the budgeted cost per unit of products A and B.

(b) Suppose that in the year to 31 March 20X3, 2,200 units of Product A are produced and 1,500 units of Product B. Direct labour hours per unit and machine hours per unit in both departments were as budgeted.

Actual production overheads are as follows.

	Machining department $	Assembly department $	Canteen $	Total $
Allocated costs	30,700	27,600	10,000	68,300
Apportioned share of general production overheads	17,000	8,000	5,000	30,000
	47,700	35,600	15,000	98,300

Calculate the under- or over-absorbed overhead in each production department and in total.

Solution

(a) **Choose absorption rates**

Since machine time appears to be more significant than labour time in the machining department, a machine hour rate of absorption will be used for overhead recovery in this department. On the other hand, machining is insignificant in the assembly department, and a direct labour hour rate of absorption would seem to be the basis which will give the fairest method of overhead recovery.

Apportion budgeted overheads

Next we need to apportion budgeted overheads to the two production departments. Canteen costs will be apportioned on the basis of the number of employees in each department. (Direct labour hours in each department are an alternative basis of apportionment, but the number of employees seems to be more directly relevant to canteen costs.)

	Machining department $	Assembly department $	Total $
Budgeted allocated costs	10,000	25,000	35,000
Share of general overheads	26,000	12,000	38,000
Apportioned canteen costs (30:20)	12,000	8,000	20,000
	48,000	45,000	93,000

Calculate overhead absorption rates

The overhead absorption rates are predetermined, using budgeted estimates. Since the overheads are production overheads, the budgeted activity relates to the volume of production, in units (the production hours required for volume of sales being irrelevant).

	Product A	Product B	Total
Budgeted production (units)	2,000	1,500	
Machining department: machine hours	6,000 hrs	6,000 hrs	12,000 hrs
Assembly department: direct labour hours	2,000 hrs	3,000 hrs	5,000 hrs

The overhead absorption rates will be as follows.

	Machining department	Assembly department
Budgeted overheads	$48,000	$45,000
Budgeted activity	12,000 hrs	5,000 hrs
Absorption rate	$4 per machine hour	$9 per direct labour hour

Determine a budgeted cost per unit

The budgeted cost per unit would be as follows.

	Product A		Product B	
	$	$	$	$
Direct materials		14		12
Direct labour:				
Machining department	16		24	
Assembly department	6		12	
		22		36
Prime cost		36		48
Production overhead:				
Machining department	12		16	
Assembly department	9		18	
		21		34
Full production cost		57		82

(b) **Apportion actual service department overhead to production departments**

When the actual costs are analysed, the 'actual' overhead of the canteen department ($15,000) would be split between the machining and assembly departments.

	Machining department $	Assembly department $	Total $
Allocated cost	30,700	27,600	58,300
Apportioned general overhead	17,000	8,000	25,000
Canteen (30:20)	9,000	6,000	15,000
	56,700	41,600	98,300

Establish the over- or under-absorption of overheads

There would be an over- or under-absorption of overheads as follows.

		Machining department $		Assembly department $	Total $
Overheads absorbed					
Product A (2,200 units)	(× $4 × 3hrs)	26,400	(× $9 × 1hr)	19,800	46,200
Product B (1,500 units)	(× $4 × 4hrs)	24,000	(× $9 × 2hrs)	27,000	51,000
		50,400		46,800	97,200
Overheads incurred		56,700		41,600	98,300
Over-/(under)-absorbed overhead		(6,300)		5,200	(1,100)

The total under-absorbed overhead of $1,100 will be written off to the income statement at the end of the year, to compensate for the fact that overheads charged to production ($97,200) were less than the overheads actually incurred ($98,300).

4.3.1 Accounting for under or over absorption

As has been noted in the example above, the under-absorbed overhead is written off to the income statement as a cost to compensate for the undercharging of overheads to that point. The double entry to correct the under-absorption in the above example is:

DEBIT	Income statement		1,100
CREDIT	Production overhead control	1,100	

To account for an over-absorption of production overheads, the double entry would be as follows:

DEBIT	Production overhead control		X
CREDIT	Income statement	X	

4.4 Inventory valuation using absorption costing and marginal costing

Marginal costing is significantly different from absorption costing. It is an **alternative method** of accounting for costs and profit, which rejects the principles of absorbing fixed overheads into unit costs.

(a) **In marginal costing**

    (i)   Closing inventories are valued at **marginal production cost**.

    (ii)   Fixed costs are charged in full against the profit of the period in which they are incurred.

(b) **In absorption costing**

    (i)   Closing inventories are valued at full production cost, and include a share of fixed production costs.

    (ii)   This means that the cost of sales in a period will include some fixed overhead incurred in a previous period (in opening inventory values) and will exclude some fixed overhead incurred in the current period but carried forward in closing inventory values as a charge to a subsequent accounting period.

4.5 Profit statements using absorption costing and marginal costing

The different treatment of overheads in the two methods are reflected in the profit statements produced. In a marginal costing system, all variable costs are deducted from the sales figure to give a **contribution** figure. All fixed costs are then deducted from this figure to give a **net profit** figure.

In absorption costing, all production costs are deducted from sales to give a **gross profit** figure. Selling and distribution and administration overheads are then deducted from this figure to give a **net** profit figure.

This is demonstrated in the following example.

4.6 Example: profits under marginal and absorption costing

TLF Company manufactures a single product, the Claud. The following **budgeted** figures relate to the Claud for a one-year period.

Activity level	100%
Sales and productions (units)	800

	$
Sales	16,000
Production costs: variable	6,400
fixed	1,600
Sales and distribution costs:	
variable	3,200
fixed	2,400

Fixed costs are incurred evenly throughout the year, and actual fixed costs are the same as budgeted.

Actual variable costs per unit are also the same as budgeted.

All of the variable production costs are direct costs (ie there are no overheads).

There were no inventories of Claud at the beginning of the year.

In the first quarter, 220 units were produced and 160 units sold.

Required

(a)   Calculate the fixed production costs absorbed by Claud in the first quarter if absorption costing is used.
(b)   Calculate the under/over recovery of overheads during the quarter.
(c)   Calculate the profit using absorption costing.
(d)   Calculate the profit using marginal costing.

Solution

(a) $$\frac{\text{Budgeted fixed production costs}}{\text{Budgeted output}} = \frac{\$1,600}{800 \text{ units}}$$

Absorption rate = $2 per unit produced.

During the quarter, the fixed production overhead absorbed was 220 units × $2 = $440.

(b)

	$
Actual fixed production overhead	400 (1/4 of $1,600)
Absorbed fixed production overhead	440
Over absorption of overhead	40

(c) **Profit for the quarter, absorption costing**

	$	$
Sales (160 × $20)		3,200
Production costs		
Variable (220 × $8)	1,760	
Fixed (absorbed overhead (220 × $2))	440	
Total (220 × $10)	2,200	
Less closing inventories (60 × $10)	600	
Production cost of sales	1,600	
Adjustment for over-absorbed overhead	40	
Total production costs		1,560
Gross profit		1,640
Less: sales and distribution costs		
variable (160 × $4)	640	
fixed (1/4 of $2,400)	600	
		1,240
Net profit		400

(d) **Profit for the quarter, marginal costing**

	$	$
Sales		3,200
Variable production costs	1,760	
Less closing inventories (60 × $8)	480	
Variable production cost of sales	1,280	
Variable sales and distribution costs	640	
Total variable costs of sales		1,920
Total contribution		1,280
Less:		
Fixed production costs incurred	400	
Fixed sales and distribution costs	600	
		1,000
Net profit		280

CHAPTER ROUNDUP

↳ **Overheads** are made up of indirect materials, indirect labour and indirect expenses.

↳ Under **absorption costing principles**, the production overheads of a business are absorbed into the cost of each of the products.

↳ The first stage of the process is the allocation of specific overheads to specific **cost centres** – then joint overheads are apportioned to each cost centre on an **appropriate basis**.

↳ The **overheads** of the **service cost centres** must then be reapportioned to the production cost centres on an appropriate basis.

↳ Once all of the production overheads have been apportioned to the production cost centres an **overhead absorption rate** is determined normally based upon direct labour hours or machine hours.

↳ The **overhead absorption rate** is then used to cost each product depending upon how many relevant hours each product takes in each production cost centre.

↳ In order for overheads to be initially allocated and apportioned to the correct cost centres all overhead invoices must be carefully coded.

↳ In absorption costing, it is usual to add overheads into products costs by applying a **predetermined overhead absorption rate**. The predetermined rate is set annually, in the budget.

↳ The **absorption rate** is calculated by dividing the budgeted overhead by the budgeted level of activity. For production overheads the level of activity is often budgeted direct labour hours or budgeted machine hours.

↳ Management should try to establish an absorption rate that provides a **reasonable 'accurate' estimate** of overhead costs for jobs, products or services.

↳ The rate of overhead absorption is based on **estimates** (of both numerator and denominator) and it is quite likely that either one or both of the estimates will not agree with what *actually* occurs. Actual overheads incurred will probably be either greater than or less than overheads absorbed into the cost of production.

(a) Over absorption means that the overheads charged to the cost of production are greater than the overheads actually incurred.

(b) Under absorption means that insufficient overheads have been included in the cost of production.

QUICK QUIZ

1 What is the name given to the costing method where the cost of goods sold and the value of closing inventory include an element of indirect costs or overheads?

    A   Absorption costing
    B   Allocation costing
    C   Apportionment costing
    D   Activity-based costing

2 Which one of the following is the formula for calculating an overhead absorption rate?

    A   Actual activity level ÷ budgeted total overhead
    B   Budgeted activity level ÷ budgeted total overhead
    C   Budgeted total overhead ÷ budgeted activity level
    D   Budgeted total overhead ÷ actual activity level

3   Put the following stages of absorption costing into the correct order.

      A   Reapportionment
      B   Allocation
      C   Absorption
      D   Apportionment

4   H Co bases its overhead absorption rate on labour hours. The following information is available for 20X9.

Budgeted overheads	$600,000
Actual overheads	$660,000
Budgeted labour hours	120,000
Actual labour hours	110,000

Calculate the over- or under-absorption of overheads for 20X9.

      A $60,000 over-absorbed
      B $60,000 under-absorbed
      C $110,000 over-absorbed
      D $110,000 under-absorbed

5   Over absorption occurs when absorbed overheads are greater than actual overheads.

      True   ☐

      False ☐

ANSWERS TO QUICK QUIZ

1   A   This is absorption costing. Absorption costing involves allocating specific overheads and apportioning any joint expenses.

2   C   Budgeted total overhead ÷ budgeted activity level. Remember that overhead absorption rates are calculated before the actual figures are known so they must use 'budgeted' figures.

3   1B, 2D, 3A, 4C. Specific overheads are first allocated to cost centres. Then joint overheads are apportioned to each cost centre on an appropriate basis. The overheads of service cost centres are then reapportioned to production cost centres. Once all of the overheads have been apportioned an overhead absorption rate can be determined and overheads can be absorbed.

4   D $$OAR = \frac{\text{Budgeted overheads}}{\text{Budgeted labour hours}} = \frac{\$600,000}{120,000} = \$5 \text{ per labour hour}$$

Overheads absorbed =   110,000 hours × $5
                    = $550,000

Overheads absorbed – actual overheads   = $550,000 – $660,000
                                         = $110,000

∴ overheads were under-absorbed by $110,000.

5   True

Now try ...

Attempt the questions below from the **Exam Question Bank**

Number

Q27-29

CHAPTER

08

Job, batch and process costing

In this chapter we will be looking at three important costing systems.

- Job costing
- Batch costing
- Process costing

A **costing system** is a system of collecting costs which is designed to suit the way that goods are processed or manufactured or the way that services are provided.

Each organisation's costing system will have unique features but **costing systems of organisations in the same line of business will have common aspects.** On the other hand, organisations involved in completely different activities, such as hospitals and car part manufacturers, will each use very different costing systems.

TOPIC LIST	SYLLABUS REFERENCE
1 Job costing	D4 (a) (i) (ii)
2 Batch costing	D4 (b) (i) (ii)
3 Process costing features	D4 (c) (i)
4 Basics of process costing	D4 (c) (ii)
5 Losses	D4 (c) (vi)
6 Closing work in progress	D4 (c) (iii) (iv) (v)

1   Job costing

Job costing is a form of specific order costing in which costs are attributed to individual jobs.

 Job costing is the costing method used where each cost unit (job) is separately identifiable.

1.1 Aim of job costing

The aim of **job costing** is simply to collect the cost information shown below.

	$
Direct materials	X
Direct labour	X
Direct expenses	X
Direct cost	X
Production overhead	X
Total production cost	X
Administration overhead	X
Selling overhead	X
Cost of sales	X

To the final figure is added a profit **'mark-up'** and the total is the selling price of the job.

In other words, all we are doing is looking at one way of putting together the pieces of information that we have studied separately so far.

1.2 What is a job?

A **job** is a cost unit which consists of a single order or contract.

With other methods of costing it is usual to **produce for inventory**. Management therefore decide in advance how many units of each type, size, colour, quality and so on will be produced during the coming period. These decisions will all be taken without taking into account the identity of the individual customers who will eventually buy the products.

In job costing on the other hand, production is usually carried out in accordance with the **special requirements** of each customer. It is therefore usual for each job to **differ in one or more respects from every other job**, which means that a separate record must be maintained to show the details of a particular job.

The work relating to a job is usually carried out within a factory or workshop and moves through processes and operations as a **continuously identifiable unit**.

1.3 Procedure for the performance of jobs

The normal procedure in jobbing concerns involves the following.

(a)   The prospective customer approaches the supplier and indicates the **requirements** of the job.

(b)   A responsible official sees the prospective customer and agrees the **precise details of the items** to be supplied, for example the quantity, quality and colour of the goods, the date of delivery and any special requirements.

(c)   The estimating department of the organisation then prepares an **estimate** for the job. The total of these items will represent the **quoted selling price**.

(d)   At the appropriate time, the job will be **'loaded'** on to the factory floor. This means that as soon as all materials, labour and equipment are available and subject to the scheduling of other orders, the job will be started.

1.4 Collection of job costs

Each job will be given a **number** to identify it. A separate record must be maintained to show the details of individual jobs. The process of collecting job costs may be outlined as follows.

(a)   Materials requisitions are sent to stores.

(b)   The materials requisition note will be used to cost the materials issued to the job concerned, and this cost may then be recorded on a job cost sheet.

(c)   The job ticket is passed to the worker who is to perform the first operation.

(d)   When the job is completed by the worker who performs the final operation, the job ticket is sent to the cost office, where the time spent will be costed and recorded on the job cost sheet.

(e)   The relevant costs of materials issued, direct labour performed and direct expenses incurred as recorded on the job cost card are charged to the job account in the work in progress ledger.

(f)   The job account is debited with the job's share of the factory overhead, based on the absorption rate(s) in operation.

(g)   On completion of the job, the job account is charged with the appropriate administration, selling and distribution overhead, after which the total cost of the job can be ascertained.

(h)   The difference between the agreed selling price and the total actual cost will be the supplier's profit (or loss).

1.5 Job account

Here is a proforma job account, which will be one of the accounts in the work in progress control account.

JOB ACCOUNT

	$		$
Materials issued	X	Finished jobs	X
Direct labour	X		
Direct expenses	X		
Production overhead at predetermined rate	X		
Other overheads	X		
	X̲		X̲

1.6 Job cost card

When jobs are completed, **job cost cards** are transferred from the **work in progress** category to **finished goods**. When delivery is made to the customer, the costs become a **cost of sale**.

1.6.1 Example: Job cost card

JOB COST CARD												Job No. B641			
Customer Mr J White					Customer's Order No.							Vehicle make Peugot 205 GTE			
Job Description Repair damage to offside front door												Vehicle reg. no. G 614 SOX			
Estimate Ref. 2599					Invoice No.										
Quoted price $338.68					Invoice price $355.05							Date to collect 14.6.X0			

Material						Labour								Overheads			
				Cost			Emp-loyee	Cost Ctre	Hrs.	Rate	Bonus	Cost				Cost	
Date	Req. No.	Qty.	Price	$	p	Date						$	p	Hrs	OAR	$	p
12.6	36815	1	75.49	75	49	12.6	018	B	1.98	6.50	-	12	87	7.9	2.50	19	75
12.6	36816	1	33.19	33	19	13.6	018	B	5.92	6.50	-	38	48				
12.6	36842	5	6.01	30	05						13.65	13	65				
13.6	36881	5	3.99	19	95												
Total C/F				158	68	Total C/F						65	00	Total C/F		19	75

Expenses						Job Cost Summary	Actual		Estimate	
				Cost			$	p	$	p
Date	Ref.	Description		$	p	Direct Materials B/F	158	68	158	68
						Direct Expenses B/F	50	00		
						Direct Labour B/F	65	00	180	00
12.6	-	N. Jolley Panel-beating		50	-	Direct Cost	273	68		
						Overheads B/F	19	75		
							293	43		
						Admin overhead (add 10%)	29	34		
						= Total Cost	322	77	338	68
						Invoice Price	355	05		
Total C/F				50	-	Job Profit/Loss	32	28		

Comments

Job Cost Card Completed by _____

1.7 Job costing and computerisation

Job cost cards exist in **manual** systems, but it is increasingly likely that in large organisations the job costing system will be **computerised**, using accounting software specifically designed to deal with job costing requirements.

Job costing systems may also be used to control the costs of **internal service departments**, eg the maintenance department.

1.8 Example: Job costing

Pansy Co is a company that carries out jobbing work. One of the jobs carried out in May was job 2409, to which the following information relates.

Direct material Y: 400 kilos were issued from stores at a cost of $5 per kilo.

Direct material Z: 800 kilos were issued from stores at a cost of $6 per kilo. 60 kilos were returned to stores.

Department P: 300 labour hours were worked, of which 100 hours were overtime.

Department Q: 200 labour hours were worked, of which 100 hours were overtime.

Overtime work is not normal in Department P, where basic pay is $6 per hour plus an overtime premium of $1 per hour. Overtime work was done in Department Q in May because of a request by the customer of another job to complete his job quickly. Basic pay in Department Q is $8 per hour and overtime premium is $1.50 per hour. Overhead is absorbed at the rate of $3 per direct labour hour in both departments.

Required

(a)   Calculate the direct materials cost of job 2409
(b)   Calculate the direct labour cost of job 2409
(c)   Calculate the full production cost of job 2409 using absorption costing

Solution

(a)

	$
Direct material Y (400 kilos × $5)	2,000
Direct material Z (800 – 60 kilos × $6)	4,440
Total direct material cost	6,440

(b)

	$
Department P (300 hours × $6)	1,800
Department Q (200 hours × $8)	1,600
Total direct labour cost	3,400

Overtime premium will be charged to overhead in the case of Department P, and to the job of the customer who asked for overtime to be worked in the case of Department Q.

(c)

	$
Direct material cost	6,440
Direct labour cost	3,400
Production overhead (500 hours × $3)	1,500
	11,340

2 Batch costing

Batch costing is a form of specific order costing in which costs are attributed to batches of products.

> **Batch costing** is similar to job costing in that each batch of similar articles is separately identifiable. The **cost per unit** manufactured in a batch is the total batch cost divided by the number of units in the batch.

Batch costing is used where common equipment is used to produce batches of different products. It is especially relevant where products are not made for a specific job, but are produced for inventory using a single production line. (If a batch of items is made to order then the costing method is classified as job

costing.) Examples of industries where batch costing is common would be food manufacturing, paint manufacturing, drug manufacturing.

2.1 Introduction

A **batch** is a cost unit which consists of a separate, readily identifiable group of product units which maintains its separate identity throughout the production process.

The procedures for **costing batches** are very similar to those for costing jobs.

> The batch is treated as a **separate cost unit** during production and the costs are collected as described earlier in this chapter.

> Once the batch has been completed, the **cost per unit** can be calculated as the total batch cost divided by the number of units in the batch.

2.2 Example: Batch costing

A company manufactures model cars and has the following budgeted overheads for the next month, based on normal activity levels.

Department	Budgeted overheads	Budgeted activity
	$	
Welding	6,000	1,500 labour hours
Assembly	10,000	1,000 labour hours

Selling and administrative overheads are 20% of production cost. Production of 250 model cars type XJS1, made as Batch 8638, incurred the following costs.

Materials	$12,000
Labour	100 hours welding shop at $8/hour
	200 hours assembly shop at $9/hour

The cost of hiring special X-ray equipment for testing the welds was $500.

Required

Calculate the cost per unit for Batch 8638.

Solution

The first step is to calculate the overhead absorption rate for the production departments.

$$\text{Welding} = \frac{\$6,000}{1,500} = \$4 \text{ per labour hour}$$

$$\text{Assembly} = \frac{\$10,000}{1,000} = \$10 \text{ per labour hour}$$

Total cost – Batch no 8638

	$	$
Direct material		12,000
Direct labour 100 × $8 =	800	
200 × $9 =	1,800	
		2,600
Direct expense		500
Prime cost		15,100
Overheads 100 × 4 =	400	
200 × 10 =	2,000	
		2,400
Production cost		17,500
Selling and administrative cost (20% of production cost)		3,500
Total cost		21,000

$$\text{Cost per unit} = \frac{\$21,000}{250} = \$84$$

QUESTION

Batch costing

Lyfsa Kitchen Units Co crafts two different sizes of standard unit and a DIY all-purpose unit for filling up awkward spaces. The units are built in batches of around 250 (although the number varies according to the quality of wood purchased), and each batch is sold to NGJ Furniture Warehouses Co.

The costs incurred in May were as follows.

	Big unit	Little unit	All-purpose
Direct materials purchased	$5,240	$6,710	$3,820
Direct labour			
Skilled (hours)	1,580	1,700	160
Semi-skilled (hours)	3,160	1,900	300
Direct expenses	$1,180	$1,700	$250
Selling price of batch	$48,980	$43,125	$25,660
Completed at 31 May	100%	80%	25%

The following information is available.

All direct materials for the completion of the batches have been recorded. Skilled labour is paid $9 per hour, semi-skilled $7 per hour. Administration expenses total $4,400 per month and are to be allocated to the batches on the basis of direct labour hours. Direct labour costs, direct expenses and administration expenses will increase in proportion to the total labour hours required to complete the little units and the all-purpose units. On completion of the work the practice of the manufacturer is to divide the calculated profit on each batch 20% to staff as a bonus, 80% to the company. Losses are absorbed 100% by the company.

Required

(a) Calculate the profit or loss made by the company on big units.
(b) Project the profit or loss likely to be made by the company on little units and all-purpose units.

ANSWER

(a) **Big units**

	$	$
Direct materials		5,240
Direct labour		
Skilled 1,580 hours at $9	14,220	
Semi-skilled 3,160 hours at $7	22,120	
		36,340
Direct expenses		1,180
Administrative expenses		
4,740 hours at $0.50 (see below)*		2,370

			45,130
Selling price			48,980
Calculated profit			3,850
Divided: Staff bonus 20%			770
Profit for company 80%			3,080

*Administrative expenses absorption rate $= \dfrac{\$4,400}{8,800}$ per labour hour

$= \$0.50$ per labour hour

(b)

		Little units			All-purpose	
		$	$		$	$
Direct materials			6,710			3,820
Direct labour						
Skilled	1,700 hrs at $9	15,300		160 hrs at $9	1,440	
Semi-skilled	1,900 hrs at $7	13,300		300 hrs at $7	2,100	
Direct expenses		1,700			250	
Administration						
expenses:	3,600 hrs at $0.50	1,800		460 hrs at $0.50	230	
		32,100			4,020	
Costs to						
completion	20/80 × 32,100	8,025		75/25 × 4,020	12,060	
			40,125			16,080
Total costs			46,835			19,900
Selling price			43,125			25,660
Calculated						
profit/(loss)			(3,710)			5,760
Divided: Staff bonus 20%			-			1,152
(Loss)/profit for company			(3,710)			4,608

Note that whilst direct labour costs, direct expenses and administration expenses increase in proportion to the total labour hours required to complete the little units and the all-purpose units, there will be no further material costs to complete the batches.

3 Process costing features

Process costing is a costing method used where there are continuous processes. Process costs are attributed to the units produced in a period.

3.1 Introduction

We have now looked at two cost accounting methods: **job costing** and **batch costing**. We will now consider another costing method, **process costing**. Process costing is applied when output consists of a continuous stream of **identical units**.

We will begin from basics and look at how to account for the most simple of processes. We will then move on to how to account for any **losses** which might occur. Next we will consider how to deal with **closing work in progress**.

EXAM FOCUS POINT

Process costing is frequently examined and it is very important you present your answers clearly.

3.2 Features of process costing

Process costing is a costing method used to determine the cost of units manufactured from a continuous process. It is common to identify process costing with **continuous production** such as the following.

- Oil refining
- Sugar refining
- Chemical processing
- Brewing

Features of process costing include the following.

(a) There is often a **loss in process** due to spoilage, wastage, evaporation and so on.

(b) The **output** of one process becomes the **input** to the next until the finished product is made in the final process.

(c) Output from production may be a single product, but there may also be one or more **by-products** and/or **joint products** (these are not covered in MA1).

4 Basics of process costing

Use our suggested four-step approach when dealing with process costing questions.

Step 1 Determine output and losses

Step 2 Calculate cost per unit of output

Step 3 Calculate total cost of completed output and WIP (step not required if no WIP)

Step 4 Complete accounts

4.1 Basic techniques

Before tackling the more complex areas of process costing, we will begin by looking at a very simple process costing example which will illustrate the basic techniques which we will build upon in the remainder of this chapter.

4.1.1 Example: Basics of process costing

Suppose that Royal Oak Co makes coloured terracotta pots. Production of the pots involves two processes, shaping and colouring. During the year to 31 March 20X3, 1,000,000 units of material worth $500,000 were input to the first process, shaping. Direct labour costs of $200,000 and production overhead costs of $200,000 were also incurred in connection with the shaping process. There were no opening or closing inventories in the shaping department. The process account for shaping for the year ended 31 March 20X3 is as follows.

Process 1

PROCESS 1 (SHAPING) ACCOUNT

	Units	$		Units	$
Direct materials	1,000,000	500,000	Output to Process 2	1,000,000	900,000
Direct labour		200,000			
Production overheads		200,000			
	1,000,000	900,000		1,000,000	900,000

You will see that a **process account** is nothing more than a **ledger account** with debit and credit entries although it does have an additional column on both the debit and credit sides showing **quantity**. When preparing process accounts, perhaps as part of your workings, you are advised to include these memorandum quantity columns and to balance them off (ie ensure they total to the same amount on both sides) **before** attempting to complete the monetary value columns since they will help you to check that you have missed nothing out. This becomes increasingly important as more complications are introduced into questions.

Process 2

When using process costing, if a series of separate processes is needed to manufacture the finished product, the **output of one process becomes the input to the next until the final output is made in the final process**. In our example, all output from shaping was transferred to the second process, colouring, during the year to 31 March 20X3. Additional material costing $300,000 was input to the colouring process. Direct labour costs of $150,000 and production overhead costs of $150,000 were also incurred. There were no opening or closing inventories in the colouring department. The process account for colouring for the year ended 31 March 20X3 is as follows.

PROCESS 2 (COLOURING) ACCOUNT

	Units	$		Units	$
Materials from process 1	1,000,000	900,000	Output to finished		
Added materials		300,000	goods	1,000,000	1,500,000
Direct labour		150,000			
Production overhead		150,000			
	1,000,000	1,500,000		1,000,000	1,500,000

Added materials, labour and overhead in Process 2 are usually **added gradually** throughout the process. Materials from Process 1, in contrast, will often be **introduced in full at the start of the second process**.

4.2 Cost per unit

The main aim of process costing is to calculate a cost per unit that gives completed units and closing inventories a value.

$$\text{Cost per unit} = \frac{\text{Costs incurred}}{\text{Output}}$$

4.2.1 Example: Cost per unit

We can calculate a cost per unit for the earlier example (Royal Oak Co) as follows.

$$\text{Cost per unit} = \frac{\text{Costs incurred}}{\text{Output}}$$

$$\text{Process 1 cost per unit} = \frac{\$900,000}{1,000,000 \text{ units}}$$

$$= \$0.90 \text{ per unit}$$

$$\text{Process 2 cost per unit} = \frac{\$1,500,000}{1,000,000 \text{ units}}$$

$$= \$1.50 \text{ per unit (this includes the process 1 cost of \$0.90 per unit).}$$

QUESTION

Cost per unit

During a period, 50,000 units of material were input to Process 1 at the production plant of Jingles Co. The following costs were incurred.

Materials	$100,000
Direct labour	$200,000
Production overhead	$100,000

50,000 units were completed in Process 1 and transferred to Process 2. There were no opening or closing work in progress inventories.

Required

Calculate the cost per unit of Process 1 output.

ANSWER

$$\text{Cost per unit} = \frac{\text{Costs incurred}}{\text{Output}}$$

Costs incurred   = $100,000 + $200,000 + $100,000

              = $400,000

Output = 50,000

$$\text{Cost per unit} = \frac{\$400,000}{50,000 \text{ units}}$$

              = $8 per unit

4.3 Framework for dealing with process costing

Process costing is centred around **four key steps**. The exact work done at each step will depend on the circumstances of the question, but the approach can always be used. Don't worry about the terms used. We will be looking at their meaning as we work through the chapter.

Step 1	Determine output and losses
	• Determine output
	• Calculate losses
	• Calculate equivalent units if there is closing work in progress

Step 2	Calculate cost per unit of output
	Calculate cost per unit or cost per equivalent unit.

Step 3	Calculate total cost of completed output and WIP (step not required if no WIP)
	In some examples this will be straightforward. In cases where there is work in progress, a statement of evaluation will have to be prepared.

Step 4	Complete accounts
	• Complete the process account
	• Write up the other accounts required by the question

EXAM FOCUS POINT

It always saves time in an exam if you don't have to think too long about how to approach a question before you begin. This four-step approach can be applied to any process costing question so it would be a good idea to memorise it now.

5 Losses

During a production process, a **loss** may occur due to wastage, spoilage, evaporation, and so on.

If loss is expected, and is an unavoidable feature of processing, it is argued by cost accountants that there is no point in charging a cost to the loss. It is more sensible to accept that the loss will occur, and

spread the costs of production over the actual units of output. An expected loss is called a 'normal loss'. The incidence of 'abnormal loss' (which **is** given a cost) as well as normal loss will be covered in paper MA2.

5.1 Example: Loss

Suppose 2,000 units are input to a process. Loss is 5% of input and there are no opening or closing inventories.

Required

Calculate the loss.

Solution

Loss = 5% × 2,000 units
     = 100 units

QUESTION   Losses

Jingles Co operates a single manufacturing process, and during March the following processing took place.

Opening inventory	nil	Closing inventory	nil
Units introduced	1,000 units	Output	900 units
Costs incurred	$4,500	Loss	100 units

Required

Determine the cost of output

ANSWER

$$\frac{\text{Costs}}{\text{Output}} = \frac{\$4,500}{900 \text{ units}}$$

$$\text{Cost per unit of output} = \frac{\$4,500}{900} = \$5$$

Normal loss is not given any cost, so that the process account would appear as follows.

PROCESS ACCOUNT

	Units	$		Units	$
Costs incurred	1,000	4,500	Normal loss	100	0
			Output units	900	4,500
	1,000	4,500		1,000	4,500

It helps to enter normal loss into the process 'T' account, just to make sure that your memorandum columns for units are the same on the debit and the credit sides of the account.

5.2 Example: Losses

Suppose 1,000 units at a cost of $4,500 are input to a process. Losses are 10% and there are no opening or closing inventories.

Required

Complete the process account.

Solution

Before we demonstrate the use of the 'four-step framework' we will summarise the way that the losses are dealt with.

- Loss is given no share of cost
- The cost of output is therefore based on the **expected** units of output, which in our example amount to 900

Step 1	Determine output and losses
	If loss is 10% (100 units), then output is 900 units.

Step 2	Calculate cost per unit of output
	The cost per unit of output and the cost per unit of loss are based on output.

$$\frac{\text{Costs incurred}}{\text{Output}} = \frac{\$4,500}{900 \text{ units}} = \$5.00 \text{ per unit}$$

Step 3	Not required (as no WIP)

Step 4   Complete accounts

PROCESS ACCOUNT

	Units	$		Units		$
Cost incurred	1,000	4,500	Output (finished goods a/c)	900	(× $5)	4,500
			Loss	100	(× $0)	0
	1,000	4,500		1,000		4,500

QUESTION

Process account

During period 3, costs of input to a process were $29,070. Input was 1,000 units and losses are 10% of input.

During the next period, period 4, costs of input were again $29,070. Input was 980 units.

There were no units of opening or closing inventory.

Required

Prepare the process account for period 3 and period 4.

ANSWER

Step 1	Determine output and losses
	Period 3

	Units
Actual output	900
Loss	100
Input	1,000

Period 4

	Units
Actual output	882
Loss	98
Input	980

Step 2   **Calculate cost per unit of output**

For each period the cost per unit is based on output.

Period 3

$$\frac{\text{Cost of input}}{\text{Units of output}} = \frac{\$29,070}{900} = \$32.30 \text{ per unit}$$

Period 4

$$\frac{\text{Cost of input}}{\text{Units of output}} = \frac{\$29,070}{882} = \$32.96 \text{ per unit}$$

Step 3   **Not required (as no WIP)**

Step 4   **Complete accounts**

PROCESS ACCOUNT

	Units	$		Units	$
Period 3					
Cost of input	1,000	29,070	Finished goods a/c (× $32.30)	900	29,070
			Loss a/c	100	0
	1,000	29,070		1,000	29,070
Period 4					
Cost of input	980	29,070	Finished goods a/c (× $32.96)	882	29,070
			Loss a/c	98	0
	980	29,070		980	29,070

6 Closing work in progress

When units are partly completed at the end of a period (ie when there is **closing work in progress**) it is necessary to calculate the **equivalent units of production** in order to determine the cost of a completed unit.

In the examples we have looked at so far we have assumed that opening and closing inventories of work in process have been nil. We must now look at more realistic examples and consider how to allocate the costs incurred in a period between completed output (ie finished units) and partly completed closing inventory.

Some examples will help to illustrate the problem, and the techniques used to share out (apportion) costs between finished output and closing work in progress.

6.1 Example: Valuation of closing inventory

Trotter Co is a manufacturer of processed goods. In one process, there was no opening inventory, but 5,000 units of input were introduced to the process during the month, and the following costs were incurred.

	$
Direct materials	16,560
Direct labour	7,360
Production overhead	5,520
	29,440

Of the 5,000 units introduced, 4,000 were completely finished during the month and transferred to the next process. Closing inventory of 1,000 units was only 60% complete with respect to materials and conversion costs.

Solution

(a) The problem in this example is to **divide the costs of production** ($29,440) between the finished output of 4,000 units and the closing inventory of 1,000 units.

(b) To apportion costs fairly and proportionately, units of production must be converted into the equivalent of completed units, ie into **equivalent units of production**.

Equivalent units are notional whole units which represent incomplete work, and which are used to apportion costs between work in progress and completed output.

Step 1 | **Determine output**

For this step in our framework we need to prepare a statement of equivalent units.

STATEMENT OF EQUIVALENT UNITS

	Total units	Completion	Equivalent units
Fully worked units	4,000	100%	4,000
Closing inventory	1,000	60%	600
	5,000		4,600

Step 2 | **Calculate cost per unit of output**

For this step in our framework we need to prepare a statement of costs per equivalent unit because equivalent units are the basis for apportioning costs.

STATEMENT OF COSTS PER EQUIVALENT UNIT

$$\frac{\text{Total cost}}{\text{Equivalent units}} = \frac{\$29,440}{4,600}$$

Cost per equivalent unit = $6.40

Step 3   **Calculate total cost of completed output and WIP**

For this stage in our framework a statement of evaluation may now be prepared, to show how the costs should be apportioned between finished output and closing inventory.

STATEMENT OF EVALUATION

	Equivalent units	Cost per equivalent unit	Valuation $
Fully worked units	4,000	$6.40	25,600
Closing inventory	600	$6.40	3,840
	4,600		29,440

Step 4   **Complete accounts**

The process account would be shown as follows.

PROCESS ACCOUNT

		Units	$		Units	$
(Stores a/c)	Direct materials	5,000	16,560	Output to next process	4,000	25,600
(Wages a/c)	Direct labour		7,360	Closing inventory c/f	1,000	3,840
(O'hd a/c)	Production o'hd		5,520			
		5,000	29,440		5,000	29,440

When preparing a process 'T' account, it might help to make the entries as follows.

(a) **Enter the units first**. The units columns are simply memorandum columns, but they help you to make sure that there are no units unaccounted for (for example as loss).

(b) Enter the costs of materials, labour and overheads next. These should be given to you.

(c) Enter your valuation of finished output and closing inventory next. The value of the credit entries should, of course, equal the value of the debit entries.

6.2 Different rates of input

In many industries, materials, labour and overhead may be added at **different rates** during the course of production.

(a) Output from a previous process (for example the output from process 1 to process 2) may be introduced into the subsequent process all at once, so that closing inventory is 100% complete in respect of these materials.

(b)   Further materials may be **added gradually** during the process, so that closing inventory is only **partially complete** in respect of these added materials.

(c)   Labour and overhead may be 'added' at yet another different rate. When production overhead is absorbed on a labour hour basis, however, we should expect the degree of completion on overhead to be the same as the degree of completion on labour.

When this situation occurs, equivalent units, and a cost per equivalent unit, should be **calculated separately for each type of material, and also for conversion costs**.

6.3 Example: Equivalent units and different degrees of completion

Suppose that Shaker Co is a manufacturer of processed goods, and that results in process 2 for a period were as follows.

Opening inventory	nil
Material input from process 1	4,000 units
Costs of input:	$
Material from process 1	6,000
Added materials in process 2	1,080
Conversion costs	1,720

Output is transferred into the next process, process 3. No losses occur in the process.

Closing work in process amounted to 800 units, complete as to:

Process 1 material	100%
Added materials	50%
Conversion costs	30%

Required

Prepare the process 2 account for the period.

Solution

Step 1   Determine output and losses

STATEMENT OF EQUIVALENT UNITS (OF PRODUCTION IN THE PERIOD)

			Equivalent units of production					
			Process 1 material		Added materials		Labour and overhead	
Input Units	Output	Total Units	Units	%	Units	%	Units	%
4,000	Completed Production	3,200	3,200	100	3,200	100	3,200	100
	Closing inventory	800	800	100	400	50	240	30
4,000		4,000	4,000		3,600		3,440	

Step 2   Calculate cost per unit of output

STATEMENT OF COST (PER EQUIVALENT UNIT)

Input	Cost $	Equivalent production in units	Cost per unit $
Process 1 material	6,000	4,000	1.50
Added materials	1,080	3,600	0.30
Labour and overhead	1,720	3,440	0.50
	8,800		2.30

Step 3 **Calculate total cost of completed output and WIP**

STATEMENT OF EVALUATION (OF FINISHED WORK AND CLOSING INVENTORIES)

Production	Cost element	Number of equivalent units	Cost per equivalent unit $	Total $	Cost $
Completed production		3,200	2.30		7,360
Closing inventory:	process 1 material	800	1.50	1,200	
	added material	400	0.30	120	
	labour and overhead	240	0.50	120	
					1,440
					8,800

Step 4 **Complete accounts**

PROCESS 2 ACCOUNT

	Units	$		Units	$
Process 1 material	4,000	6,000	Process 3 a/c	3,200	7,360
Added material		1,080	(finished output)		
Conversion costs		1,720	Closing inventory c/f	800	1,440
	4,000	8,800		4,000	8,800

QUESTION

Equivalent units

A chemical producer manufactures Product XK by means of two successive processes, Process 1 and Process 2. The information provided below relates to the most recent accounting period, period 10.

	Process 1	Process 2
Opening work in progress	Nil	Nil
Material input during period	2,400 units – cost $5,280	2,200 units (from Process 1)
Added material		$9,460
Direct labour	$2,260	$10,560
Factory overhead	100% of labour cost	2/3 of labour cost
Transfer to Process 2	2,200 units	
Transfer to finished goods		2,200 units
Closing work in progress	200 units 100% complete with respect to materials and 30% complete with respect to labour and production overhead.	Nil

Required

(a)   Calculate the value of the goods transferred from Process 1 to Process 2 during period 10.

(b)   Calculate the value of the closing work in progress left in Process 1 at the end of period 10.

(c)   Calculate the value of the goods transferred from Process 2, to finished goods, during period 10, and the value of one unit of production.

ANSWER

(a)   The value of goods transferred from Process 1 to Process 2 during period 10 was $9,240.

(b)   The value of closing work in progress left in Process 1 at the end of Period 10 was $560.

Workings

Remember that when closing WIP is partly completed, it is necessary to construct a statement of equivalent units in order to apportion costs fairly and proportionately.

STATEMENT OF EQUIVALENT UNITS

Input Units	Output	Total Units	Process 1 material	Labour	Overheads
2,400	Completed production (transfer to Process 2)	2,200	2,200 (100%)	2,200 (100%)	2,200
	Closing work in progress	200	200 (100%)	60 (30%)	60 (30%)
2,400		2,400	2,400	2,260	2,260

STATEMENT OF COST PER EQUIVALENT UNIT

Input		Cost	Equivalent units produced	Cost per unit
	$	$		$
Process 1 materials		5,280	2,400	2.20
Labour	2,260			
Overhead	2,260	4,520	2,260	2.00
		9,800		4.20

STATEMENT OF EVALUATION

Output	Number of equivalent units	Cost per unit		Value
			$	$
Transfers to Process 2	2,200	4.20		9,240
Closing work in progress				
Process 1 materials	200	2.20	440	
Labour and overhead	60	2.00	120	
				560
				9,800

PROCESS 1 ACCOUNT

	Units	$		Units	$
Process 1	2,400	5,280	Transfers to Process 2	2,200	9,240
Labour and overheads		4,520	Closing WIP	200	560
	2,400	9,800		2,400	9,800

(c)   STATEMENT OF EQUIVALENT UNITS

Input Units	Output	Total	Materials	Labour and overhead
2,200	Transferred from Process 1	2,200	2,200 (100%)	2,200 (100%)
2,200		2,200	2,200	2,200

NB. No opening or closing WIP in Process 2.

STATEMENT OF COST PER EQUIVALENT UNIT

Input		Cost	Equivalent units produced	Cost per unit
	$	$		
Transfers from Process 1		9,240	2,200	4.20
Added materials		9,460	2,200	4.30
Labour	10,560			
Overhead	7,040	17,600	2,200	8.00
Value of one unit of production =				16.50

Value of goods transferred from Process 2 to finished goods = 2,200 units × $16.50 = $36,300.

QUICK QUIZ

1   Which of the following are not characteristics of job costing?

   I   Customer driven production
   II   Complete production possible within a single accounting period
   III   Homogeneous products

   A   I and II only
   B   I and III only
   C   II and III only
   D   III only

2   How would you calculate the cost per unit of a completed batch?

3   A job cost estimate includes 630 productive labour hours. In addition, it is anticipated that idle time will be 10% of the total hours paid for the job. The wage rate is $12 per hour.

   What is the total estimated labour cost for the job?

   A $6,804
   B $7,560
   C $8,316
   D $8,400

4 A firm uses job costing. Details of the three jobs worked on during a period are:

	Job BA	Job DC	Job FE
	$	$	$
Opening work-in-progress	22,760	3,190	–
Direct materials in the period	4,620	11,660	14,335
Direct labour in the period	12,125	10,520	7,695

Overheads are absorbed at 40% of prime cost in each period. Jobs DC and FE remained incomplete at the end of the period.

What is the value of the closing work-in-progress?

A $61,894
B $65,084
C $66,360
D $68,952

5 Process costing is centred around four key steps.

Step 1 _____

Step 2 _____

Step 3 _____

Step 4 _____

6 When there is closing WIP at the end of a process, what is the first step in the four-step approach to process costing questions and why must it be done?

7 The following information relates to a production process for a period:

Input costs $194,860
Completed output 11,400 units
Closing work-in-progress 1,200 units (60% complete)
There were no process losses or opening work-in-progress.

What was the cost per unit for the process?

A $15.47
B $16.08
C $16.40
D $17.09

ANSWERS TO QUICK QUIZ

1   D

2    $$\frac{\text{Total batch cost}}{\text{Number of units in the batch}}$$

3   D $(630 \div 0.9 \text{ hours}) \times \$12/\text{hour}) = \$8,400$.

4   B   Job BA is completed so can be ignored

     Total costs $= (11,660 + 10,520 + 14,335 + 7,695) \times 1.4$

          $= \$61,894$

     Closing work in progress value $= 61,894 + 3,190$

                    $= \$65,084$

5

Step 1	Determine output and losses

Step 2	Calculate cost per unit of output

Step 3	Calculate total cost of completed output and WIP (not required if no WIP)

Step 4	Complete accounts

6   It is necessary to calculate the equivalent units of production (by drawing up a statement of equivalent units). Equivalent units of production are notional whole units which represent incomplete work and which are used to apportion costs between work in progress and completed output.

7   B $\$194,860 \div [11,400 + (1,200 \times 0\cdot6) \text{ units}] = \$16.08$

Now try ...

Attempt the questions below from the **Exam Question Bank**

Number

Q30-33

Providing management information

Providing management information

We saw earlier in the study text that management information helps managers plan, control and make decisions. We have also discussed how managers obtain actual data for the current period.

We now go on to discuss how managers make comparisons between actual data and other data. In doing so they can assess the **significance** of the actual data for the period. Comparing current results with other data can make the information more useful. Comparisons may also help to show up any errors that have occurred.

Information for comparison

Study Guide | Intellectual level

E Providing management information

1 Information for comparison

(a) Explain the purpose of making comparisons. K

(b) Identify relevant bases for comparison: previous period data, corresponding period data, forecast/budget data. S

(d) Explain the concept of flexible budgets. S

(e) Use appropriate income and expenditure data for comparison. S

One of the technical competences for FPER that relates to paper MA1 is to provide basic information on costs and revenues. You can apply the knowledge you obtain from this chapter of the text to help to demonstrate this competence.

---

1 Types of comparison

Comparing actual results with **other information** helps to put them in context.

```
   ┌──────────┐   ┌───────────────┐              ┌───────────┐
   │ Previous │   │ Corresponding │              │ Forecasts │
   │ periods  │   │   periods     │              └───────────┘
   └──────────┘   └───────────────┘

              ┌───────────────┐   ┌──────────┐
              │  COMPARISONS  │───│ Budgets  │
              └───────────────┘   └──────────┘
```

Comparisons may be **financial** or **non-financial**.

Common comparisons include the following.

1.1 Comparisons with previous periods

The most common comparison of a previous period is when **one year's final figures** are **compared** with the **previous year's**. A business's statutory financial accounts contain comparative figures for the previous year as well as the figures for the actual year. As financial accounts are sent to shareholders, this comparison is obviously of great interest to them.

For management accounting purposes, however, year-on-year comparisons are insufficient by themselves. Management will wish to pick up problems a lot sooner than the end of the financial year. Hence comparisons are often made for management accounting purposes **month-by-month** or **quarter-by-quarter**. This can either be a comparison with the previous period (eg comparing June 20X2 with May 20X2), or with the corresponding period (eg comparing June 20X2 with June 20X1).

Making comparisons month-by-month or quarter-by-quarter is most useful when you expect figures to be reasonably even over time. However demand for many products fluctuates **season-by-season**.

1.2 Example: seasonal fluctuations

A company making Christmas decorations had sales for the quarter ended 31 December that were considerably greater than sales for the previous quarter ended 30 September. For the quarter ended the following 31 March its sales decreased significantly again. Should its managers be concerned?

Based on the information given, we cannot tell. All the information tells us is that most people buy Christmas decorations in the three months leading up to Christmas. Comparing the December quarter's sales with the quarters either side is not very useful, because we are not comparing like with like. People are far more likely to buy Christmas decorations in the December quarter.

A far more meaningful comparison would therefore be to compare the December quarter's sales with those of the December quarter of the previous year, since the demand conditions would be similar.

This example demonstrates where comparisons with corresponding periods can be very useful, in businesses where the trade is **seasonal** (you would expect significant variations between adjacent periods).

Another example is heating bills. If the heating bill for the summer quarter is less than that for the winter quarter, the difference does not tell you anything about organisational performance, only about the weather.

1.3 Comparisons with forecasts

Businesses make forecasts for a number of purposes. A very common type of forecast is a **cash flow forecast.**

1.4 Example: cash flow forecast

GEORGE LIMITED: CASH FLOW FORECAST FOR FIRST QUARTER

	Jan $	Feb $	Mar $
Estimated cash receipts			
From credit customers	14,000	16,500	17,000
From cash sales	3,000	4,000	4,500
Proceeds on disposal of non-current assets	–	2,200	–
Total cash receipts	17,000	22,700	21,500
Estimated cash payments			
To suppliers of goods	8,000	7,800	10,500
To employees (wages)	3,000	3,500	3,500
Purchase of non-current assets	–	12,500	–
Rent and rates	–	–	1,000
Other overheads	1,200	1,200	1,200
Repayment of loan	2,500	–	–
	14,700	25,000	16,200
Net surplus/(deficit) for month	2,300	(2,300)	5,300
Opening cash balance	1,200	3,500	1,200
Closing cash balance	3,500	1,200	6,500

The purpose of making this forecast is for the business to be able to see how likely it is to have problems **maintaining** a **positive cash balance**. If the cash balance becomes negative, the business will have to obtain a loan or overdraft and have to pay interest costs.

At the end of the period management will **compare** the **actual figures** with the **forecast figures**, and try to assess why they differ. Differences are likely to be a sign that some of the **assumptions** made when drawing up the original forecast were **incorrect**. Hence management, when making forecasts for future periods, may wish to change the assumptions that are made.

1.5 Non-financial comparisons

As well as being made in **financial terms** (costs and revenues), you may make comparisons in other ways. For example you may compare units produced or sold. Other possible comparisons include measures of quality/customer satisfaction, time taken for various processes etc.

1.6 Example: a hospital casualty department

A hospital casualty department will aim to deal with incoming patients quickly, efficiently and effectively but numbers and types of patients are hard to predict. Comparing waiting times or cases dealt with per day will be misleading if one day includes the victims of a serious train crash and another covers only minor injuries. Long term comparisons might give a clearer picture and help to identify usage patterns (for example busy Saturday nights). Comparisons with other casualty departments might be even more revealing.

EXAM FOCUS POINT

You must be able to compare sets of data for the exam and be able to draw conclusions such as the fact that there were greater profits or higher levels of efficiency in one period versus the other.

1.7 Comparison with budgets

Most organisations have long-term goals which can be divided into:

- **Objectives** (measurable steps towards achieving their goals)
- **Action plans** (detailed steps for achieving their objectives)

The action plans are often expressed in money and provide:

- An overall view for management
- Assurance that different departments' plans co-ordinate with each other

The financial plan is usually called a **budget**.

A budget is an organisation's plan for a forthcoming period, expressed in monetary terms.

Budget comparisons are popular because they show whether budget holders are **achieving** their **targets**.

Budget reports may be **combined** with **other information** such as non-financial information, ratios etc.

Budgets, like forecasts, represent a view of the future. However the two are not identical. Forecasts represent a prediction of what is **likely to happen**, the most likely scenario. Budgets may be a **target** rather than a prediction. The target may be a very stiff one and it may be far more likely that the business fails to reach the target than that it does achieve the target. However management may feel that setting a stiff target may keep staff 'on their toes'.

You can use budgets to check that the organisation's financial plan is working by **comparing** the **budgeted results** for the day, week, month or year to date **with** the **actual results**. Differences between these are known as **variances**.

The ways in which managers use budgets is a part of a continuous process of planning, monitoring performance and taking action on variances. This is sometimes called the **control cycle** and can be illustrated as follows.

1.8 The control cycle

```
                    ┌─────────────────┐
                    │ 1: DECIDE GOALS │
                    │ AND OBJECTIVES  │
                    └─────────────────┘
┌─────────────────┐                    ┌─────────────┐
│ 6: COMPARE GOALS│                    │ 2: DEVELOP  │
│ AND OBJECTIVES  │                    │    PLAN     │
│ ACHIEVED WITH   │                    └─────────────┘
│ THOSE DEFINED   │
└─────────────────┘                    ┌──────────────────┐
                                       │ 3: DECIDE        │
┌─────────────────┐                    │ RESOURCES        │
│ 5: COMPARE      │                    │ NEEDED AND       │
│ ACTUAL          │                    │ PERFORMANCE      │
│ PERFORMANCE     │                    │ STANDARDS        │
│ WITH PLAN       │                    └──────────────────┘
└─────────────────┘
                    ┌─────────────────┐
                    │ 4: START        │
                    │ OPERATIONS      │
                    └─────────────────┘
```

Stages of the control cycle is what we are looking at here.

2 Identifying differences

2.1 Variances and flexed budgets

> Variances can be calculated by comparing the budget with the actual results (total variance) or comparing the flexed budget with the actual results (efficiency of usage and price variance).
>
> You should report differences in such a way that managers can **understand them** and pick out **vital information easily**. Comparisons should not be cluttered with irrelevant information or too much detail.

There are two ways of looking at variances. The first way is to compare the budget figures to the actual figures achieved and this is called a total cost variance (or total sales variance).

For example, XYZ Ltd produces a product M. The following information is available for June.

	Budget	Actual	Variance
Material Cost	$5,000	$7,000	$2,000 (adverse)

The total cost variance comparing budget to actual cost is $2,000 adverse.

The problem with this type of variance calculation is that the volume of production may be different from the budgeted volume. This means that variance may not be very helpful for management making decisions on the product M.

In the example above, more was spent on materials than we budgeted for so we have an adverse variance. At first sight this may seem like a bad thing and management may decide product M is costing too much. However, it turns out that there was such a large demand for product M in June that twice as many units of M were produced and sold. The materials were brought from an alternative supplier and cost only 35c per units instead of 50c per unit. This means that XYZ Ltd produced and sold more units and paid less per unit for the materials than budgeted. This is a good thing!

To make a useful comparison between the actual and budgeted figures for direct/variable costs we can use the second type of variance calculation. We can **adjust** or **flex** the budget to reflect the same production levels as was actually achieved. The new budget, flexed to the actual production level is known as the **flexed budget.** The differences between the actual figures and the new flexed budged give us variances which we will examine further in the next chapter. These take out the effects of volume changes between actual and budget, and focus instead on the variances resulting from changes in the efficiency with which resources are used, and from the price of the resources.

Flexed budgets should be used for comparison of direct/variable costs if the actual level of production is different from the original budget.

A **flexed budget** is a budget which recognises different cost behaviour patterns and is designed to change as volume of activity changes.

2.2 Example: flexed budget

Here is a production cost report for week 32 for the department making cartons.

	Actual	Budget	Variance	
Production (units)	5,000	4,800		
	$	$	$	
Direct materials	1,874	1,850	24	Adverse
Direct labour	825	810	15	Adverse
Prime cost	2,699	2,660	39	Adverse
Fixed overheads	826	840	14	Favourable
TOTAL COST	3,525	3,500	25	Adverse

Required

Prepare a flexed budget for week 32 for the department making cartons.

Solution

The figures above illustrate how easy it is to gain a misleading picture of performance if like is not compared with like. At first glance, it would seem that the results are generally worse than expected. An adverse difference, or variance, indicates that the actual cost was more than expected, and this was the case for direct costs, and the overall cost.

But if you were reminded that the budget was for a production level of 4,800 units, whilst 5,000 units were actually produced, this would change the picture. We might now suspect that the performance was better than expected, but to quantify and confirm that suspicion, we need to flex the original budget and make a new comparison.

All variable costs, such as direct materials and direct labour, will change in line with the change in production level, but fixed costs will remain the same.

	Actual	Flexed budget		Variance	
Production (units)	5,000	5,000			
	$	$		$	
Direct materials	1,874	1,927	$\left(\dfrac{1,850 \times 5,000}{4,800}\right)$	53	Favourable
Direct labour	825	844	$\left(\dfrac{810 \times 5,000}{4,800}\right)$	19	Favourable
Prime cost	2,699	2,771		72	Favourable
Fixed overheads	826	840		14	Favourable
Total cost	3,525	3,611		86	Favourable

Comparisons with budget are an extremely important aspect of management accounting, and need to be considered in more detail. This is done in the next chapter.

QUESTION

Flexed budgets

Here is a production cost report for MWR Ltd for the three month period January-March 20X2.

	Actual	Budget
Production and sales (units)	3,000	2,000
	$	$
Sales revenue	30,000	20,000
Direct materials	8,500	6,000
Direct labour	4,500	4,000
Fixed overheads		
– Depreciation	2,200	2,000
– Rent and rates	1,600	1,500
Total cost	16,800	13,500
Profit	13,200	6,500

Required

Prepare a flexed budget for MWR Ltd for the three month period January-March 20X2.

ANSWER

FLEXED BUDGET MWR LTD JANUARY-MARCH 20X2

	Actual	Flexed budget	Variance	
Production and sales (units)	3,000	3,000		
	$	$	$	
Sales revenue	30,000	30,000		
Direct materials (W1)	8,500	9,000	500	Favourable
Direct labour (W2)	4,500	6,000	1,500	Favourable
Fixed overheads (W3)				
– Depreciation	2,200	2,000	200	Adverse
– Rent and rates	1,600	1,500	100	Adverse
Total cost	16,800	18,500	1,700	Favourable
Profit	13,200	11,500	1,700	Favourable

Workings

(1) **Direct materials**

Cost per unit = $\dfrac{\$6,000}{2,000\,\text{units}}$ = $3 per unit

Therefore 3,000 units = 3,000 × $3 = 9,000

(2) **Direct labour**

Cost per unit = $\dfrac{\$4,000}{2,000\,\text{units}}$ = $2 per unit

Therefore 3,000 units = 3,000 × $2 = $6,000

(3) **Fixed overheads**

The flexed budget for fixed overheads will be the same as the original budget as overheads are **fixed costs**.

QUESTION

Flexible budgets

Which of the following best describes a flexible budget?

A   A budget which is designed to be easily updated to reflect recent changes in unit costs or selling prices

B   A budget which can be flexed when actual costs are known, to provide a realistic forecast for the forthcoming period

C   A budget which, by recognising different cost behaviour patterns, is designed to change as the volume of activity changes

D   A budget which is prepared on a spreadsheet, with the flexibility to add new cost items to prepare new forecasts as circumstances change during the year

ANSWER

C   A flexible budget identifies fixed costs separately from variable costs. The allowance for variable costs can be flexed to derive a realistic target in the light of the actual activity level achieved.

2.3 Other uses of comparisons with budgets

Businesses obviously need to be **co-ordinated**. For example you cannot increase sales if you do not have the goods available, or increase inventories if you don't have the money to pay for them. Variance reporting is important in alerting management to unplanned changes in one area of the business which may affect another. For example an unplanned decrease in production will affect future sales unless it can be made up.

CHAPTER ROUNDUP

↳ **Comparing actual results** with **other information** helps to put them in context and may show up errors.

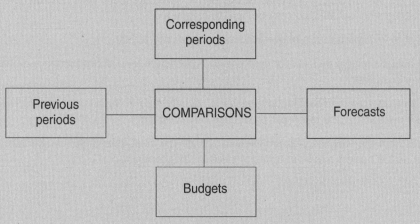

↳ Comparisons may be **financial** or **non-financial**.

↳ Choice of the comparison to make depends on the **characteristics** of the organisation, the **individual** and the **activity** being reported.

↳ Budget comparisons are popular because they show whether budget holders are **achieving** their **targets**.

↳ Budget reports may be **combined** with **other information** such as non-financial information, ratios etc.

↳ Variances can be calculated by comparing the fixed budget with the actual results (total variance) or comparing the flexed budget with the actual results (usage or price variance).

↳ You should report differences in such a way that managers can **understand them** and pick out **vital information easily**. Comparisons should not be cluttered with irrelevant information or too much detail.

↳ Flexed budgets should be used for comparison if the actual level of production is different from the original budget.

QUICK QUIZ

1 Which one of the following options is a financial comparison?

    A   Number of units produced compared to last year
    B   Number of units sold compared to last year
    C   Profit compared to last month
    D   Customer satisfaction compared to last month

2 A budget is expressed in monetary terms. Is this true or false?

3 When are flexed budgets used?

    A   When the actual level of production is different from the original budget
    B   When the actual level of production is the same as the original budget
    C   Neither of the above.

4 List possible non-financial comparisons that could be made by a manufacturing company

5 A company selling Christmas trees has its sales figures for December. Which sales figures would provide the most meaningful comparison?

1   C   Comparisons made in financial terms (costs and revenues) are financial comparisons. Options A, B and D are non-financial comparisons. Sometimes these are more difficult to compare, for example customer satisfaction may be hard to measure.

2   True   A budget is an organisation's plan, expressed in monetary terms.

3   A   Flexed budgets should be used for comparison if the actual level of production is different from the original budget.

4   Your list may include: customer satisfaction measures, quality reports (eg number of defective units), units produced, units sold, time taken per production run, wastage.

5   December sales from the previous year are likely to provide the most meaningful comparison, since December will be the busiest month in terms of sales for this company.

Now try ...

Attempt the questions below from the **Exam Question Bank**

Number

Q34-37

We stated in the last chapter that budgets can be used to check whether management's action plan is working. You compare the planned results for the day, week, month or year-to-date with actual results. Differences between actual figures and the budget are called **variances**.

Variance reporting is the reporting of differences between budgeted and actual performance.

Variances

1 Calculating variances

> **Variance reports** help budget holders to perform their function of **control**. The reports are especially useful if they separate controllable from non-controllable variances.

Variances are:

- **Favourable** if the business has more money as a result
- **Adverse** if the business has less money as a result

Favourable variances are not always good for the organisation. For example failure to recruit necessary staff will result in a favourable variance (less wages). It may, however, mean that business does not reach its production targets.

Reporting variances to the appropriate person draws attention to areas which are not running according to plan.

1.1 Example: Calculation of variances as a percentage

Here is an extract from a monthly cost report for a residential care home.

	Budgeted $	Actual $	Variance $	Variance %
Laundry	1,000	1,045	45 (A)	4.5
Heat and light	1,500	1,420	80 (F)	5.3
Catering	8,500	8,895	395 (A)	4.6
Nursing staff	7,000	6,400	600 (F)	8.6
Ancillary staff	10,600	10,950	350 (A)	3.3

$$\text{Variance \%} = \frac{\text{Actual costs} - \text{Budgeted costs}}{\text{Budgeted costs}} \times 100\%$$

We noted in the last chapter that the differences between the actual figures and the flexed budget give us variances. The flexed budget enables the total cost variance to be divided into two sub variance called the activity variance and the price/efficiency variance. The total variance, activity variance and price/efficiency variance are the subject of the next two sections of this chapter.

2 Sales revenue variance calculations

There are **three types** of **sales revenue variance**. These are the total sales revenue variance, the activity (or volume) variance and the selling price variance.

2.1 Introduction

Total sales revenue variance = activity variance + selling price variance.

Now we will look at the variance calculations using fixed and flexed budgets.

2.2 Total sales revenue variance

The total sales revenue variance measures the combined effect of the following.

• The actual selling price being different to standard selling price
• The actual sales volume being different to budgeted sales volume

The following example will illustrate how the total sales revenue variance is calculated.

2.3 Example

The following budgeted cost and selling price data relate to SM Limited's single product.

	$ per unit	$ per unit
Selling price		21.00
Direct cost	12.25	
Overhead cost	1.75	
		14.00
Budgeted profit		7.00

Data for last period were as follows.

Budgeted sales units	740	
Actual sales units	795	
Actual sales revenue	$16,200	

Solution

	$
Sales revenue should have been (740 × $21)	15,540
Sales revenue actually was	16,200
	660 (F)

QUESTION

Total sales revenue variance

Jasper Ltd has the following budget and actual figures for 20X4.

	Budget	Actual
Sales units	600	620
Selling price per unit	$30	$29

Budgeted full cost of production = $28 per unit.

Calculate the total sales revenue variance.

ANSWER

	$
Sales revenue should have been (600 × $30)	18,000
Sales revenue actually was (620 × $29)	17,980
Total sales revenue variance	20 (A)

2.4 Activity (or volume) variance

As mentioned in 2.2, the total sales revenue variance measures the combined effect of a difference in selling price and a difference in quantity sold. The activity (or volume) variance looks at the difference in quantity sold.

Remember that when we looked at flexed budgets, it was to take into account that the activity level was different from budgeted. In effect we were removing the variance which arose because of a difference in the quantity sold. This means that a comparison between actual figures and flexed budget figures gives us the price/efficiency variance only.

2.5 Example

The budgeted sales of SM Ltd were 740 units at a selling price of $21. The actual sales were 795 units at a total sales revenue of $16,200. What is the activity variance?

Solution

	Units
Budgeted sales volume	740
Actual sales volume	795
Activity variance in units	55 (F)
× Budgeted sales price per unit	× $21
Activity variance	$1,155 (F)

QUESTION   Activity variance

Jasper Ltd has the following budget and actual figures for 20X4.

	Budget	Actual
Sales units	600	620
Selling price per unit	$30	$29

Calculate the activity (or volume) variance.

ANSWER

	Units
Budgeted sales volume	600
Actual sales volume	620
Activity variance in units	20 (F)
× Budgeted sales price per unit	× $30
Activity variance	$600 (F)

2.6 Selling price variance

The selling price variance is shown in the example in 2.7. Note that the total sales revenue variance is the activity variance added to the selling price variance.

2.7 Example

The budgeted sales of SM Ltd were 740 units at a selling price of $21 per unit. The actual sales were 795 units at a total sales revenue of $16,200.

What was the selling price variance?

Solution

	$
Sales revenue from 795 units should have been (× $21)	16,695
But was	16,200
Selling price variance	495 (A)

The total sales revenue variance calculated in example 2.3 was $660 favourable. The activity (quantity) variance calculated in example 2.5 was $1,155 favourable. The selling price variance calculated in example 2.7 was $495 adverse.

Note that $660 (F) = $1,155 (F) + $495 (A)

QUESTION

Selling price variance

Jasper Ltd has the following budget and actual figures for 20X4.

	Budget	Actual
Sales units	600	620
Selling price per unit	$30	$29

Calculate the selling price variance.

ANSWER

	$
Sales revenue from 620 units should have been (× $30)	18,600
But was	17,980
Selling price variance	620 (A)

3 Cost variance calculations

3.1 Total direct cost variance

There are **three types** of **cost variance**. These are the total direct cost variance, the activity variance and the purchase price/efficiency of usage variance.

There are three types of cost variance. These are the total direct cost variance, the activity variance and the purchase price/efficiency of usage variance.

Total direct cost variance = activity variance + purchase price/efficiency of usage variance

The total direct cost variance measures the combined effect of the following

- The actual quantity produced being different to budgeted production volume
- The actual cost price being different to budgeted cost price
- The actual efficiency in which resources are used being different to budgeted efficiency.

3.2 Example

The budgeted materials for CTF Ltd were 800 units at a cost of $20 each. Actual material costs for the month were $17,600.

Solution

	$
Materials should have cost (800 × $20)	16,000
But did cost	17,600
Total direct cost variance	1,600 (A)

QUESTION

Total cost variance

The budgeted materials for HMF Ltd were 500 units at a cost of $15 each. Actual material costs for the month were $5,000.

Calculate the total direct cost variance.

ANSWER

	$
Materials should have cost (500 × $15)	7,500
But did cost	5,000
Total direct cost variance	2,500 (F)

3.3 Activity (or volume) variance

The activity (or volume) variance looks at the difference in the quantity produced.

It is worth mentioning again that when we looked at flexed budgets, it was to take into account that the activity level was different from budgeted. In effect we were removing the variance which arose because of a difference in quantity produced. This means that a comparison between actual figures and flexed budget figures give us the price/efficiency variance only.

3.4 Example

The budgeted materials for CTF were 800 units at a cost of $20 each. Actual materials costs for the month were $17,600 and 820 units were produced.

Solution

	Units
Budgeted production volume	800
Actual production volume	820
Activity variance in units	20 (A)
× Budgeted cost per unit	× $20
Activity variance	$400 (A)

QUESTION

Volume variance

The budgeted materials for HMF Ltd were 500 units at a cost of $15 each. Actual material costs for the month were $5,000 and 550 units were produced.

Calculate the activity variance.

ANSWER

	Unit
Budgeted production volume	500
Actual production volume	550
Activity variance in units	50 (A)
× Budgeted cost per unit	× $15
Activity variance	$750 (A)

3.5 Purchase price/efficiency of usage variance

This variance is shown in example 3.6. Note that the total cost variance is the activity variance added to the purchase price/efficiency of usage variance (for direct materials) or the rate of pay/efficiency variance (for direct labour).

3.6 Example – Materials

The budgeted materials for CTF Ltd were 800 units at a cost of $20 each. Actual materials costs for the month were $17,600 and 820 units were produced. Calculate the price/efficiency variance.

Solution

	$
Production of 820 units should have cost (× $20)	16,400
But did cost	17,600
Price/efficiency variance	1,200 (A)

QUESTION

Purchase price variance

The budgeted materials for HMF Ltd were 500 units at a cost of $15 each. Actual material costs for the month were $5,000 and 550 units were produced.

Calculate the price/usage variance.

ANSWER

	$
Production of 550 units should have cost (× $15)	8,250
But did cost	5,000
Price/efficiency variance	3,250 (F)

Note that:

Total direct cost variance = Activity variance + purchase price/usage variance.

Using examples 3.2, 3.4 and 3.6, the variances are $1,600 adverse, $400 adverse and $1,200 adverse.

$1600(A) = $400(A) + $1200(A)

3.7 Example – Labour

The budgeted labour cost for Blob Co was $10.20 per unit for 20,000 units. Actual labour costs were $10.50 per unit for 22,000 units. Calculate the rate/efficiency variance and the activity variance.

Solution

	$
Production of 22,000 units should have cost (× $10.20)	224,400
But did cost	231,000
Rate/efficiency variance	6,600 (A)

	Units
Budgeted production volume	20,000
Actual production volume	22,000
Activity variance in units	2,000 (A)
× budgeted cost per unit	× $10.20
Activity variance	$20,400 (A)

Note again that:

Total direct cost variance = Activity variance + rate/efficiency variance
= $20,400 (A) + $6,600 (A)
= $27,000 (A)

You can check this by calculating the total direct cost variance as follows:

Should have cost	($10.20 × 20,000 units)	204,000
But did cost	($10.50 × 22,000 units)	231,000
		27,000 (A)

4 The reasons for cost variances

There are a wide range of **reasons** for the occurrence of adverse and favourable cost **variances.**

The following is not an exhaustive list and an exam question might suggest other possible causes. You should review the information provided and select any causes that are consistent with the reported variances.

Variance	Favourable	Adverse
(a) Material price	Unforeseen discounts received More care taken in purchasing	Price increase Careless purchasing
(b) Material usage	Material used of higher quality than standard More effective use made of material Errors in allocating material to jobs	Defective material Excessive waste Theft Stricter quality control Errors in allocating material to jobs
(c) Labour rate	Use of apprentices or other workers at a rate of pay lower than standard	Wage rate increase Use of higher grade labour
(d) Labour efficiency	Output produced more quickly than expected because of work motivation, better quality of equipment or materials, or better methods. Errors in allocating time to jobs	Lost time in excess of standard allowed Output lower than standard set because of deliberate restriction, lack of training, or sub-standard material used Errors in allocating time to jobs

5 Exception reporting and investigating variances

Exception reporting highlights variances which might need investigating.

5.1 Exception reporting

Budgets are also used to allocate financial responsibility to individual managers. For example, the training manager will be responsible for expenditure on training. These responsible people are called **budget holders** and will have to decide what action to take if costs are higher or revenues lower than forecast. Reporting to them is sometimes called **responsibility accounting**.

Budget holders need to be informed of any variances that require investigation. They need not be pestered with immaterial variances, but they will need to look at larger variances. They should also investigate variances which are showing a worrying trend. For this reason, many businesses operate a system of **exception reporting**.

Exception reporting is the reporting only of those variances which exceed a certain amount or %.

It is like a central heating thermostat with the budget as the temperature setting. Thermostats allow small variations around the setting but if the variation gets larger, they will take appropriate action (switch the boiler on or off) to control the temperature.

5.2 Investigating variances

The decision to investigate a variance can also depend on whether it is **controllable** or **non-controllable**.

- **Controllable**: can be rectified by managers
- **Non-controllable:** are due to external factors beyond the managers' control

Budget holders may be required to explain why either type of variance has occurred and should take whatever action is needed. If the variance is controllable, management can take action to rectify problems. If the variance is non-controllable, management may wish to revise their plan. Either way budget holders are not necessarily to **blame** for the variance.

Finally, a variance will only be investigated if the cost of the investigation is to be outweighed by the benefits.

EXAM FOCUS POINT

You may need to be able to distinguish between controllable and non-controllable variances.

5.3 Example: investigation of variances

A manufacturer of copper pipes has budgeted for expenditure of $25,000 on copper in month 6 but actual expenditure is $28,000. Possible reasons for this $3,000 adverse variance include:

(a) **Price increase** by supplier. This may be controllable. The purchasing officer should try alternative suppliers.

(b) **World price rise** for copper. This is non-controllable. The budget may need revising for the rest of the year.

(c) **Higher factory rejection rate** of finished pipes. This is probably controllable but needs investigation. Is the raw material quality satisfactory? (if not, is this due to supplier, purchasing, warehousing?) Is the factory process at fault? (if so why? Poor supervision? Inadequate training? Machinery wearing out? – find out from the factory supervisors/managers).

You can see that reporting variances puts managers on the alert but only gives clues as to where the real problems lie.

Variances can be **interdependent**.

It is important to understand that variances can be **interdependent**, with a single factor affecting more than one variance. Two examples are given below.

- Buying a better quality of material may increase the cost of materials due to its higher price, but usage of the material may be improved as there is less wastage. It could also decrease the labour cost for a given level of production as fewer hours may be needed to process the material if it is easier to work with, or fewer rejects are produced.

- Using unskilled labour rather than skilled labour for a particular task may cut the cost of labour in terms of rate of pay, but they may take longer to complete the job which will increase the labour cost again. Unskilled workers may also use more material than skilled labour, causing an adverse material variance.

To summarise, significant variances will be reported to the manager responsible who will then investigate the cause of the variance and act by either correcting an operational problem if the variance is controllable, or adjusting the budget if it is non-controllable and expected to continue. This system is known as **feedback control**.

Sometimes, if a variance is foreseen, the manager might take corrective action in advance of the problem in order to avoid a variance. This is known as **feedforward control**.

QUESTION

A hospital decides to cut costs by reducing the number of cleaners employed by 10%. This results in a favourable variance in the budget reports. Is it good for the hospital?

Helping hand. Think of any other impacts a drop in a number of cleaners might have.

ANSWER

Helping hand. This illustrates not only the importance of non-financial objectives, but also how failure to meet non-financial objectives may impact upon financial objectives.

This is only good if the necessary standards of cleanliness can be maintained. If they can be, then there were probably too many cleaners before. If standards fall, there will be other effects (like more patient infections) which will cost more in the long term and damage the chief goal of improving health.

QUESTION

Here is an extract from a sales report for Region 3 in month 4 of the budget year.

		$ actual	$ budgeted
Salesperson	Green	8,500	8,000
	Brown	7,600	8,000

Brown is more junior than Green, and has attended fewer training courses. The more 'difficult' customers are shared between the two salespeople.

Brown's variance for month 4 is

A   Favourable and controllable
B   Adverse and controllable
C   Favourable and non-controllable
D   Adverse and non-controllable

ANSWER

Answer B

Brown's actual sales were $400 less than the budget which is an adverse variance. The information in the question leads us to the conclusion that the variance is controllable as he has been given the same target as the more experienced salesperson. Brown could be sent on more training courses.

QUESTION

A ward sister in a private hospital has the following changes in ward costs reported as exceptional.

	Actual $	Budget $	Variance $	
Nursing salaries	4,500	4,750	250	Favourable
Drugs and dressings	237	370	133	Favourable

Which of these costs do you think the sister can control?

A   Nursing salaries
B   Drugs
C   Dressings
D   None of the costs

ANSWER

Helping hand. The key to this activity is determining who makes the decisions about which costs.

(a) Nursing salaries would probably be centrally controlled by the hospital and influenced by NHS salaries. Drugs would be determined by a doctor and administered by a nurse. Dressings are probably the only item the ward sister has any control over.

(b) The $300 drugs cost for March looks quite different from the normal pattern of cost. You should look at the ledger account and purchase documents to see if it is correct.

(c) Combining drugs and dressings costs does not seem helpful in a ward report since only one is likely to be a controllable cost for the ward sister.

QUESTION

Performance reports

A company produces the following performance report.

PERFORMANCE REPORT		
PRODUCTION COST CENTRES		
TOTAL COSTS – APRIL 20X1		
	YEAR TO DATE 30.04.X1	
	Actual	**Budget (flexed)**
	$	$
Materials	39,038	35,000
Labour	89,022	85,000
Expenses	18,781	15,000

Which cost variances would be brought to the attention of the production managers responsible, if the company reports by exception any variances that vary by more than 10% from budget?

A   Materials only
B   Materials and labour
C   Expenses only
D   Expenses and materials

ANSWER

D.

VARIANCE REPORT PRODUCTION COST CENTRES APRIL 20X1	
	Year to 30 April 20X1 $
Materials	4,038 (A)
Labour	4,022 (A)
Expenses	3,781 (A)

Comment

The significant variances which are more than 10% from budget are:

- Materials $4,038 (A) = 11.5% $\left(\dfrac{4,038}{35,000}\right)$

- Expenses $3,781 (A) = 25.2% $\left(\dfrac{3,781}{15,000}\right)$

The labour variance is not more than 10% from budget.

- Labour $4,022 (A) = 4.7% $\left(\dfrac{4,022}{85,000}\right)$

CHAPTER ROUNDUP

↪ **Variance reports** help budget holders to perform their function of **control**. The reports are especially useful if they separate controllable from non-controllable variances.

↪ There are **three types** of **sales revenue variance**. These are the total sales revenue variance, the activity variance and the selling price variance.

↪ There are **three types** of **cost variance**. These are the total direct cost variance, the activity variance and the purchase price/efficiency of usage variance.

↪ There are a wide range of **reasons** for the occurrence of adverse and favourable cost **variances**.

↪ **Exception reporting** highlights variances which might need investigating.

↪ **Variances** can be **interdependent**.

QUICK QUIZ

1   A difference between planned and actual results which results in the organisation having less money than forecast is called:

   A   A favourable variance
   B   An adverse variance
   C   A loss
   D   A profit

2   Statement 1   An adverse variance is always good for the business
     Statement 2   An adverse variance is always bad for the business

   A   Both statements are false
   B   Both statements are true
   C   Statement 1 is true but statement 2 is false
   D   Statement 1 is false but statement 2 is true

3   Which of the following statements about exception reporting is false?

   A   It avoids information overload
   B   It makes it easier for managers to spot important variances
   C   It reports variances which exceed a certain amount or %
   D   All variances highlighted should be investigated

4   What is the name given when a variance is foreseen and the manager takes corrective action in advance of the problem to avoid a variance?

   A   Feedforward control
   B   Feedback control
   C   Neither of the above

5   Which of the following options describes an activity variance?

   A   The actual efficiency in which resources are used being different to budgeted efficiency
   B   The actual quantity produced being different to budgeted production volume
   C   The actual cost pricing being different to budgeted cost price
   D   The budgeted efficiency in which resources are used being different to actual efficiency.

1	B	This is an adverse variance.
2	A	An adverse variance is not always good or bad. Whether it is good or bad depends on the reasons for the variance. For example, recruiting extra staff may result in an adverse labour variance but may mean that increased demand required higher levels of production (and higher revenue).
3	D	Not all variances should necessarily be investigated. For example a variance should only be investigated if the cost of the investigation is to be outweighed by the benefits.
4	A	Feedforward control (Feedback control involves acting after the cause of the variance has been investigated.)
5	B	The activity (or volume) variance looks at the difference in the quantity produced.

Now try ...

Attempt the questions below from the **Exam Question Bank**

Number

Q38-41

Earlier in the study text we discussed how you obtain and code management information.

In this chapter we shall talk about **different ways** of communicating and presenting information. We also discuss when you should not communicate information – when you should keep it confidential.

Reporting management information

TOPIC LIST	SYLLABUS REFERENCE
1 Deciding who needs what	N/A
2 Types of communication	E2 (a), (b), (d)
3 Confidentiality	E2 (c)

Study Guide | **Intellectual level**

E **Providing management information**

2 **Reporting management information**

(a) Describe methods of analysing, presenting and communicating information — K

(b) Identify suitable formats for communicating management information according to purpose and organisational guidelines including informal business reports, letter and email or memo. — S

(c) Identify the general principles of distributing reports (eg procedures, timing, recipients) including the reporting of confidential information — K

(d) Interpret information presented in management reports — S

One of the essential competences you require for FPER is to communicate effectively. You can apply the knowledge you obtain from this chapter of the text to help to demonstrate this competence.

1 Deciding who needs what

Management information should be **relevant to** and **understood** by the individual who receives it.

You learnt in Chapter 2 that management information should be **relevant** to the organisation and the individual.

The person receiving management information should be able to understand it. Understandability can be helped by:

- Avoiding unexplained technical terms
- Cutting out unnecessary detail
- Using charts, diagrams, tables and good report layouts
- Asking the users' views on required information and presentation

In many organisations standard reports are issued regularly. The information system may produce the reports directly. Alternatively the reports may need special preparation. They will tell the managers responsible for various activities how they are performing. They may be used as a basis for extra rewards such as bonuses, promotions etc.

Ideally the reports should distinguish between **controllable** and **non-controllable** factors. This is not always easy in practice however.

Managers may also need **ad hoc** reports to help them with particular problems. For example they may want more detail than is given by the regular reports on a particular aspect of the business. If you have to provide this type of information you must understand **exactly what is required**, including the **format** required for presenting it.

2 Types of communication

Types of communication include:

- – Letters
- – Memos
- – E-mails
- – Formal reports

It is important to choose the right one for a given purpose.

Choosing the right method of communication is important. Many organisations have standard sets of regular reports in prescribed formats. Many also have a standard **house style** for other documents, that is a particular way of setting things out. The aim of this is to:

- • Make it easier for employees to read, locate and produce information
- • Present a consistent image to people outside the organisation

Charts, graphs and tables can be used to communicate management information, these are covered in Chapter 13.

Different situations suit different methods of communication. Some relevant considerations are outlined in the following table.

Choosing a communication method	
Factor	**Considerations**
Time	How long will be needed to prepare the message, and how long will it take to transmit it in the chosen form? This must be weighed against the urgency with which the message must be sent.
Complexity	The method used for relaying a complex piece of information must be chosen carefully. A written document may make it easier for the reader to take their time over digesting the information. On the other hand, a conversation would allow for instant clarification where necessary.
Distance	How far is the message required to travel? Must it be transmitted to an office on a different floor of the building, or across town, or to the other end of the country?
Written record	A written record may be needed as proof, confirming a transaction, or for legal purposes, or as an aid to memory. It can be duplicated and sent to many recipients. It can be stored and later retrieved for reference and analysis as required.
Feedback/ interaction	How quickly is the feedback required? If an instant response is needed then a conversation may be appropriate. How many responses are required? If there are many responses needed then talking to each individual may take too long.
Confidentiality	Telephone calls may be overheard; faxed messages can be read by whoever is standing by the fax machine; internal memos may be read by colleagues or by internal mail staff; highly personal letters may be read by the recipient's secretary. On the other hand a message may need to be spread widely and quickly to all staff: the notice-board, or a public announcement or the company newsletter may be more appropriate.
Recipient	It may be necessary to be reserved and tactful, warm and friendly, or impersonal, depending upon the desired effect on the recipient. If you are trying to impress him, a high quality document may be needed.
Cost	Cost must be considered in relation to all of the above factors. The aim is to achieve the best possible result at the least possible expense.

2.1 Letters

You are most likely to use a letter when communicating with someone **outside your organisation.**

Letters should be polite, accurate, clear, logical and concise; and should give appropriate references. Spelling and punctuation should, of course, be impeccable! Also, if your company has a house-style, your letter should conform to that.

2.2 Example: a letter

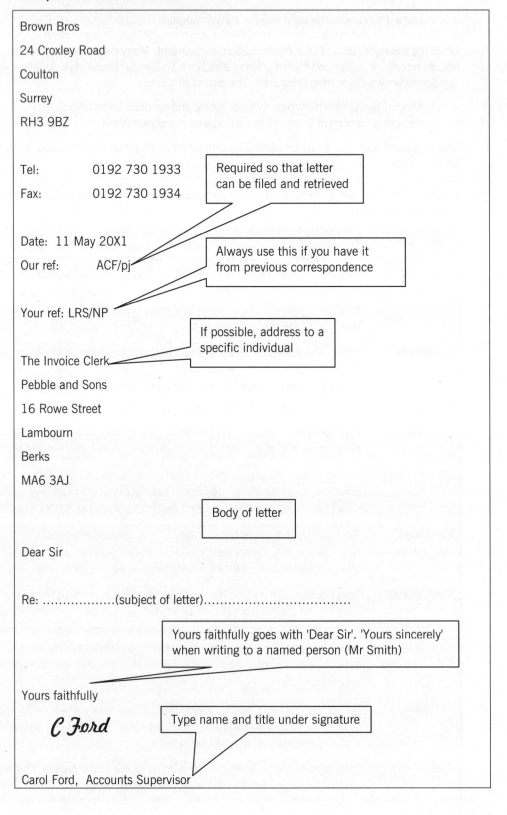

BPP
LEARNING MEDIA

QUESTION

If you begin a letter 'Dear Sir', you should sign the letter

A   Yours sincerely
B   Yours faithfully
C   Yours truly
D   Yours gratefully

ANSWER

B   Yours faithfully is the formal ending if the recipient's name is not used. A would be used if the recipients name had been referred to, e.g. 'Dear Mr Jackson'. C and D are not generally used in business letters.

2.3 Memos

The **memorandum** or **memo** performs internally the same function as a letter does in communication externally. It can be used for any kind of communication that is best conveyed in writing such as reports, brief messages or notes.

Memos need less detail than a formal letter.

2.4 Example: a memo

Forrest Fire Extinguishers Ltd

MEMORANDUM

To: All Staff   **Ref:** PANC/mp

From: D B Gavaskar, Managing Director   **Date:** 13 January 20X0

Subject: Overtime arrangements for January/February ⟶ Main theme

I would like to remind you that thanks to Pancake Day on and around 12 February, we can expect the usual increased demand for small extinguishers. I am afraid this will involve substantial overtime hours for everyone.   Reason for writing

In order to make this as easy as possible, the works canteen will be open all evening for snacks and hot drinks. The works van will also be available in case of transport difficulties late at night.

I realise that this period puts pressure on production and administrative staff alike, but I would appreciate your co-operation in working as many hours of overtime as you feel able.

Copies to: All staff   No need to   Finish by stating clearly what is
                                sign off   required of recipient in response

---

QUESTION

A memorandum is

A   Signed by the person sending it
B   Generally used for the communication of short messages between different organisations
C   Not used if important information is to be communicated
D   For any written communication within an organisation

ANSWER

D   A memo can be used for internal communication of information that is presented in writing, so B
     and C are incorrect. A is incorrect as it does not have to be signed.

2.5 E-mails

If available, you can use **e-mails** in the same way as a memo, or for external communications. It is
possible for emails to be used for documents to be signed electronically, or else for documents to be
scanned, signed and then sent as email attachments.

2.5.1 Advantages of e-mail

E-mail has the following **advantages**.

(a)   **Speed** (transmission, being electronic, is almost instantaneous). E-mail is far faster than post. It
       is a particular time-saver when communicating with people overseas.

(b)   **Economy** (no need for stamps etc). E-mail is reckoned to be 20 times cheaper than fax.

(c)   **Efficiency** (a message is prepared once but can be sent to thousands of employees at the touch
       of a button).

(d)   **Security** (access can be restricted by the use of passwords).

(e)   Documents can be attached from **word-processing** and other packages.

(f)   Electronic **delivery and read receipts** can be requested.

2.5.2 Dangers of e-mail

E-mail has the following dangers:

- **Confidentiality** – passwords must be safeguarded
- Used to **replace** other communications that may be more appropriate (eg conversation)
- Too much going to **people who don't need it** as it is so easy to send to many recipients

2.6 Reports

Standard reports are a regular part of the management information system.

Ad-hoc reports deal with a one-off issue or problem.

A formal **report** may be needed where a comprehensive investigation has taken place.

ELEMENTS OF A FORMAL REPORT	
Title	Subject of report
Terms of reference	Clarify what has been requested
Introduction	Who the report is from and to
	How the information was obtained
Main body	Divided into sections with sub-headings to aid reader
	Logical order
Conclusions	Summarises findings
Recommendations	Based on information and evidence
	May be combined with conclusion

ELEMENTS OF A FORMAL REPORT	
Signature	Of writer
Executive summary	Saves time for managers receiving a long report
	No more than one page

One example of a short formal report is shown below.

2.7 Example: short formal report

REPORT ON PROPOSED UPDATING OF COMPANY POLICY MANUAL

To: Board of Directors, BCD Ltd
From: J Thurber, Opus Management Consultants
Status: Confidential
Date: 3 October 20X8

I   INTRODUCTION AND TERMS OF REFERENCE

This report details the results of an investigation commissioned by the Board on 7 September 20X8. We were asked to consider the current applicability of the company's policy manual and to propose changes needed to bring it into line with current practice.

II   METHOD

The following investigatory procedures were adopted:

1   Interview all senior staff regarding use of the policy manual in their departments
2   Observe working practices in each department

III   FINDINGS

The manual was last updated 10 years ago. From our observations, the following amendments are now needed:

1   The policy section on computer use should be amended. It deals with safe storage of disks, which is no longer applicable as data is now stored on a server. Also, it does not set out the company's e-mail policy.

2   The company's equal opportunities policy needs to be included.

3   The coding list in the manual is now very out of date. A number of new cost centres and profit centres have been set up in the last 10 years and the codes for these are not noted in the manual.

4   There is no mention of the provisions of the Data Protection Act as they relate to the company.

IV   CONCLUSIONS

We discovered upon interviewing staff that very little use is made of the policy manual. When it has been amended as above, it can be brought back into use, and we recommend that this should be done as soon as possible.

Signed J Thurber, Opus Management Consultants

A formal report like this will of course be **word-processed**.

QUESTION

Communication methods

In each of the cases below, select the form of communication which will generally be the most appropriate.

1   A complaint to a supplier about the quality of goods supplied.

       A   Letter
       B   Memo
       C   Formal report
       D   E-mail

2   A query to a supervisor about the coding of an invoice.

       A   E-mail
       B   Memo
       C   Face-to-face
       D   All of the above are equally suitable if available

3   An investigation into the purchasing costs of your company.

       A   Letter
       B   Memo
       C   Formal report
       D   E-mail

4   Notification to customers of a change of the company's telephone number.

       A   Letter
       B   Memo
       C   E-mail
       D   All of the above are equally suitable if available

5   Reply to an e-mail.

       A   Letter
       B   Memo
       C   E-mail
       D   Face-to-face

6   Query to the sales department about an expenses claim.

       A   Memo
       B   E-mail
       C   Telephone
       D   All of the above are equally suitable if available

ANSWER

1   A
2   D
3   C
4   A
5   C
6   D

EXAM FOCUS POINT

In the exam you might be required to determine the most appropriate form of communication as in the activity above.

BPP
LEARNING MEDIA

3 Confidentiality

> Some information will be **confidential**, maybe because of the Data Protection Act or because of company policy. Access to it will be restricted.

Keeping some information confidential is an important **legal requirement.** It may also be part of your organisation's **policy**.

Some requirements are pure common sense. For example most of us would expect details of our wages, salaries, health etc to be kept confidential. Others are less obvious. For example some information about your organisation may be valuable to competitors. This is known as **commercially sensitive information**.

> The **Data Protection Act 1998** aims to protect the rights of **individuals** in relation to information organisations hold about them.

3.1 Why is privacy an important issue?

In recent years, there has been a growing popular fear that **information** about individuals which was stored on computer files and processed by computer could be **misused**. In the UK the current legislation is the **Data Protection Act 1998**.

Privacy is the right of a person to be free of unwanted intrusion by others into their lives or activities.

3.2 The Data Protection Act 1998

The Data Protection Act 1998 is an attempt to protect the **individual**. The Act covers manual and computer systems.

3.2.1 Definitions of terms used in the Act

In order to understand the Act it is necessary to know some of the technical terms used in it.

(a)   **Personal data** is information about a living individual, including expressions of opinion about him or her. The 'living individual' could come from within the organisation or from outside eg job applicant, person who works for a supplier, person who works for a customer etc.

(b)   **Data users** are organisations or individuals who control personal data and the use of personal data.

(c)   A **data subject** is an individual who is the subject of personal data.

3.2.2 The rights of data subjects

The Act includes the following rights for data subjects.

(a)   A data subject may seek **compensation** through the courts for damage and any associated distress caused by the **loss, destruction** or **unauthorised disclosure** of data about himself or herself or by **inaccurate data** about himself or herself.

(b)   A data subject may apply to the courts for **inaccurate data** to be **put right** or even **wiped off** the data user's files altogether. Such applications may also be made to the Registrar.

(c)   A data subject may obtain **access** to personal data of which he is the subject. (This is known as the 'subject access' provision.) In other words, a data subject can ask to see his or her personal data that the data user is holding.

(d)   A data subject can **sue** a data user for any **damage or distress** caused to him by personal data about him which is **incorrect** or **misleading** as to matter of **fact** (rather than opinion).

The Act applies to information held in any form. Therefore it does not matter whether the information is held on paper, in computer files or in another form – it is all covered by the Act.

The strictest requirements of the Act apply to 'sensitive data' such as racial origin, health, sexual orientation or political or religious beliefs. The processing of sensitive data is generally forbidden without the consent of the subject.

Data users are organisations or individuals which use personal data covered by the Act.

The most obvious use is actually **processing the data**. However use also includes **controlling** the **contents** of **personal data files**.

Data users must apply to the Data Protection Registrar to be **registered** for holding personal data for a particular purpose. Registered users are only allowed to hold and use personal data for the registered purposes.

Data subjects are individuals on whom personal data is held.

Data subjects can **sue** data users for **damage** or **distress** caused by inaccurate data, loss of data or unauthorised disclosure. They also have a legal right to see their own personal data.

3.3 Internal requirements

Within an organisation, the policy manual will often lay down other confidentiality rules. For example some organisations forbid employees to talk to the press without authorisation, or to publish their research results. You can imagine that businesses planning large redundancies or the launch of a new product will not want the information to become public prematurely.

Paper files with **restricted access** should be

- Listed
- Stored securely
- Only accessible by specific people

Computer systems often use **passwords** to restrict access to information that is held on computer. You should never divulge your password to an unauthorised person or keep it in view on your desk. Think of your password as needing as much secrecy as your bank PIN number.

Use of the **Internet** can pose particular problems in maintaining confidentiality. Many companies have a policy on the purposes for which the Internet should and should not be used. The law surrounding Internet information and its protection is still developing.

If you have access to restricted information in any form, you are responsible for protecting it to comply with company policy and the law. You should lock confidential papers or computer disks away when you are not using them. You should not leave them lying around on your desk (or in the photocopier!).

You should also **not provide confidential information** to **others** outside your department without checking with a supervisor.

QUESTION

Your company's planning department asks for a copy of the monthly research cost reports for the last six months. Your computer password does not give you access to this information. What should you do?

A   Refer the query to your supervisor

B   Ask someone what the password is that will access the information

C   Ask for your password to be changed so that it will access the information

D   Try and find a hard copy of the information

ANSWER

A   Access to this information is restricted. B, C and D are therefore not appropriate.

CHAPTER ROUNDUP

↳ Management information should be **relevant to** and **understood** by the individual who receives it.

↳ **Types of communication** include:

- ° Letters
- ° Memos
- ° E-mails
- ° Formal reports

It is important to choose the right one for a given purpose.

↳ **Standard reports** are a regular part of the management information system.

↳ **Ad-hoc reports** deal with a one-off issue or problem.

↳ Some information will be **confidential**, maybe because of the Data Protection Act or because of company policy. Access to it will be restricted.

↳ The **Data Protection Act 1998** aims to protect the rights of individuals in relation to information organisations hold about them.

QUICK QUIZ

1 Which one of the following options would **not** help management information to be understood?

A Avoiding unexplained technical terms
B Using charts, diagrams and tables
C Asking the users' view on required information and presentation
D Lots of detail

2 Which one of the following is **not** an aim of house style for documents?

A To make it easier to read the documents
B To make it easier to locate information
C To control costs
D To present a consistent image to people outside the organisation

3 Information about an organisation which may be valuable to competitors is known as:

A Cost sensitive information
B Commercially sensitive information
C Commercially secure information
D Cost secure information

4 Data users are individuals on whom personal data is held. Is this true or false?

5 List five considerations when choosing a communication method.

6 Which one of the following is a possible disadvantage/danger of e-mail?

A Economy
B Speed
C Delivery and read receipts
D Large volumes of information

7 What would be the most appropriate method of communication in each of the following circumstances?

(a) Explaining to a customer that a cash discount that has been deducted was not valid, as the invoice was not paid within the discount period.
(b) Requesting customer balances from a colleague in the sales ledger department.
(c) Arranging your holiday period with the HR manager.
(d) A complaint to a supplier regarding the delivery times of goods, which are not as agreed.
(e) Information to be provided to the sales director regarding the breakdown of sales geographically for the last two years.

ANSWERS TO QUICK QUIZ

1	D	Cutting out unnecessary detail can greatly benefit understandability
2	C	Controlling costs is not one of the aims of house style
3	B	This is known as commercially sensitive information
4	False	Data subjects are individuals on whom personal data is held. Data users are organisations or individuals which use personal data.

5   Answers could include: Time, complexity, distance, written record, feedback/interaction, confidentiality, recipient, cost

6   D   The danger with e-mail is that too much information will go to people who don't need it because it is so easy to send to many recipients.

7   (a)   Telephone, followed-up in writing if required.

(b)   Note or e-mail.

(c)   E-mail to request dates, perhaps followed-up by face-to-face discussion or phone call if negotiation is required.

(d)   Letter.

(e)   E-mail or possibly a more formal report.

Now try ...

Attempt the questions below from the **Exam Question Bank**

Number

Q42-45

part

F

The spreadsheet system

12

Much of the information used for management control today is analysed or presented using spreadsheet software. This chapter covers the basics of using spreadsheets. The next chapter will look at using spreadsheets to present information.

The basics of using spreadsheets

TOPIC LIST	SYLLABUS REFERENCE
1 Spreadsheets	F1 (a), F2 (g)
2 Basic spreadsheet skills	F2 (a), (b)
3 Spreadsheet formulae	F2 (d)
4 Identifying and correcting errors in formulae	F2 (e)

Study Guide	Intellectual level
F **The spreadsheet system**	
1 **Spreadsheet system overview**	
(a) Describe a spreadsheet system	K
2 **Using computer spreadsheets**	
(a) Identify what numerical and other information is needed in spreadsheets and how it should be structured	S
(b) Describe the process of entering and editing information	K
(d) Identify a wide range of formulae to meet calculations requirements (addition, subtraction, multiplication, division, average and relative and absolute cell references)	S
(e) Describe and correct errors in formulae	S
(g) Describe how spreadsheet files are stored and retrieved	K
3 **Presenting information in spreadsheets**	
(d) Describe how to print information including page layout	K

One of the essential competences you require for FPER is to use information and communication technology. You can apply the knowledge you obtain from this chapter of the text to help demonstrate this competence.

1 Spreadsheets

A **spreadsheet** is basically an electronic piece of paper divided into **rows** and **columns**. The intersection of a row and a column is known as a **cell**.

Much of the information presented to management in the modern office is produced and/or presented using spreadsheet software. You should be able to produce clear, well-presented spreadsheets that utilise basic spreadsheet functions such as simple formulae.

EXAM FOCUS POINT

In the examiner's report for the December 2011 exam, the examiner singled out this area of the syllabus as being "relatively poorly answered". Although spreadsheets may appear to be one of the simpler parts of the paper, the reality is that candidates often do not score well on exam questions in this area.

1.1 What is a spreadsheet?

A spreadsheet is essentially an electronic piece of paper divided into rows (horizontal) and columns (vertical). The rows are numbered 1, 2, 3 . . . etc and the columns lettered A, B C . . . etc. Each individual area representing the intersection of a row and a column is called a 'cell'.

A cell address consists of its row and column reference. For example, in the spreadsheet below the word Jan is in cell B2. In the same spreadsheet the **active cell** is D7. This is shown by the box around the cell. A cell must be active for data to be input to that cell.

The main examples of spreadsheet packages are Lotus 1 2 3 and Microsoft Excel. We will be referring to Microsoft Excel 2003, as this is the most widely-used spreadsheet. (Microsoft Excel 2007 and 2010 are now available but these are not yet used by the majority of businesses. The 2007 and 2010 versions look slightly different.) A simple Microsoft Excel spreadsheet, containing budgeted sales figures for three geographical areas for the first quarter of the year, is shown below.

	A	B	C	D	E	F
1	BUDGETED SALES FIGURES					
2		Jan	Feb	Mar	Total	
3		$'000	$'000	$'000	$'000	
4	North	2,431	3,001	2,189	7,621	
5	South	6,532	5,826	6,124	18,482	
6	West	895	432	596	1,923	
7	Total	9,858	9,259	8,909	28,026	
8						

1.2 Why use spreadsheets?

Spreadsheets provide a tool for calculating, analysing and manipulating numerical data. Spreadsheets make the calculation and manipulation of data easier and quicker. For example, the spreadsheet above has been set up to calculate the totals **automatically.** If you changed your estimate of sales in February for the North region to $3,296, when you input this figure in cell C4 the totals (in E4, C7 and E7) would change accordingly.

1.3 File: Open

With Excel open, click on the word File and a menu will drop down which includes the item Open. If you click on this, a window like the following will appear.

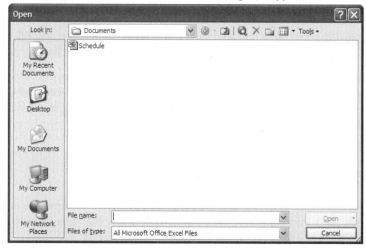

To open an existing file, click on the Look in box arrow and then locate the file by navigating through the folder structure. When you locate the document, click on the file name and then click on OK to open the file. Double-clicking on a file name has the effect of both selecting it and clicking on OK to open it.

1.4 File: Save As

If you open an existing file (that will obviously already have an existing file name), then make some changes to it which you want to save, but you also wish to leave the original document intact, you should use the File, Save As option, and give the amended file a new name.

The file you originally opened will remain in its original form, and the file with the new name will include all of your changes. For example, you could open a file containing Sales information during November

called Nov Sales.xls, add information for December, and save it as Nov Dec Sales.xls. You would end up with two files – one called Nov Sales.xls and the other called Nov Dec Sales.xls.

1.5 File: Save

If you open an existing file, then make some changes to it which you want to save and you wish to save this over the original document you should use the File, Save option.

2 Basic spreadsheet skills

> Essential basic **skills** include how to **move around** within a spreadsheet, how to **enter** and **edit** data, how to **fill** cells, how to **insert** and **delete** columns and rows and how to improve the basic **layout** and **appearance** of a spreadsheet.

In this section we explain some **basic spreadsheet skills**. We give instructions for Microsoft Excel, the most widely used package. Our examples should be valid with all versions of Excel. You should read this section while sitting at a computer and trying out the skills we describe, '**hands-on**'. Come back to this section later if you cannot do this right now.

2.1 Examples of useful spreadsheet skills

Start Microsoft Excel by double-clicking on the Excel **icon** or button (it will look like an X), or by choosing Excel from the **Start** menu (maybe from within the **Microsoft Office** option**).**

2.1.1 Moving about

A single cell can be accessed by clicking on the cell using the mouse or by using the arrow keys on the keyboard.

Pressing **Enter** will move you to the cell below in the same column. Pressing **Shift** and **Enter** together will move you to the cell above in the same column.

The F5 key is useful for moving about large spreadsheets. If you press the function key **F5,** a **Go To** dialogue box will allow you to specify the cell address you would like to move to. Try this out.

Also experiment by holding down Ctrl and pressing each of the direction arrow keys in turn to see where you end up. Try using the **Page Up** and **Page Down** keys and also try **Home** and **End** and Ctrl + these keys. Try **Tab** and **Shift + Tab**, too. These are all useful shortcuts for moving quickly from one place to another in a large spreadsheet.

2.1.2 Cell contents

The contents of any cell can be one of the following.

(a) **Text**. A text cell usually contains **words**. Numbers that do not represent numeric values for calculation purposes (eg a Part Number) may be entered in a way that tells Excel to treat the cell contents as text. To do this, enter an apostrophe before the number eg '451.

(b) **Values**. A value is a **number** that can be used in a calculation.

(c) **Formulae**. A formula **refers to other cells** in the spreadsheet, and performs some sort of computation with them. For example, if cell C1 contains the formula =A1-B1, cell C1 will display the result of the calculation subtracting the contents of cell B1 from the contents of cell A1. In Excel, a formula always begins with an equals sign: = . There are a wide range of formulae and functions available.

2.1.3 Range of cells

A **range** of cells can be specified in Excel by two cell references separated by a colon. The two cell references are the upper left and lower right corners of the range. For example B2:D7 would specify the **range** of cells highlighted below.

	A	B	C	D	E
1					
2					
3					
4					
5					
6					
7					
8					
9					

2.1.4 Filling a range of cells

Start with a blank spreadsheet. Type the number 1 in cell A1 and the number 2 in cell A2. Now *select* cells A1: A2, this time by positioning the mouse pointer over cell A1, holding down the left mouse button and moving the pointer down to cell A2. When cell A2 goes black you can release the mouse button.

Now position the mouse pointer at the **bottom right hand corner** of cell A2. (You should be able to see a little black lump in this corner: this is called the **'fill handle'**.) When you have the mouse pointer in the right place it will turn into a black cross.

Hold down the left mouse button again and move the pointer down to cell A10. You will see an outline surrounding the cells you are trying to 'fill'.

Release the mouse button when you have the pointer over cell A10. You will find that the software **automatically** fills in the numbers 3 to 10 below 1 and 2.

Try the following variations of this technique.

(a)   Delete what you have just done and type in **Jan** in cell A1. See what happens if you select cell A1 and fill down to cell A12: you get the months **Feb, Mar, Apr** and so on.

(b)   Type the number 2 in cell A1. Select A1 and fill down to cell A10. What happens? The cells should fill up with 2's.

(c)   Type the number 2 in cell A1 and 4 in cell A2. Then select A1: A2 and fill down to cell A10. What happens? You should get 2, 4, 6, 8, and so on.

(d)   Try **filling across** as well as down. In Excel you can fill in any direction.

(e)   What happens if you click on the bottom right hand corner using the **right mouse button**, drag down to another cell and then release the button? You should get a menu giving you a variety of different options for how you want the cells to be filled in.

2.1.5 Editing cell contents

Suppose cell A2 currently contains the value 456. If you wish to **change the entry** in cell A2 from 456 to 123456 there are four options – as shown below.

(a)   Activate cell A2, **type** 123456 and press **Enter**. (To undo this and try the next option press **Ctrl + Z**: this will always undo what you have just done.)

(b)   **Double-click** in cell A2. The cell will keep its thick outline but you will now be able to see a vertical line flashing in the cell. You can move this line by using the direction arrow keys or the Home and the End keys. Move it to before the 4 and type 123. Then press Enter.

After you have tried this, press Ctrl + Z to undo it.

(c) **Click once** on the number 456 in the line that shows the active cell reference and cell contents at the top of the screen. Again you will get the vertical line and you can type in 123 before the 4. Then press Enter, then Ctrl + Z.

(d) Press the **function key F2**. The vertical line cursor will be flashing in cell A2 at the *end* of the figures entered there (after the 6). Press Home to get to a position before the 4 and then type in 123 and press Enter, as before.

(e) Under the default settings in Excel, any formulae referring to cell A2 will be recalculated using the new value in A2.

2.1.6 Deleting cell contents

You may delete the contents of a cell simply by making the cell the active cell and then pressing **Delete**. The contents of the cell will disappear. You may also highlight a range of cells to delete and then delete the contents of all cells within the range.

For example, enter any value in cell A1 and any value in cell A2. Move the cursor to cell A2. Now hold down the **Shift** key (the one above the Ctrl key) and keeping it held down press the ↑ arrow. Cell A2 will stay white but cell A1 will go black. What you have done here is **selected** the range A1 and A2. Now press Delete. The contents of cells A1 and A2 will disappear.

2.1.7 The Sum button Σ

Start with a blank spreadsheet, and then enter the following figures in cells A1:B5.

	A	B
1	400	582
2	250	478
3	359	264
4	476	16
5	97	125

Make cell B6 the active cell and click *once* on the sum button (the button with a Σ symbol on the toolbar – the Σ symbol is the mathematical sign for 'the sum of'). A formula will appear in the cell saying =SUM(B1:B5). Above cell B6 you will see a flashing dotted line encircling cells B1:B5. Accept the suggested formula by hitting the Enter key. The formula =SUM(B1:B5) will be entered, and the number 1465 will be appear in cell B6.

Next, make cell A6 the active cell and **double-click** on the sum button. The number 1582 should show in cell A6.

2.1.8 Multiplication

Continuing on with our example, next select cell C1. Type in an = sign then click on cell A1. Now type in an **asterisk** * (which serves as a **multiplication sign**) and click on cell B1. Watch how the formula in cell C1 changes as you do this. (Alternatively you can enter the cell references by moving the direction arrow keys.) Finally press Enter. Cell C1 will show the result (232,800) of multiplying the figure in Cell A1 by the one in cell B1.

Your next task is to select cell C1 and **fill in** cells C2 to C5 automatically using the filling technique described earlier. If you then click on each cell in column C and look above at the line showing what the cell contains you will find that the software has automatically filled in the correct cell references for you: A2*B2 in cell C2, A3*B3 in cell C3 and so on.

(**Note**: The forward slash / is used to represent division in spreadsheet formulae).

2.1.9 Copy, cut and paste

If you wish to duplicate cells within a spreadsheet you can use copy and paste. This can be done by selecting the relevant cells and choosing Edit > Copy from the menu. Then use Edit > Paste to insert them at the appropriate point.

If you wish to move cells within a spreadsheet you can use cut and paste. This can be done by selecting the relevant cells and choosing Edit > Cut from the menu. Then use Edit > Paste to insert them at the appropriate point.

2.1.10 Inserting columns and rows

Suppose we want to create a sum for the contents in a row, for example cells A1 and B1. The logical place to do this would be cell C1, but what if column C already contains data? We have three options that would enable us to place this total in column C.

(a) Highlight cells C1 to C5 and position the mouse pointer on one of the **edges**. (It will change to an arrow shape.) Hold down the **left** mouse button and drag cells C1 to C5 into column D. There is now space in column C for our next set of sums. Any **formulae** that need to be changed as a result of moving cells using this method should be changed **automatically** – but always check them.

(b) The second option is to highlight cells C1 to C5 as before, position the mouse pointer anywhere **within** column C and click on the **right** mouse button. A menu will appear offering you an option **Insert...** . If you click on this you will be asked where you want to shift the cells that are being moved. In this case you want to move them to the *right* so choose this option and click on OK.

(c) The third option is to **insert a whole new column**. You do this by clicking on the letter at the top of the column (here C) to highlight the whole of it then proceeding as in (b). The new column will be inserted to the left of the one you highlight.

You can now display the sum of each of the rows in column C.

You can also insert a **new row** in a similar way (or stretch rows).

(a) To insert **one** row – for headings say – click on the row number to highlight it, click with the right mouse button and choose insert. One row will be inserted **above** the one you highlighted. Try putting some headings above the figures in columns A to C.

(b) To insert **several** rows click on the row number **immediately below** the point where you want the new rows to appear and, holding down the left mouse button select the number of extra rows you want – rows 1, 2 and 3, say, to insert three rows above the current row 1. Click on the highlighted area with the right mouse button and choose insert.

2.1.11 Changing column width

You may occasionally find that a cell is not wide enough to display its contents. When this occurs, the cell displays a series of hashes ######. There are two options available to solve this problem.

(a) One is to **decide for yourself** how wide you want the columns to be. Position the mouse pointer at the head of the affected column, directly over the little line dividing that column from the one to the right. The mouse **pointer** will change to a sort of **cross**. Hold down the left mouse button and, by moving your mouse, stretch the column to the right, until the words you typed fit.

(b) Often it is easier to **let the software decide for you**. Position the mouse pointer over the little dividing line as before and get the cross symbol. Then double-click with the left mouse button. The column automatically adjusts to an appropriate width to fit the widest cell in that column.

You can either adjust the width of each column individually or you can do them all in one go. To do the latter click on the button in the top left hand corner to **select the whole sheet** and then **double-click** on just one of the dividing lines: all the columns will adjust to the **'best fit'** width.

2.1.12 Changing row height

You may occasionally find that a cell is not tall enough to display the full contents. Again there are two options available to solve this problem.

(a) One is to **decide for yourself** how tall you want the rows to be. Position the mouse pointer at the far left hand side of the affected row (where the row numbers are) directly over the little line dividing that row from the one below. The mouse **pointer** will change to the **cross**. Hold down the

left mouse button and, by moving your mouse, stretch the row downwards, until the words you typed fit.

(b)   Often it is easier to **let the software decide for you**. Position the mouse pointer over the little dividing line as before and get the cross symbol. Then double-click with the left mouse button. The row automatically adjusts to an appropriate height to fit the tallest cell in that row.

2.1.13 Find and replace

If you are searching for a particular value or piece of text in a spreadsheet, you can use the find tool. This is accessed by selecting Edit > Find from the menu. The following window will appear

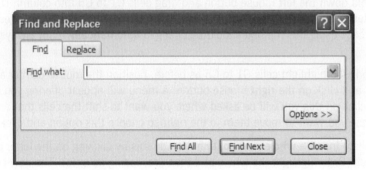

The text or value that you are searching for can be entered and Excel will search for it. Excel can be made to search for all occurrences in one go (Find All) or it will stop at the next instance it finds (Find Next).

If you wish to replace an entry in a large spreadsheet it is probably more efficient to use find and replace. By clicking on the replace tab in the window shown before, the following window appears.

You can do this in two ways. One way is by pressing the "Find All" button, which will find all occurrences of the entry you have typed. The other method is by using the "Find Next" button, which will find the next occurrence of the text. Choose the desired option and, when you find text to replace, click on the "Replace" button to replace it. You can also click on "Replace All" to replace all occurrences of the text inside of the spreadsheet.

2.1.14 Keyboard shortcuts and toolbar buttons

Finally a few tips to improve the **appearance** of your spreadsheets and speed up your work. To do any of the following to a cell or range of cells, first **select** the cell or cells and then:

(a)   Press Ctrl + B to make the cell contents **bold.**

(b)   Press Ctrl + I to make the cell contents *italic.*

(c)   Press **Ctrl + C** to **copy** the contents of the cells.

(d)   Move the cursor and press **Ctrl + V** to **paste** the cell you just copied into the new active cell or cells.

(e)   Ctrl + P will bring up the print options.

There are also **buttons** in the Excel toolbar (shown below) that may be used to carry out these and other functions. The best way to learn about these features is to use them – enter some numbers and text into a spreadsheet and experiment with keyboard shortcuts and toolbar buttons.

3 Spreadsheet formulae

EXAM FOCUS POINT

The April 2012 edition of *student accountant* featured a useful article entitled 'Getting to grips with spreadsheets'. You should make sure you read it after you have finished working through this Interactive Text. It is relevant to both chapters 12 and 13.

Formulae can be used in spreadsheets to perform a wide range of calculations, all of which are performed much quicker than manual calculations.

The following illustration shows the formula bar in an Excel spreadsheet. The formula bar allows you to see and edit the contents of the active cell. The bar also shows the cell address of the 'active cell' (C3 in this example), which is the cell that the cursor is currently in.

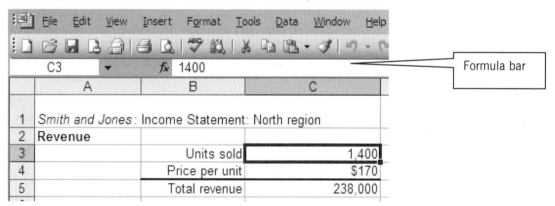

3.1 Examples of spreadsheet formulae

Formulas in Microsoft Excel follow a specific syntax that includes an equal sign (=) followed by the elements to be calculated (the operands) and the calculation operators. Each operand can be a value that does not change (a constant value), a cell or range reference, a label, a name, or a worksheet function.

Formulae can be used to perform a variety of calculations.

3.1.1 Addition and subtraction formulae

(a) =C4+5. This formula **adds** 5 to the value in C4.

(b) =C4+C5. This formula **adds** the value in C4 to the value in C5. Note that this method is fine for addition of a small number of cells, but when larger numbers of cells are added the SUM function is better.

(c) =SUM(C4,C5,C6). This formula adds the values in cells C4, C5 and C6 together. Alternatively the following formula can also be used.

(d) =SUM(C4:C6). This formula sums the range of cells between C4 and C6. This method is more efficient when long lists of cells need to be added together.

(e)   =C4-5. This formula **subtracts** 5 from the value in C4.

(f)   =C4-C5. This formula **subtracts** the value in C5 from the value in C4.

(g)   =C4-C5-C6-C7-C8-C9. This formula **subtracts** the values in C5, C6, C7, C8 and C9 from the value in C4.

(h)   =C4-SUM(C5:C9). This formula **subtracts** the values in C5, C6, C7, C8 and C9 from the value in C4. The use of the SUM function is more efficient than listing the cells separately.

3.1.2 Multiplication and division formulae

(a)   =C4*5. This formula **multiplies** the value in C4 by 5. The result will appear in the cell holding the formula.

(b)   =C4*B10. This **multiplies** the value in C4 by the value in B10.

(c)   =C4/E5. This **divides** the value in C4 by the value in E5. (* means multiply and / means divide by.)

(d)   =C4*B10-D1. This **multiplies** the value in C4 by that in B10 and then subtracts the value in D1 from the result. Note that generally Excel will perform multiplication and division before addition or subtraction. If in any doubt, use brackets (parentheses): =(C4*B10)–D1.

(e)   =C4*117.5%. This **adds** 17.5% to the value in C4. It could be used to calculate a price including 17.5% sales tax.

3.1.3 Use of brackets and averages

(a)   =(C4+C5+C6)/3. Note that the **brackets** mean Excel would perform the addition first. Without the brackets, Excel would first divide the value in C6 by 3 and then add the result to the total of the values in C4 and C5. Excel calculates a formula from left to right, starting with the equals. You can control how calculation is performed by changing the syntax of the formula. For example, the formula =5+2*3 gives a result of 11 because Excel calculates multiplication before addition. Excel would multiply 2 by 3 (resulting in 6) and would then add 5.

(b)   You may use parentheses to change the order of operations. For example =(5+2)*3 would result in Excel firstly adding the 5 and 2 together, then multiplying that result by 3 to give 21.

(c)   To divide one sums of cells by another requires the use of brackets. For example =(C4+C5+C6)/(D4+D5+D6) will divide the sum of cells C4 to C6 by the sum of cells D4 to D6.

(d)   =AVERAGE(C4,C5,C6) or =AVERAGE(C4:C6). These formulae will calculate the average (arithmetic mean) of the values in cells C4,C5 and C6. Although the average can also be calculated by other formulae, this method is the most efficient, particularly with large ranges of numbers.

(e)   If the AVERAGE function is referred to a blank cell or one containing text it will ignore this for calculation purposes. If the cell contains a 0 value this will be included in the calculation.

QUESTION

Spreadsheets

	A	B	C	D	E	F
1	BUDGETED SALES FIGURES					
2		Jan	Feb	Mar	Total	
3		$'000	$'000	$'000	$'000	
4	North	2,431	3,001	2,189	7,621	
5	South	6,532	5,826	6,124	18,482	
6	West	895	432	596	1,923	
7	Total	9,858	9,259	8,909	28,026	
8						

(a)   In the spreadsheet shown above, which of the cells have had a number typed in, and which cells display the result of calculations (ie which cells contain a formula)?

(b)   What formula would you put in each of the following cells?

(i)   Cell B7

(ii)   Cell E6

(iii)   Cell E7

(c)   If the February sales figure for the South changed from £5,826 to £5,731, what other figures would change as a result? Give cell references.

ANSWER

(a)   Cells into which you would need to enter a value are: B4, B5, B6, C4, C5, C6, D4, D5 and D6. Cells which would perform calculations are B7, C7, D7, E4, E5, E6 and E7.

(b)   (i)   =B4+B5+B6 or better =SUM(B4:B6)

(ii)   =B6+C6+D6 or better =SUM(B6:D6)

(iii) =E4+E5+E6 or better =SUM(E4:E6) Alternatively, the three monthly totals could be added across the spreadsheet: = SUM (B7: D7)

(c)   The figures which would change, besides the amount in cell C5, would be those in cells C7, E5 and E7. (The contents of E7 would change if any of the sales figures changed.)

QUESTION

Actual sales compared with budget sales

	A	B	C	D	E
1	Sales team comparison of actual against budget sales				
2	Name	Sales (Budget)	Sales (Actual)	Difference	% of budget
3		$	$	$	$
4	Northington	275,000	284,000	9,000	3.27
5	Souther	200,000	193,000	(7,000)	(3.50)
6	Weston	10,000	12,000	2,000	20.00
7	Easterman	153,000	152,000	(1,000)	(0.65)
8					
9	Total	638,000	641,000	3,000	0.47
10					

Give a suitable formula for each of the following cells.

(a)   Cell D4

(b)   Cell E6

(c)   Cell E9

ANSWER

(a)   =C4-B4.

(b)   =(D6/B6)*100.

(c)   =(D9/B9)*100. Note that in (c) you **cannot simply add up the individual percentage differences**, as the percentages are based on different quantities.

QUESTION

Formulae

The following spreadsheet shows sales, exclusive of sales tax, in row 6.

	A	B	C	D	E	F	G	H	
1	**Taxable supplies Co**								
2	*Sales analysis - Branch C*								
3	*Six months ended 30 June 200X*								
4		Jan	Feb	Mar	Apr	May	Jun	Total	
5		$	$	$	$	$	$	$	
6	Net sales	2,491.54	5,876.75	3,485.01	5,927.7	6,744.52	3,021.28	27,546.80	
7	Sales tax								
8	Total								
9									

Your manager has asked you to insert formulae to calculate sales tax at 17½% in row 7 and also to produce totals.

Devise a suitable formula for cell B7 and cell E8.

ANSWER

(a)   For cell B7   =B6*0.175   For cell E8   =SUM(E6:E7)

EXAM FOCUS POINT

Identifying the correct formula for a cell could easily be a question in the exam.

---

4 Identifying and correcting errors in formulae

There are a number of **types of error** in Excel, which you need to know how to **identify** and **correct**.

4.1 Removing circular references

Circular references usually (but not always) represent a mistake in the logic of the spreadsheet, for example a formula that includes a reference to its own cell address.

Here's an example of a circular reference error.

	A	B
1		
2	Jan	2,100
3	Feb	2,500
4	Mar	2,600
5	Quarter 1	=SUM(B2:B5)

The formula held in cell B5 refers to cell B5 – a circular reference.

When a formula that contains a circular reference is entered, Excel displays the following warning.

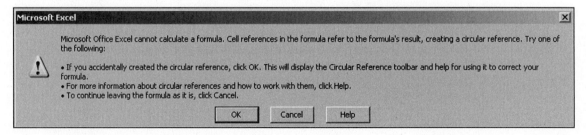

If this warning appears, Click OK to bring up the Circular Reference toolbar (shown below together with the meaning of the toolbar buttons).

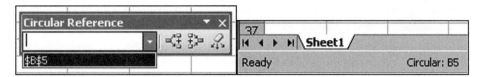

A warning (the word 'Circular') appears in the status bar. The cell address of the circular reference is also shown eg B5 in this example.

If 'Circular' appears without a cell reference, it means the workbook contains a circular reference but it isn't in the active worksheet.

Excel only provides one warning at a time, regardless of how many circular references are in the spreadsheet. When all circular references have been removed, the 'Circular' warning will disappear.

4.1.1 Using Trace precedents and trace dependents

A precedent is a cell that is referred to by another cell. To trace cells that provide data to a formula, click on the cell containing the formula, then from the menu select Tools > Formula Auditing > Trace Precedents. A tracer arrow then appears linking the active cell with precedent cells.

	A	B	C	D
1		**Revenue**	**Costs**	**Gross Profit**
2	North	2,543	890	1,653
3	South	5,487	1,920	3,567
4	East	2,855	999	1,856
5	West	3,642	1,275	2,367
6		14,527	5,084	9,443
7				

To identify the next level of precedents, remain in the active cell and select Tools > Formula Auditing > Trace Precedents again.

To remove the arrows, select _Tools > Formula Auditing > Remove All Arrows_. Rather than navigating through the menus, you may prefer to use the _Formula Auditing_ toolbar. To display the toolbar, select _View > Toolbars > Formula Auditing_, or select _Tools > Formula Auditing > Show Formula Auditing Toolbar_.

A **dependent** is the opposite of a precedent. It is a cell that contains a formula that refers to another cell. To identify the dependent cells from a particular cell in a spreadsheet from the menu select Tools > Formula Auditing > Trace Dependents. A tracer arrow then appears linking the active cell with dependent cells.

4.2 Identifying and correcting error values

Errors should be identified, investigated and corrected. An understanding of Excel's error values is an important part of this process.

If Excel is unable to calculate a formula, it will return an error value. Common error values are explained in the table below.

Error value	Explanation
#DIV/0!	Commonly caused by a formula attempting to divide a number by zero (perhaps because the divisor cell is blank or a formula including division may refer to a cell that is blank). Check the cells referenced by the formula to look for any zero values being used as a divisor. If either the zero value is incorrect or the cell reference is incorrect, correct this to remove the error.
#VALUE!	Occurs when a mathematical formula refers to a cell containing text, eg if cell A2 contains text the formula =A1+A2+A3 will return #VALUE!. Functions that operate on ranges (eg SUM) will not result in a #VALUE! error as they ignore text values.

Error value	Explanation
	If the error results from a cell that appears to be blank, it's likely the cell holds one or more 'spaces' (ie entered by pressing the space bar). To clear the contents, use either the delete key - or select Edit > Clear > All (this option clears formats too).
	#VALUE! is a 'data type' error and can be corrected by change text values for number values where applicable, or removing the cell reference to the cell with text from the formula.
#NULL!	The cell references within the formula are not separated correctly. This may occur by separating cell references by a space rather than a mathematical operator or entering a range but not separating the range ends by a colon. To investigate the error, click on the cell displaying #NULL! and then on the error button that appears ⬦.
#REF!	The formula includes an invalid cell reference, for example a reference to cells that have subsequently been deleted.
	If you notice the reference immediately after a deletion, use Edit > Undo Delete. Otherwise, investigation and editing of the formula to correct it is required. The Formula Auditing toolbar (View > Toolbars > Formula Auditing) may help with this process. The auditing toolbar and other options to help investigate errors may also be accessed by clicking on the error and then on the error button that appears ⬦.

You should also be aware of the #### error. This is a display feature rather than an error value. It's usually caused by a column not being wide enough to display its contents. #### also occurs when a negative number is formatted as a date or time.

4.2.1 Finding and correcting cell reference errors

The formula in cell D41 is intended to calculate taxation at 22% on the Profit before tax. The result in D41 is obviously wrong, as it is greater than the profit.

C41	▾	*fx* =C40*B41		
	A	B	C	D
3			**Jan**	**Feb**
40	Profit before tax		4,905	5,175
41	Taxation	22%	1,079	5,584,343
42	Profit after tax		3,826	-5,579,168
43				

To investigate, first display formulas by selecting Tools > Options from the menu, and selecting the Formulas box on the View tab. This also brings up the Formula Auditing toolbar (or use View > Toolbars > Formula Auditing).

The formula in cell C41 refers to cell B41. The formula in D41 does not refer to the taxation rate in B41, resulting in an incorrect calculation.

C41	▾	*fx* =C40*B41		
	A	B	C	D
3			**Jan**	**Feb**
40	Profit before tax		4905	5175
41	Taxation	0.22	=C40*B41	=D40*C41
42	Profit after tax		=C40-C41	=D40-D41
43				
44		Formula Auditing		
45				
46				

If we select B41 and then click the *Trace Dependents* button on the *Formula Auditing* toolbar, this confirms that only cell C41 is using the *Taxation* rate.

After correcting this formula, D41 calculates correctly.

	C41 ▼		*fx* =C40*$B41	
	A	B	C	D
3			Jan	Feb
40	Profit before tax		4,905	5,175
41	Taxation	22%	1,079	1,139
42	Profit after tax		3,826	4,037

CHAPTER ROUNDUP

- A **spreadsheet** is basically an electronic piece of paper divided into **rows** and **columns**. The intersection of a row and a column is known as a **cell**.

- Essential basic **skills** include how to **move around** within a spreadsheet, how to **enter** and **edit** data, how to **fill** cells, how to **insert** and **delete** columns and rows and how to improve the basic **layout** and **appearance** of a spreadsheet.

- **Formulae** can be used in spreadsheets to perform a wide range of calculations, all of which are performed much quicker than manual calculations

- There are a number of **types of error** in Excel, which you need to know how to **identify** and **correct**.

QUICK QUIZ

1   Which one of the following statements about spreadsheets is incorrect?

    A   Spreadsheets make calculations easier and quicker
    B   Data can be manipulated more easily
    C   'Totals' figures can be calculated automatically
    D   The information will always be accurate

2   Cell C4 contains a sales price net of sales tax of 17.5%. Which one of the following formulae would NOT give the gross sales price?

    A   C4* 117.5%
    B   C4* 1.175
    C   C4* (1 + 0.175)
    D   C4 + 17.5%

3   In order to move quickly from one place to another in a large spreadsheet, which one of the following key controls would be unhelpful.

    A   F2
    B   Page up
    C   F5
    D   Ctrl and an arrow key

4   If a spreadsheet column is not wide enough to display its contents, which of the following would appear?

    A   #REF!
    B   #NUM!
    C   #####
    D   #DIV/O!

5   Which of the following options would perform the 'paste' function?

    A   Ctrl + P
    B   Ctrl + R
    C   Ctrl + T
    D   Ctrl + V

6   When a cell displays the error #REF!, what has caused this?

ANSWERS TO QUICK QUIZ

1   D   The spreadsheet itself won't make errors but it is still subject to human error. If, for example, the data which is input is incorrect then the output information will be incorrect.

2   D   Try this using a figure of 100 in cell C4.

             The first three options will return a figure of 117.50. Option D will return a figure of 100.175 because Excel has added 0.175 to the 100.

3   A   F2 will not be helpful as this is an edit key.

4   C   When this occurs, the cell displays a series of hashes.

5   D   Ctrl + V will paste.

6   This error is caused by a formula containing an invalid cell reference, which may be because the cell has been deleted.

Now try ...

Attempt the questions below from the **Exam Question Bank**

Number

Q46-49

13

Much of the information used for management control today is analysed or presented using spreadsheet or software. This chapter covers the basics of using spreadsheets to present information.

Using spreadsheets to present information

Study Guide	Intellectual level
F The spreadsheet system	
1 Spreadsheet system overview	
(b) Explain the role of spreadsheets in management accounting	K
(c) Describe advantages and limitations of spreadsheets	K
2 Using computer spreadsheets	
(c) Explain and illustrate formatting tools	S
(f) Describe how data from different sources are linked and combined	K
3 Presenting information in spreadsheets	
(a) Explain methods of summarising and analysing spreadsheet data (including sorting, ranking and filter)	K
(b) Explain and interpret charts and graphs (bar, line, pie and scatter)	S
(c) Describe how to present and format information to meet particular needs	S

1 Charts, graphs and tables

Charts and **graphs** and tables are often excellent ways of communicating information.

In many cases, communication may best be achieved if information is presented in a visual form such as a chart or a graph.

Graphs and charts can be complex and highly technical, so they should, like any other medium of communication, be adapted to suit the understanding and information needs of the intended recipient: they should be simplified and explained as necessary, and include only as much data as can clearly be presented and assimilated.

1.1 Charts

The **bar or column chart** is one of the most common methods of presenting data in a visual display. It is a chart in which data is shown in the form of a **bar** (two dimensional, or three dimensional for extra impact), and is used to **demonstrate and compare amounts or numbers of things**. The bars are the same width but variable in height and are read off a vertical scale as you would read water levels or a thermometer. A horizontal presentation is also possible.

The bar chart is very **versatile**. Each block may represent a different (identified) item, for example the annual production cost of a different product (to compare costs of a range of products), or the total sales turnover of a company for a year (to compare success over a period of years), or the number of hours required to produce a product in a particular country (to compare efficiency in a group of industrial nations).

A simple barchart is a chart consisting of one or more bars, in which the length of each bar indicates the magnitude of the corresponding data item.

A simple bar chart is a visually appealing way of illustration.

1.2 Example: simple bar chart

A company's total expenditure for the years from 20X4 to 20X9 are as follows.

Year	$'000
20X4	800
20X5	1,200
20X6	1,100
20X7	1,400
20X8	1,600
20X9	1,700

The data could be shown on a simple bar chart as follows.

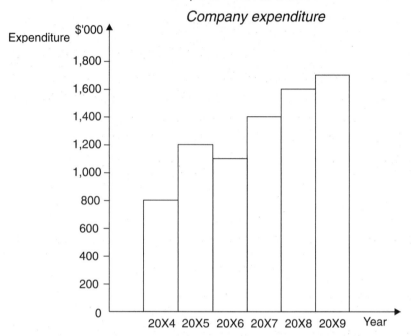

1.3 Component bar chart

A **component bar chart** (also known as a stacked bar chart) is a bar chart that shows component information in each bar on a percentage basis. For example company revenue may be shown for a number of years, split by geographical region. This type of graph is a good way to compare relative percentages, but also showing absolute amounts as well – it is possible to produce a component bar chart showing either ('stacked' or 'per cent stacked'). In the example that follows a company has two selling divisions East and West. The West division is shaded with diagonal lines and the east division portion is unshaded. Looking at this chart, it is easy to see that most of the revenue comes from the West division in each year and also to see the total revenue in each year.

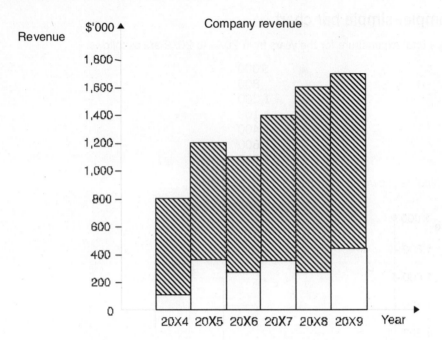

1.4 Line graphs

Line graphs are often used in commercial contexts, to display a wide variety of information. They are particularly useful for **demonstrating trends**: the progress of events or the fluctuation over time of variables such as profits, prices, sales totals, customer complaints.

This is done by plotting points of information on a grid, usually something like this.

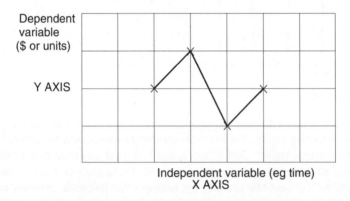

1.4.1 Dependent and independent variables

If you are given two variables, the examiner might not tell you which is x and which is y. You need to be able to work this out for yourself.

y is the dependent variable, depending for its value on the value of x

x is the independent variable whose value helps to determine the corresponding value of y. Time is usually an independent variable.

For example, the total cost of materials purchases depends on the budgeted number of units of production. The number of production units is the independent (x) variable and the total cost is the dependent variable (y).

In the graph above, the points are joined by a line which thus reflects the 'ups and downs' of the variable, over a period of time. Two or three such lines may comfortably be drawn on a spacious graph before it gets too overcrowded, allowing several trends (for example the performance of several competing products over a period of time) to be compared. An example is shown below.

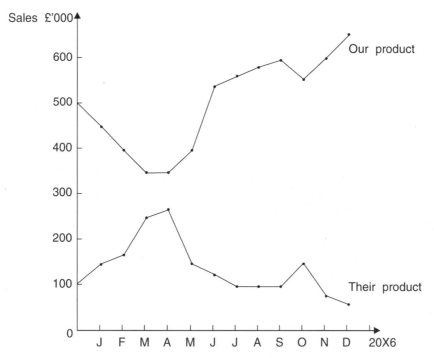

The scale of the vertical axis is large enough for you to tell with reasonable accuracy the price at any given point during the period. (This is important, because the eye cannot distinguish fractions of inches which might represent a large leap on a scale marked for example by units of ten or a hundred).

Despite peaks and troughs, the overall trend is also obvious, in a way that would not be possible in a table of fluctuating figures. This will be helpful, for example, in demonstrating the success of a productivity scheme to encourage employees, or in spotting potentially disastrous declines in sales (or increases in absenteeism).

EXAM FOCUS POINT

You will not be required to prepare a graph in the exam but there may be a question about how you would prepare one.

1.5 Pie charts

A **pie chart** is a chart which is used to show pictorially the relative size of component elements of a total.

It is called a pie chart because it is **circular**, and so has the **shape of a pie** in a round pie dish. The 'pie' is then cut into slices with each slice representing part of the total.

Pie charts have sectors of varying sizes, and you need to be able to draw sectors fairly accurately. To do this, you need a **protractor**. Working out sector sizes involves converting parts of the total into **equivalent degrees of a circle**. A complete 'pie' = 360°: the number of degrees in a circle = 100% of whatever you are showing. An element which is 50% of your total will therefore occupy a segment of 180°, and so on.

1.5.1 Using shading and colour

Two pie charts are shown as follows.

Breakdown of air and noise pollution complaints, 1

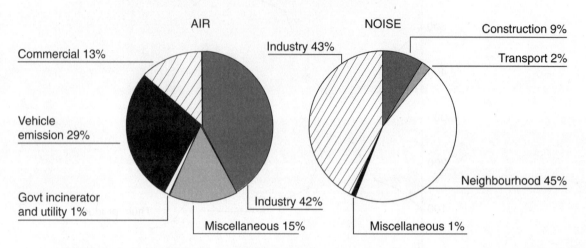

- **Shading** distinguishes the segments from each other
- **Colour** can also be used to distinguish segments

1.5.2 Example: Pie charts

The costs of materials at the Cardiff Factory and the Swansea Factory during January 20X0 were as follows.

	Cardiff factory		Swansea factory	
	$'000	%	$'000	%
Material W	70	35	50	20
Material A	30	15	125	50
Material L	90	45	50	20
Material E	10	5	25	10
	200	100	250	100

Show the costs for the factories in pie charts.

Solution

To convert the components into degrees of a circle, we can use either the **percentage figures** or the **actual cost figures**.

Using the percentage figures

The total percentage is 100%, and the total number of degrees in a circle is 360°. To convert from one to the other, we multiply each percentage value by 360/100% = 3.6.

	Cardiff factory		Swansea factory	
	%	Degrees	%	Degrees
Material W	35	126	20	72
Material A	15	54	50	180
Material L	45	162	20	72
Material E	5	18	10	36
	100	360	100	360

Using the actual cost figures

	Cardiff factory		Swansea factory	
	$'000	Degrees	$'000	Degrees
Material W (70/200 × 360°)	70	126	50	72
Material A	30	54	125	180
Material L	90	162	50	72
Material E	10	18	25	36
	200	360	250	360

A pie chart could be drawn for each factory.

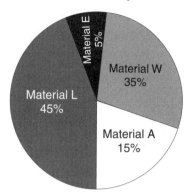

Cardiff Factory

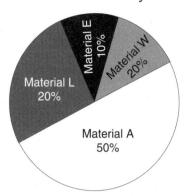

Swansea Factory

(a) If the pie chart is drawn manually, a protractor must be used to measure the degrees accurately to obtain the correct sector sizes.

(b) Using a computer makes the process much simpler, especially using a spreadsheet. You just draw up the data in a spreadsheet and click on the chart button to create a visual representation of what you want. Note that you can only use colour effectively if you have a colour printer!

1.5.3 Advantages of pie charts

- They give a simple pictorial display of the relative sizes of elements of a total
- They show clearly when one element is much bigger than others
- They can clearly show differences in the elements of two different totals

1.5.4 Disadvantages of pie charts

(a) They only show the relative sizes of elements. In the example of the two factories, for instance, the pie charts do not show that costs at the Swansea factory were $50,000 higher in total than at the Cardiff factory.

(b) It is often **difficult to compare sector sizes** easily. For example, suppose that the following two pie charts are used to show the elements of a company's sales.

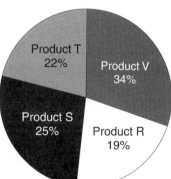

20X0

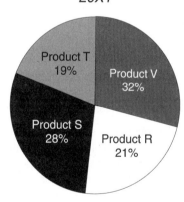

20X1

Without the percentage figures, it would not be easy to see how the distribution of sales had changed between 20X0 and 20X1.

QUESTION

Pie charts

The European division of Scent to You, a flower delivery service has just published its accounts for the year ended 30 June 20X0. The sales director made the following comments.

'Our total sales for the year were $1,751,000, of which $787,000 were made in the United Kingdom, $219,000 in Italy, $285,000 in France and $92,000 in Germany. Sales in Spain and Holland

amounted to $189,000 and $34,000 respectively, whilst the rest of Europe collectively had sales of $145,000 in the twelve months to 30 June 20X0.'

Required

Present the above information in the form of a pie chart. Show all of your workings.

ANSWER

Workings

	Sales $'000		Degrees
United Kingdom	787	(787/1,751 × 360)	162
Italy	219		45
France	285		58
Germany	92		19
Spain	189		39
Rest of Europe	145		30
Holland	34		7
	1,751		360

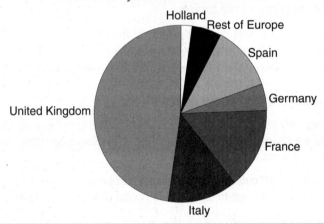

Scent to You
Sales for the year ended 30 June 20X0

1.6 Scatter diagram

Scatter diagrams are graphs which are used to exhibit data, (rather than equations) in order to compare the way in which two variables vary with each other. The x axis of a scatter diagram is used to represent the independent variable and the y axis represents the dependent variable.

To construct a scatter diagram or scattergraph, we must have several pairs of data, with each pair showing the value of one variable and the corresponding value of the other variable. Each pair is plotted on a graph. The resulting graph will show a number of pairs, scattered over the graph. The scattered points might or might not appear to follow a trend.

1.6.1 Example: Scatter diagram

The output at a factory each week for the last ten weeks, and the cost of that output, were as follows.

Week	1	2	3	4	5	6	7	8	9	10
Output (units)	10	12	10	8	9	11	7	12	9	14
Cost ($)	42	44	38	34	38	43	30	47	37	50

Required

Plot the data given on a scatter diagram.

Solution

The data could be shown on a scatter diagram as follows.

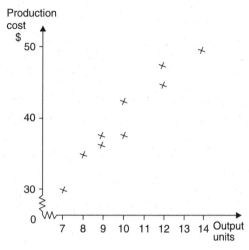

(a) The cost depends on the volume of output: volume is the independent variable and is shown on the x axis.

(b) You will notice from the graph that the plotted data, although scattered, lie approximately on a rising trend line, with higher total costs at higher output volumes. (The lower part of the axes have been omitted, so as not to waste space. The break in the axes is indicated by the jagged lines.)

1.6.2 The trend line

For the most part, scatter diagrams are used to try to identify **trend lines**.

If a trend can be seen in a scatter diagram, the next step is to try to draw a trend line.

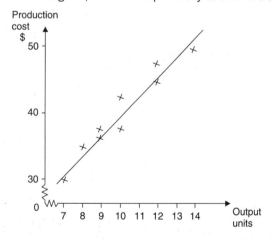

QUESTION

Scatter diagrams

The quantities of widgets produced by WDG Co during the year ended 31 October 20X9 and the related costs were as follows.

Month	Production Thousands	Factory cost $'000
20X8		
November	7	45
December	10	59
20X9		
January	13	75
February	14	80
March	11	65
April	7	46

Month	Production Thousands	Factory cost $'000
May	5	35
June	4	30
July	3	25
August	2	20
September	1	15
October	5	35

You may assume that the value of money remained stable throughout the year.

Required

(a) Draw a scatter diagram related to the data provided above, and plot on it the line of best fit.

(b) Now answer the following questions.

(i) What would you expect the factory cost to have been if 12,000 widgets had been produced in a particular month?

(ii) What is your estimate of WDG's monthly fixed cost?

ANSWER

Your answers to parts (b)(i) and (ii) may have been slightly different from those given here, but they should not have been very different, because the data points lay very nearly along a straight line.

(a) WDG Co – Scatter diagram of production and factory costs, November 20X8 – October 20X9

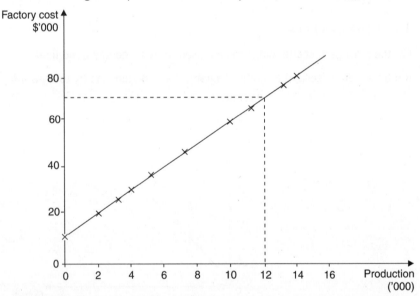

(b) (i) The estimated factory cost for a production of 12,000 widgets is $70,000.

(ii) The monthly fixed costs are indicated by the point where the line of best fit meets the vertical axis (costs at zero production). The fixed costs are estimated as $10,000 a month.

1.7 Tables

Tables are a simple way of presenting **numerical information**. Figures are displayed, and can be compared with each other: relevant totals, subtotals, percentages can also be presented as a summary for analysis.

A table is **two-dimensional** (rows and columns): so it can only show two variables: a sales chart for a year, for example, might have rows for products, and columns for each month of the year.

SALES FIGURES FOR 20--													
Product	Jan	Feb	Mar	Apr	May	Jun	Jul	Aug	Sep	Oct	Nov	Dec	Total $'000
A													
B													
C													
D													
Total													

You are likely to be presenting data in tabular form very often, in doing so, be aware of the following guidelines.

- The table should be given a **clear title**.

- All columns should be **clearly labelled**.

- Where appropriate, there should be **clear sub-totals** and a right-hand **total column** for comparison.

- A **total figure** is often advisable at the bottom of each column of figures also, for comparison.

- Tables should not be packed with too much data so that the information presented is difficult to read.

2 Using Excel to produce charts and graphs

Using Microsoft Excel, it is possible to use data held in a spreadsheet to generate a variety of charts and graphs.

Today, the vast majority of **charts** and **graphs** produced in a business setting are prepared using **spreadsheet software**.

2.1 Using Microsoft Excel to produce charts and graphs

Using Microsoft Excel, it is possible to display data held in a range of spreadsheet cells in a variety of charts or graphs. We will use the Discount Traders Ltd spreadsheet shown below to generate a chart.

	A	B	C	D	
1	Discount Traders				
2	Sales analysis April 20X0				
3	Customer	Sales	5% discount	Sales (net)	
4		$	$	$	
5	Arthur	956.00	0.00	956.00	
6	Dent	1423.00	71.15	1351.85	
7	Ford	2894.00	144.70	2749.30	
8	Prefect	842.00	0.00	842.00	
9					

The data in the spreadsheet could be used to generate a chart, such as those shown below. We explain how later in this section.

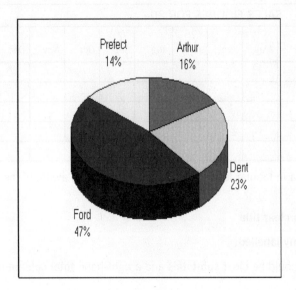

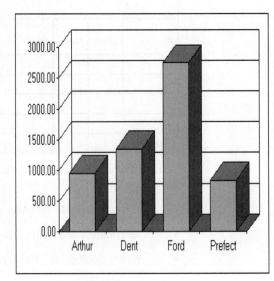

The Chart Wizard, which we explain in a moment, may also be used to generate a line graph. A line graph would normally be used to track a tend over time. For example, the chart below graphs the Total Revenue figures shown in Row 6 of the following spreadsheet.

	A	B	C	D	E	F
1		Revenue 20X0 - 20X3				
2						
3	Net revenue	20X0	20X1	20X2	20X3	
4	Products	24,001	27,552	34,823	39,205	
5	Services	5,306	5,720	6,104	6,820	
6	Total	29,307	33,272	40,927	46,025	
7						

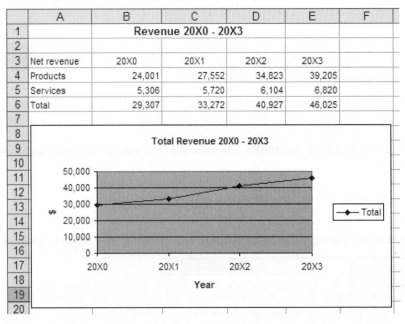

2.2 The Chart Wizard

Charts and graphs may be generated simply by **selecting the range** of figures to be included, then using Excel's Chart Wizard. The Discount Traders spreadsheet referred to earlier is shown again below.

	A	B	C	D
1	**Discount Traders**			
2	*Sales analysis April 20X0*			
3	Customer	Sales	5% discount	Sales (net)
4		$	$	$
5	Arthur	956.00	0.00	956.00
6	Dent	1423.00	71.15	1351.85
7	Ford	2894.00	144.70	2749.30
8	Prefect	842.00	0.00	842.00
9				

To chart the **net sales** of the different **customers**, follow the following steps.

Step 1	Highlight cells A5:A8, then move your pointer to cell D5, hold down **Ctrl** and drag to also select cells D5:D8.

Step 2	Look at the **toolbar** at the top of your spreadsheet. You should see an **icon** that looks like a small bar chart. Click on this icon to start the 'Chart Wizard'.

The following steps are taken from the Excel 2003 Chart Wizard. Other versions may differ slightly.

Step 3	Pick the type of chart you want. We will choose chart type **Column** and then select the sub-type we think will be most effective. (To produce a graph, select a type such as **Line**).

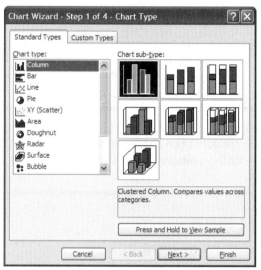

Step 4	This step gives us the opportunity to confirm that the data we selected earlier was correct and to decide whether the chart should be based on **columns** (eg Customer, Sales, Discount etc) or **rows** (Arthur, Dent etc). We can accept the default values and click Next.

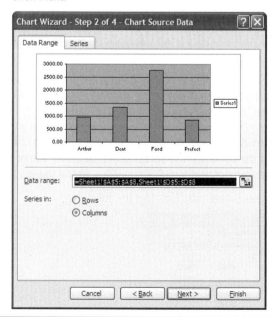

Step 5   Next, specify your chart **title** and axis **labels**. Incidentally, one way of remembering which is the **X axis** and which is the **Y axis** is to look at the letter Y: it is the only letter that has a vertical part pointing straight up, so it must be the vertical axis! Click Next to move on.

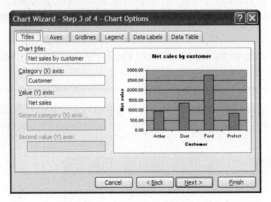

As you can see, there are other index tabs available. You can see the effect of selecting or deselecting each one in **preview** – experiment with these options as you like then click Next.

Step 6   The final step is to choose whether you want the chart to appear on the same worksheet as the data or on a separate sheet of its own. This is a matter of personal preference – for this example choose to place the chart as an object within the existing spreadsheet.

2.3 Changing existing charts

Even after your chart is 'finished', you can change it.

(a)   You can **resize it** simply by selecting it and dragging out its borders.

(b)   You can change **each element** by **double clicking** on it then selecting from the options available.

(c)   You could also select any item of **text** and alter the wording, size or font, or change the **colours** used.

3 Spreadsheet format and appearance

A spreadsheet should be given a **title** which clearly defines its purpose. The contents of rows and columns should also be clearly **labelled**. **Formatting** should be used to make the data held in the spreadsheet easy to read and interpret.

It is important that the information provided in a spreadsheet is easy to understand. Good presentation can help people understand the contents of a spreadsheet. Sensible use of formatting will help aid understanding and make the spreadsheet visually appealing to the users.

Without any formatting a spreadsheet may look like the following.

	A	B	C	D	E	F
1	Sales team salaries and commissions - 20X0					
2	Name	Sales	Salaries	Commissi	Total earnings	
3		$	$	$	$	
4	Northingto	284000	14000	5680	19680	
5	Souther	193000	14000	3860	17860	
6	Weston	12000	14000	240	14240	
7	Eastermar	152000	14000	3040	17040	
8						
9	Total	641000	56000	12820	68820	
10						

3.1 Titles and labels

A spreadsheet should be headed up with a title which **clearly defines its purpose**. Examples of titles are follows.

(a)   Income statement for the year ended 30 June 20X0

(b)   (i)   Area A: Sales forecast for the three months to 31 March 20X0
         (ii)   Area B: Sales forecast for the three months to 31 March 20X0
         (iii)   Combined sales forecast for the three months to 31 March 20X0

(c)   Salesmen: Analysis of earnings and commission for the six months ended 30 June 20X0

Row and **column** headings (or labels) should clearly identify the contents of the row/column. Any assumptions made that have influenced the spreadsheet contents should be clearly stated.

3.2 Formatting

Numbers can be **formatted** in several ways, for instance with commas, as percentages, as currency or with a certain number of decimal places.

There are a wide range of options available under the **Format** menu. Some of these functions may also be accessed through toolbar **buttons**. Formatting options include the ability to:

(a)   Add **colour, shading** or **borders** to cells. These can all be used to highlight important cells containing key information. Borders can be used to create tables or add total or sub total lines around a cell as shown below.

	A	B	C
1			
2		5,500	
3		658	
4		73	
5		52	
6		6,283	
7			

(b)   Use **different sizes of text** and different **fonts**.

(c)   Choose from a range of options for presenting values, for example to present a number as a **percentage** (eg 0.05 as 5%), or with commas every third digit, or to a specified number of **decimal places** etc.

(d)   **Alignment** of text or values within cells. Sometimes text contents are easier to view if they are aligned in the centre or to the right of the cell. With a column of values, however, the numbers are often easier to compare if they are aligned to the right hand side of the cells.

(e)   **Wrap text** is an important formatting function. Where the text entered in a cell is bigger than the cell, this option increases the height of the row containing that cell so that the whole of the text is visible. This is similar to changing the height of the cell which was covered in Chapter 12.

Experiment with the various formatting options yourself.

3.3 Formatting numbers

Most spreadsheet programs contain facilities for presenting numbers in a particular way. In Excel you simply select **Format** and then **Cells ...** to reach these options.

(a)   **Number format** displays the number in the cell rounded off to the number of decimal places you select. Negative numbers can be shown in red if desired.

(b)   **Currency format** displays the number with a '$' in front, with commas and a default of two decimal places, eg $10,540.23. Negative numbers can be shown in red if desired.

(c) **General format** is the format assumed unless another format is specified. In general format the number is displayed with no commas and with as many decimal places as entered or calculated that fit in the cell.

(d) **Percent format** multiplies the number in the display by 100 and follows it with a percentage sign. For example the number 0.548 in a cell would be displayed as 54.8%.

(e) **Accounting format** is similar to the currency format, but the decimal points will be aligned, the currency symbol and any minus sign are always displayed on the far left of the cell. Also all negative values are always displayed in black.

(f) **Hidden format** is a facility by which values can be entered into cells and used in calculations but are not actually displayed on the spreadsheet. The format is useful for hiding sensitive information. This can be achieved by selecting custom and entering three semi-colons in the type box.

3.4 Gridlines

One of the options available under the **Tools**, **Options** menu, on the **View** tab, is an option to remove the gridlines from your spreadsheet.

Compare the following two versions of the same spreadsheet. Note how the formatting applied to the second version has improved the spreadsheet presentation.

	A	B	C	D	E		A	B	C	D	E
1	Sales team salaries and commissions - 20X0						Sales team salaries and commissions - 20X0				
2	Name	Sales	Salaries	Commissic	Total earnings		Name	Sales	Salaries	Commission	Total earnings
3		$	$	$	$			$	$	$	$
4	Northingto	284000	14000	5680	19680		Northington	284,000	14,000	5,680	19,680
5	Souther	193000	14000	3860	17860		Souther	193,000	14,000	3,860	17,860
6	Weston	12000	14000	240	14240		Weston	12,000	14,000	240	14,240
7	Eastermar	152000	14000	3040	17040		Easterman	152,000	14,000	3,040	17,040
8											
9	Total	641000	56000	12820	68820		Total	641,000	56,000	12,820	68,820
10											

3.5 Data manipulation

Data manipulation refers to a number of techniques available in Excel for summarising, analysing, sorting and presenting data.

3.5.1 Sorting

The data below is currently not arranged in any order. The horizontal rows are records: one record for each inventory type. The vertical columns are attributes (qualities) relating to each record.

	A	B	C	D	E	F	G
1	STK						
2	Part number	Supplier	Quantity	Reorder level	Unit price	Value	
3					$	$	
4	125684	B	201	120	10.00	2,010	
5	127544	A	25	25	15.00	375	
6	123673	B	42	30	5.00	210	
7	125445	C	86	60	6.00	516	
8	125421	C	400	150	7.00	2,800	
9	123548	D	20	12	12.00	240	
10	125687	A	5	3	60.00	300	
11	124587	C	63	70	14.00	882	
12	124895	B	52	40	8.00	416	
13	126874	B	117	85	9.00	1,053	
14							
15							

To sort the part number data into descending value order.

Step 1   Select the data range A4:F13

Step 2   Select Data > Sort. The following window then appears

Step 3   Choose to sort by column A, descending

Step 4   Click OK

You will see that the data has been sorted by descending value of part numbers.

	A	B	C	D	E	F
1	STK					
2	Part number	Supplier	Quantity	Reorder level	Unit price	Value
3					$	$
4	127544	A	25	25	15.00	375
5	126874	B	117	85	9.00	1,053
6	125687	A	5	3	60.00	300
7	125684	B	201	120	10.00	2,010
8	125445	C	86	60	6.00	516
9	125421	C	400	150	7.00	2,800
10	124895	B	52	40	8.00	416
11	124587	C	63	70	14.00	882
12	123673	B	42	30	5.00	210
13	123548	D	20	12	12.00	240

3.5.2 Filtering

Filtering data allows you to select and display just some of it in the table. This is useful if the table consists of many records but you only wish to view some of them.

The data above shows inventory information including supplier details.

Let's say we just want to find inventory records relating to suppliers B and C.

Step 1   Select Data > Filter > Autofilter, the spreadsheet should now appear as follows

	A	B	C	D	E	F
1	STK					
2	Part numb ▾	Suppli ▾	Quantit ▾	Reorder lev ▾	Unit pri ▾	Value ▾
3					$	$
4	125684	B	201	120	10.00	2,010
5	127544	A	25	25	15.00	375
6	123673	B	42	30	5.00	210
7	125445	C	86	60	6.00	516
8	125421	C	400	150	7.00	2,800
9	123548	D	20	12	12.00	240
10	125687	A	5	3	60.00	300
11	124587	C	63	70	14.00	882
12	124895	B	52	40	8.00	416
13	126874	B	117	85	9.00	1,053

Step 2   Click on the drop-down arrow that has appeared at the top of the Supplier column

Step 3   Select Custom then complete the dialogues as follows:

Step 4   Click OK

	A	B	C	D	E	F
1	STK					
2	Part numb ▾	Supplie ▾	Quanti ▾	Reorder lev ▾	Unit pri ▾	Value ▾
4	125684	B	201	120	10.00	2,010
6	123673	B	42	30	5.00	210
7	125445	C	86	60	6.00	516
8	125421	C	400	150	7.00	2,800
11	124587	C	63	70	14.00	882
12	124895	B	52	40	8.00	416
13	126874	B	117	85	9.00	1,053

Note that the other records are still there and are included in the total value figure. It's simply that they have been obscured for presentation.

Filter can also be used for identifying items contained in large spreadsheets. For example it could be used to isolate the information relating to one part number from a list of 10,000.

3.5.3 Ranking

If you wanted to rank the data in the above example by inventory value, then you can use the RANK function. The function uses the syntax RANK(number,ref,order).

BPP
LEARNING MEDIA

To rank the data by inventory value:

Step 1   In cell G4 enter the formula =RANK(F4,$F$4:$F$13,0).

Entering zero means the ranking goes from highest to lowest value. Any non-zero value would give the ranking from lowest to highest.

Step 2   Copy the formula into cells G5 to G13, by dragging the bottom right of the box around G4 down to cell G13.

The data is now ranked as follows

	A	B	C	D	E	F	G
1	STK						
2	Part number	Supplier	Quantity	Reorder level	Unit price	Value	Rank
3					$	$	
4	125684	B	201	120	10.00	2,010	2
5	127544	A	25	25	15.00	375	7
6	123673	B	42	30	5.00	210	10
7	125445	C	86	60	6.00	516	5
8	125421	C	400	150	7.00	2,800	1
9	123548	D	20	12	12.00	240	9
10	125687	A	5	3	60.00	300	8
11	124587	C	63	70	14.00	882	4
12	124895	B	52	40	8.00	416	6
13	126874	B	117	85	9.00	1,053	3

This data could also be ranked by unit price by changing all Fs to Es in the formula, or by quantity by changing all Fs to Cs.

4 Linking spreadsheets

4.1 Using spreadsheets with word processing software

Spreadsheets can be **linked** to and exchange data with **word processing documents** – and vice versa.

There may be a situation where you wish to incorporate the contents of all or part of a spreadsheet into a **word processed report**. There are a number of options available to achieve this.

(a)   The simplest, but least professional option, is to **print out** the spreadsheet and interleave the page or pages at the appropriate point in your word processed document.

(b)   A neater option if you are just including a small table is to select and **copy** the relevant cells from the spreadsheet to the computer's clipboard by selecting the cells and choosing Edit, Copy. Then switch to the word processing document, and **paste** them in at the appropriate point.

(c)   Office packages, such as Microsoft Office, allow you to **link** spreadsheets and word processing files.

For example, a new, blank spreadsheet can be '**embedded**' in a document by selecting Insert, Object then, from within the Create New tab, selecting Microsoft Excel worksheet. The spreadsheet is then available to be worked upon, allowing the easy manipulation of numbers using all the facilities of the spreadsheet package. Clicking outside the spreadsheet will result in the spreadsheet being inserted in the document.

The contents of an existing spreadsheet may be inserted into a Word document by choosing Insert, Object and then activating the Create from File tab. Then click the Browse button and locate the spreadsheet file. Highlight the file, then click Insert, and then OK. You may then need to move and resize the object, by dragging its borders, to fit your document.

4.2 Creating and maintaining links

Formulae that span more than one file require particular care to ensure the links are set up correctly and remain valid. Links may need to be modified to cope with changes relating to file names, location, workbook structure and worksheet structure.

During formula entry, links are best created by navigating to, and then selecting, the required range. As well as helping with accurate range identification, this also ensures the correct syntax is used. When linking to ranges in separate files (ie a separate workbook), ensure the file or files you wish to link to are open before starting to enter the formula.

4.2.1 Referring to a different worksheet in the same file

A reference to a range in a different worksheet (in the same file) displays the worksheet name with an exclamation mark. For example, if a formula in a sheet named *Summary* added the values in the range C10:C25 in a sheet named *Jan*, the reference would appear as **=SUM(Jan!C10:C25)**.

4.2.2 Referring to a different spreadsheet file

Links to external files display in two ways, depending on whether the source workbook is open or closed.

When the source file is open, the link displays the file name in square brackets, the worksheet name with an exclamation mark, and the range. The default format for references to ranges in other files is absolute references. Here's an example of a reference to an open file,
=SUM([Annual.xls]Jan!$C$10:$C$25).

When the source file is closed, the link also includes the path (the source file location). Single quotes are also added, one at the start of the path the other after the sheet name, eg
=SUM('C:\Sales\[Annual.xls]Jan'!$C$10:$C$25).

4.2.3 Maintaining links between files

As explained above, a formula that links to a range in a different spreadsheet file includes the source file location and file name. If the source file is closed, its location is displayed in the formula eg
=SUM('C:\Sales\[Annual.xls]Jan'!$C$10:$C$25)

Changes to file name or location made in Excel

If linked workbook files are opened simultaneously in Excel and then saved using different names and/or locations, Excel will automatically update the links.

Changes to file name or location made outside Excel

If source file names or locations are changed outside Excel (or if files are deleted), the links within Excel aren't updated and will therefore be pointing to an incorrect location. If subsequently a different file is renamed to the original name and location, the links would be pointing at a different workbook.

4.2.4 Checking links

When links between files are established it's essential they are checked thoroughly. Use the techniques mentioned elsewhere in this book (eg range names, absolute cell references, formula auditing, cross-checks etc) to ensure links operate as intended.

The spreadsheet documentation should identify links and explain the logic behind them.

If changes are required to file names or location, these should be made with all relevant files open in Excel, so links are updated. Checks should be carried out after changes have been made to ensure the links operate as intended.

5 Three dimensional (multi-sheet) spreadsheets

Spreadsheet packages permit the user to work with **multiple sheets** that refer to each other.

5.1 Background

In early spreadsheet packages, a spreadsheet file consisted of a single worksheet. Excel provides the option of multi-sheet spreadsheets, consisting of a series of related sheets. Excel files which contain more than one worksheet are often called **workbooks**.

For example, suppose you were producing a profit forecast for two regions, and a combined forecast for the total of the regions. This situation would be suited to using separate worksheets for each region and another for the total. This approach is sometimes referred to as working in **three dimensions**, as you are able to flip between different sheets stacked in front or behind each other. Cells in one sheet may **refer** to cells in another sheet. So, in our example, the formulae in the cells in the total sheet would refer to the cells in the other sheets.

Excel has a series of 'tabs', one for each worksheet at the foot of the spreadsheet.

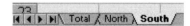

5.2 How many sheets?

Excel can be set up so that it always opens a fresh file with a certain number of worksheets ready and waiting for you. Click on **Tools ... Options ...** and then the **General** tab and set the number *Sheets in new workbook* option to the number you would like each new spreadsheet file to contain (sheets may be added or deleted later).

If you subsequently want to insert more sheets you just **right click** on the index tab after which you want the new sheet to be inserted and choose **Insert ...** and then **Worksheet**. By default sheets are called **Sheet 1, Sheet 2** etc. However, these may be changed. To **rename** a sheet in **Excel, right click** on its index tab and choose the rename option.

5.3 Pasting from one sheet to another

When building a spreadsheet that will contain a number of worksheets with identical structure, users often set up one sheet, then copy that sheet and amend the sheet contents. [To copy a worksheet in Excel, from within the worksheet you wish to copy, select Edit, Move or Copy sheet, and tick the Create a copy box.] A 'Total' sheet would use the same structure, but would contain formulae totalling the individual sheets.

5.4 Linking sheets with formulae

Formulae on one sheet may refer to data held on another sheet. The links within such a formula may be established using the following steps.

Step 1	In the cell that you want to refer to a cell from another sheet, type =.
Step 2	Click on the index tab for the sheet containing the cell you want to refer to and select the cell in question.
Step 3	Press Enter or Return.

5.5 Uses for multi-sheet spreadsheets

There are a wide range of situations suited to the multi-sheet approach. A variety of possible uses follow.

(a)   A model could use one sheet for variables, a second for calculations, and a third for outputs.

(b)   To enable quick and easy **consolidation** of similar sets of data, for example the financial results of two subsidiaries or the budgets of two departments.

(c)   To provide **different views** of the same data. For instance you could have one sheet of data sorted in product code order and another sorted in product name order.

6   Uses of spreadsheets by management accountants

Spreadsheets are used in a **variety of accounting contexts**.

Some common applications of spreadsheets are:

*   Preparation of management accounts
*   Cash flow analysis, budgeting and forecasting
*   Account reconciliation
*   Revenue and cost analysis
*   Comparison and variance analysis
*   Sorting, filtering and categorising large volumes of data

Management accountants will use spreadsheet software in activities such as budgeting, forecasting, reporting performance and variance analysis.

Spreadsheet packages for management accounting have a number of advantages.

(a)   Spreadsheet packages have a facility to perform **'what if' calculations** at great speed. For example, the consequences throughout the organisation of sales growth per month of nil, $1/2$%, 1%, $1^1/2$% and so on can be calculated very quickly.

(b)   Preparing budgets may be complex; budgets may need to go through several drafts. If one or two figures are changed, the **computer will automatically make all the computational changes to the other figures**.

(c)   A spreadsheet model will **ensure that the preparation of the individual budgets is co-ordinated**. Data and information from the production budget, for example, will be automatically fed through to the material usage budget (as material usage will depend on production levels).

These advantages of spreadsheets make them ideal for taking over the **manipulation of numbers**, leaving staff to get involved in the real planning process.

7   Printing and proofing

There are a number of **printing options** that can be used to make a spreadsheet more **visually appealing**.

Spreadsheet output will often be printed. Printed output should be inspected before circulation to ensure it contains what was intended and presents information clearly.

The default printing options in Excel are to print with a portrait orientation on A4 paper. The gridlines from the spreadsheet are not shown on the printout.

The printing options available within Excel are extremely flexible. The material below includes some tips that may be applied to print spreadsheet content in such a way that aids communication and understanding. If you require further guidance, please refer to Excel's Help facility (eg search Help using 'printing').

7.1 Use print preview

Before you print, preview your worksheet. To open print preview, select Print Pre\u0332view from the \u0332File menu, or click the Print Preview button on the standard toolbar. This can be used to show how the

BPP LEARNING MEDIA

printout will look, without actually printing, so that you can experiment with different print options without wasting paper.

7.2 Print margins

Altering the margins will affect how much of the spreadsheet will fit onto a single page. This is accessed by selecting File > Page Setup, Margins tab. A window like the following will appear.

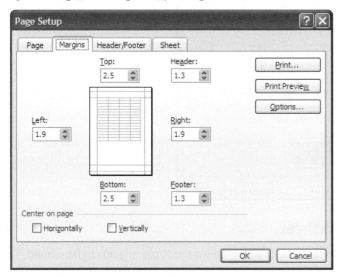

If the current content is just too wide to fit on a page, the left and right margins can be reduced in order to get the information to fit.

7.3 Paper orientation and size

The orientation of the paper can be changed from portrait to landscape from the options in select File > Page Setup. This can be useful as a method of fitting the information on the spreadsheet onto one page when there are too many columns to fit using a portrait orientation.

7.4 Fit output on one page

To fit output to one page, select File > Page Setup, Page tab and under Scaling, click Fit to 1 page(s) wide by 1 page(s) tall. Avoid using this setting if as a result the output print size is too small to be read easily. This can be checked by using print preview.

7.4.1 Fit output to a specific number of pages

To fit output to a specific number of pages, select File > Page Setup, Page tab and under Scaling, experiment with the Fit to x page(s) wide by x page(s) tall setting. Check that the result looks sensible using print preview.

7.5 Create or amend page breaks

Page breaks show where the content of the spreadsheet will be split onto another page. To adjust the page breaks in a spreadsheet, on the View menu, click Page Break Preview. Drag the dotted blue line (the automatic page break) you wish to change to the desired location.

To reset an individual page break, drag the line to the left and off the print area. To reset all page breaks, right-click and then select Reset All Page Breaks.

7.6 Print gridlines

If you wish to include the gridlines from the spreadsheet in the printout, this feature can be enabled by selecting File > Page Setup, Sheet tab and checking the box marked Gridlines as can be seen in the following picture.

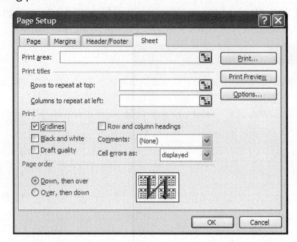

7.7 Print part of a worksheet

A spreadsheet may contain a lot of data, of which only a small piece needs to be printed. To set a specific area as the print area, select the area then click File > Print Area, and then click Set Print Area. To clear the set print area select File > Print Area >Clear Print Area.

To print a selection as a 'one-off', select the area to be printed, then click File > Print and under Print what click Selection.

7.8 Print row and / or column headings on every page

From the File menu click Page Setup, in the Sheet tab enter details in the Rows to repeat at top and Columns to repeat at left boxes. This is a useful feature to ensure that after the first page the data can still be easily understood.

7.9 Add headers and / or footers

If you want to add the same text at the top or bottom of each page, this can be done by using headers and / or footers. From the File menu click Page Setup and select the Header/Footer tab. Click the Custom Header or Custom Footer button, then either the Left, Center or Right section box. Experiment with the buttons (eg file name, date, page number etc).

8 | Advantages and disadvantages of spreadsheets

8.1 Advantages of spreadsheets

- Excel is easy to learn and to use
- Spreadsheets make the calculation and manipulation of data easier and quicker
- They enable the analysis, reporting and sharing of financial information
- They enable 'what-if' analysis to be performed very quickly

8.2 Disadvantages of spreadsheets

- A spreadsheet is only as good as its original design, garbage in = garbage out!

- Formulae are hidden from sight so the underlying logic of a set of calculations may not be obvious

- A spreadsheet presentation may make reports appear infallible

- Research shows that a high proportion of large models contain critical errors

- A database may be more suitable to use with large volumes of data

- Spreadsheets can easily be corrupted and it is difficult to find errors in large models

QUESTION

Spreadsheet advantages

An advantage of a spreadsheet program is that it

A   Can answer 'what if?' questions
B   Checks for incorrect entries
C   Automatically writes formulae
D   Can answer 'when is?' questions

ANSWER

The correct answer is A.

CHAPTER ROUNDUP

↳ **Charts** and **graphs** and tables are often excellent ways of communicating information.

↳ Using Microsoft Excel, it is possible to use data held in a spreadsheet to generate a variety of charts and graphs.

↳ A spreadsheet should be given a **title** which clearly defines its purpose. The contents of rows and columns should also be clearly **labelled**. **Formatting** should be used to make the data held in the spreadsheet easy to read and interpret.

↳ **Numbers** can be **formatted** in several ways, for instance with commas, as percentages, as currency or with a certain number of decimal places.

↳ Spreadsheets can be **linked** to and exchange data with **word processing documents** – and vice versa.

↳ Spreadsheet packages permit the user to work with **multiple sheets** that refer to each other.

↳ Spreadsheets are used in a **variety of accounting contexts**.

↳ There are a number of **printing options** that can be used to make a spreadsheet more **visually appealing**.

QUICK QUIZ

1   List five possible changes that may improve the appearance of a spreadsheet.

2   List five activities for which a management accountant could use spreadsheets.

3   What would be the most effective way of demonstrating the trend in new car sales from January to December 20X8?

A   Line graph
B   Bar chart
C   Table
D   Pie chart

4   When a spreadsheet contains a significant amount of data, but only a small percentage is required to be presented, _____ the data is the most appropriate Excel tool.

5   Which of the following is a disadvantage of a spreadsheet?

A   They cannot answer "what if" questions
B   They cannot check for incorrect entries
C   They are difficult to learn to use
D   They make calculations more difficult

6   List three possible uses for a multi-sheet (3D) spreadsheet.

7   Which one of the following is not a reason for formatting a spreadsheet

A   To make it visually appealing
B   To organise the data for analysis
C   To make the numbers more representative

ANSWERS TO QUICK QUIZ

1   Removing gridlines, adding shading, adding borders, using different fonts and font sizes, presenting numbers as percentages or currency or to a certain number of decimal places.

2   Answers include budgeting, forecasting, reporting performance, variance analysis, revenue and cost analysis and reconciliations.

3   A   Line graph. Line graphs are particularly useful for demonstrating **trends.**

4   When a spreadsheet contains a significant amount of data, but only a small percentage is required to be presented, **filtering** the data is the most appropriate Excel tool.

5   B   Spreadsheets accept the data that is entered into them and cannot identify incorrect entries.

6   The construction of a spreadsheet model with separate Input, Calculation and Output sheets. They can help consolidate data from different sources. They can offer different views of the same data.

7   B   Organising data for analysis is not an issue of formatting.

Now try ...

Attempt the questions below from the **Exam Question Bank**

Number

Q50-52

Exam question and answer bank

1   What is the most appropriate definition of an office?

   A   A centre for exchanging information between businesses
   B   A centre for information and administration
   C   A place where information is stored
   D   A room where many people using IT work

2   Which is a disadvantage of office manuals?

   A   Strict interpretation of instructions creates inflexibility
   B   The quality of service received from suppliers is reduced
   C   They create bureaucracy and demotivate staff
   D   They do not facilitate the induction and training of new staff

3   Which function is **least** likely to be carried out by an accounts department?

   A   Arrangement of payment of accounts payable
   B   Calculation of wages and salaries to be paid
   C   Despatch of customer orders
   D   Preparation of company financial records

4   The following relate to batch processing or real-time processing of data:

   1.   Audit trails are easily made since the processing of data occurs at pre-determined times.

   2.   Customer queries can be responded to immediately.

   3.   Processing can be performed during the evening when the computer is not being used interactively.

   4.   The data is always up-to-date

What are the advantages of real-time processing?

   A   1 and 2 only
   B   1 and 3 only
   C   2 and 4 only
   D   1, 3 and 4 only

5   What is the main purpose of prime entry records?

   A   Calculate the cash received and spent by a business
   B   Prevent a large volume of unnecessary detail in the ledgers
   C   Provide a monthly check on the double-entry bookkeeping
   D   Separate the taxable and exempt VAT transactions

6   Which **one** of the following is **not** a quality of good information?

   A   Accuracy
   B   Completeness
   C   Complexity
   D   Relevance

7   Which is an example of internal information for the wages department of a large company?

   A   A Code of Practice issued by the Institute of Directors
   B   A new national minimum wage
   C   Changes to tax arrangements issued by the tax authorities
   D   The company's employees' schedule of hours worked

8   Which of the following would be included in the financial accounts, but may be excluded from management accounts?

    A   Bank interest and charges
    B   Depreciation of storeroom handling equipment
    C   Direct material costs
    D   Factory manager's salary

9   Which of the following would be data rather than information?

    A   Sales increase/decrease per product in last quarter
    B   Total sales value per product
    C   Sales made per salesman as a percentage of total sales
    D   Salesmen's' commission as a percentage of total sales

10   Which type of cost is illustrated by the graph below

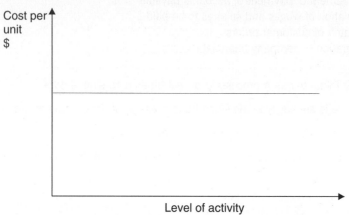

    A   Fixed cost
    B   Variable cost
    C   Stepped-fixed cost
    D   Mixed cost

11   Which item would most likely be treated as an indirect cost by a furniture manufacturer?

    A   Fabric to cover the seat of the chair
    B   Metal used for the legs of the chair
    C   Staples to fit the fabric to the seat of the chair
    D   Wood used to make the frame of the chair

12   Which of the following would be classified as a fixed cost in the operation of a motor vehicle?

    A   Oil change every 10,000 kilometres
    B   Petrol
    C   Insurance
    D   Tyre replacement

13   Prime cost is

    A   All costs incurred in manufacturing a product
    B   The total of all direct costs
    C   The material cost of a product
    D   The cost of operating a department

14   Which of the following departments listed is **not** a service cost centre in a manufacturing company?

    A   Accounting
    B   Assembly
    C   Maintenance
    D   Human resources

15   Which of the following costs would **not** be the concern of the supervisor of a production department?

    A   Labour costs
    B   Material costs
    C   Maintenance costs
    D   Finance lease payments

16   Asset turnover is the basis used to assess performance in a company. The results are

	$
Sales	40,000
Cost of sales	(15,000)
Gross profit	25,000
Expenses	(5,000)
Net profit	20,000
Capital employed	20,000

What is the asset turnover?

    A   1
    B   1.25
    C   2
    D   0.5

17   A division achieved the following results:

	$
Profit before interest and tax	61,050
Capital employed	555,000

Assuming a notional interest charge of 9%, what is the division's residual income?

    A $11,100
    B $111,000
    C   ($11,100)
    D   ($111,000)

18   A company uses a unique code top identify its customers: the first four letters of each name are followed by four digits.

The letters of the name uses which type of coding?

    A   Hierarchical
    B   Block
    C   Mnemonic
    D   Sequential

19   A company maintains an inventory control database. What is most likely to occur when suppliers cannot deliver goods on time?

    A   Customer demand will rise accordingly
    B   Customer orders will not be satisfied
    C   Inventory levels will become too high
    D   Suppliers' delivery quantities will be lowered

20   What is the sequential flow of documents to complete the purchase of goods on credit?

    A   Goods received note, purchase order, payment requisition, invoice, delivery note
    B   Purchase order, delivery note, goods received note, invoice, payment requisition
    C   Purchase order, goods received note, delivery note, payment requisition, invoice
    D   Purchase order, invoice, goods received note, payment requisition, delivery note

21   A company has 3,000 litres of a raw material in inventory. 1,250 of these litres have been committed for future use and 760 litres have been ordered but not arrived. What is the free inventory?

    A   3,000 litres
    B   3,490 litres
    C   3,760 litres
    D   2,510 litres

22   Aspects of payroll include:

    1.   Employer's benefit contribution
    2.   Employee's benefit contribution
    3.   Income tax
    4.   Salaries

Which of the above are costs to the employer?

    A   1 and 4 only
    B   2 and 4 only
    C   2,3 and 4 only
    D   1, 2, 3 and 4

23   An employee is paid on a piecework basis. The scheme operates as follows:

1 – 100 units per day	$0.20 per unit
101 – 200 units per day	$0.30 per unit
>200 units per day	$0.40 per unit

Only the additional units qualify for the higher rates. Rejected units do not qualify for payment. The employee produced 210 units in a day of which 17 were rejected as faulty.

How much did the employee earn for the day?

    A $47.90
    B $54.00
    C $57.90
    D $84.00

24   Consider the following statements.

    1   Overtime payments are generally treated as indirect costs
    2   The cost of idle time is generally treated as an indirect cost

Which one of the following is correct regarding the above statements?

    A   Both statements are correct
    B   Both statements are incorrect
    C   Statement 1 is correct but statement 2 is incorrect
    D   Statement 1 is incorrect but statement 2 is correct

25   The following purchases and issues from inventory occurred in May 20X4

1 May	Opening stock	200 units	$4.20
5 May	Purchase	100 units	$4.50
7 May	Issue	250 units	
17 May	Purchase	125 units	$4.30
24 May	Issue	75 units	

What is the value of the closing inventory on 31 May using FIFO?

A $430
B $425
C $420
D $450

26   A company employs 20 direct production operatives and 10 indirect staff in its manufacturing department. The normal operating hours for all employees is 38 hours per week and all staff are paid a basic rate of $5 per hour. Overtime hours are paid at the basic rate plus 50%. During a particular week all employees worked for 44 hours to meet the company's general production requirements.

What amount is charged to production overheads?

A $300
B $450
C $2,350
D $2,650

27   What term is used to describe charging an item of overhead expenditure in its entirety to one specific cost centre?

A   Absorption
B   Allocation
C   Apportionment
D   Re-apportionment

28   What would be the most appropriate basis for apportioning machinery insurance costs to cost centres within a factory?

A   Floor space occupied by the machinery
B   Number of machines
C   Operating hours of machinery
D   Value of machinery

29   Which of the following correctly describes the treatment of selling and distribution overheads in marginal costing?

A   All selling and distribution overheads are included in the inventory valuation

B   All selling and distribution overheads are deducted after contribution has been calculated

C   Fixed selling and distribution overheads are deducted after contribution has been calculated

D   Variable selling and distribution overheads are deducted after contribution has been calculated

30   Which of the following are not characteristics of job costing?

I   Customer driven production
II   Complete production possible within a single accounting period
III   Homogeneous products

A   I and II only
B   I and III only
C   II and III only
D   III only

---

31   A batch cost estimate includes 630 productive labour hours. In addition, it is anticipated that idle time will be 10% of the total hours paid for the batch. The wage rate is $12 per hour.

What is the total estimated labour cost for the batch?

A $6,804
B $7,560
C $8,316
D $8,400

---

32   A process requires the input of a single raw material at the start of the process. There are no process losses. 10,000 units of the material were input to the process in a period. At the end of the period, processing was only 75% complete on 800 units of the material. There was no work-in-progress at the beginning of the period.

What were the equivalent units of production?

	Raw material	Conversion costs
A	9,400	9,400
B	9,800	9,800
C	10,000	9,400
D	10,000	9,800

---

33   The following information relates to a production process for a period:
Input costs $194,860
Completed output 11,400 units
Closing work-in-progress 1,200 units (60% complete)
There were no process losses or opening work-in-progress.
What was the cost per unit for the process?

A $15.47
B $16.08
C $16.40
D $17.09

---

34   Which is the correct description of a flexible budget?

A   A budget that can be changed according to circumstances
B   A budget that is adjusted according to actual activity
C   A budget that is open to negotiation
D   A budget that is used for planning purposes only

---

35   A large hotel has bars, restaurants and banqueting facilities. They are used by hotel residents and outside users. The manager of the hotel is responsible for encouraging residents to use the hotel's catering facilities.

Which report will show how effective the manager has been in achieving this objective?

A   A report analysing the utilisation of hotel services per room occupied
B   A report showing the amount of money spent in the hotel's catering facilities
C   A report showing the number of residents in the hotel at any given time
D   A report showing the occupancy of the various catering facilities

---

36   The following statements relate to the application of feedback and feedforward control:

1.   Feedback and feedforward are both applied in budgetary planning and control.
2.   Feedback is used in the analysis of variances.
3.   Feedforward enables budgeted data for a period to be amended for the next period.
4.   Feedforward relates to the setting of performance standards

Which of the above statements are true?

A   1 and 2 only
B   3 and 4 only
C   1, 2 and 4 only
D   1, 3 and 4 only

---

37   Which of the following is a non-financial comparison?

A   Number of units sold compared to last year
B   Net profit compared to last year
C   Gross profit compared to last year
D   ROCE compared to last month

---

38   A product has a budgeted direct material cost of $5 per unit. In a specific period the production information was:
Budget   9,000 units
Actual   8,800 units

$44,380 was incurred on direct materials for the period's production

What was the direct material variance, comparing actual with the flexed budget?

A $380 Adverse
B $380 Favourable
C $620 Adverse
D $620 Favourable

---

39   Which of the following is **not** a factor that should affect a decision whether to investigate a variance?

A   Controllability of variance
B   Cost of investigation
C   Personnel involved
D   Trend of variance

---

40   Which of the following would help to explain a favourable direct material usage variance?

(i)   The material purchased was of a higher quality than standard
(ii)   Losses due to evaporation were less than expected
(iii)   Activity levels were lower than budget therefore less material was used

A   All of them
B   (i) and (ii) only
C   (ii) and (iii) only
D   (i) and (iii) only

---

41   The budgeted sales of SM Ltd were 800 units at a selling price of $20. The actual sales were 775 units at a total sales revenue of $17,050. What is the activity variance?

A $500 (A)
B $550 (A)
C $500 (F)
D $550 (F)

42   When communicating information, which of the following determine the choice of method used?

    1.   Comparative cost.
    2.   Degree of confidentiality.
    3.   Speed of delivery.

    A   1 only
    B   3 only
    C   1 and 2 only
    D   1, 2 and 3

43   In relation to effective communication of management information, which of the following statements is **false**?

    A   An ad hoc report can be less concise than one that is regularly produced because its purpose is less clear

    B   Management reports should avoid swamping the reader with too much detail

    C   The use of visuals can enhance the clarity of the report and therefore make it easier to understand

    D   An executive summary, giving the main points of the report, both saves the time of the managers and makes the report more understandable

44   Different managers will require different information in order to facilitate decision-making depending on the nature of the organisation and individual responsibilities.

    Which of the following is least likely to be true?

    A   Senior management will be interested in the financial statements, probably on a monthly basis to help make strategic decisions

    B   The human resources manager will require information on absenteeism analysed by department and reason for absence

    C   A factory supervisor will want details of order enquiries taken by the sales team each day in order to help plan production levels

    D   A sales manager will want a weekly report of orders achieved by each sales team to help assess their effectiveness

45   You are working in the finance department of a company. A colleague from the sales department has requested some accounting information that the sales department does not normally receive. They assure you that the head of the finance department is aware of the request. What should you do?

    A   Give them access to the information
    B   Print out the information and give it to them
    C   Ignore the request
    D   Refer the matter to the head of finance

46   Which of the following is not a valid spreadsheet cell input?

    A   Number
    B   Graph
    C   Text
    D   Formula

47   What does an error value of #VALUE! in an Excel spreadsheet indicate?

    A   A formula is attempting to divide a number by zero
    B   The formula contains text that is an invalid cell reference or function name
    C   The formula refers to a cell that contains text
    D   The formula has invalid numeric values supplied (eg trying to square root a negative number)

48   The following statements relate to spreadsheet formulae

    I   The formula =C4*B10 multiplies the value in C4 by the value in B10
    II   The formula =C4*117.5% adds 17.5% to the value in C4
    III   The formula =C4+C5+C6/3 adds C4, C5 and C6 together and divides the result by 3

    Which statements are correct?

    A   I and II only
    B   I and III only
    C   II and III only
    D   I, II and III

49   Which of the following keyboard shortcuts in Excel will copy the selected cell(s)?

    A   Ctrl + X
    B   Ctrl + C
    C   Ctrl + P
    D   Ctrl + Z

50   Which of the following is **not** a possible use for a spreadsheet by a management accountant?

    A   Preparation of management accounts
    B   Filtering data
    C   Account reconciliation
    D   Creating a report for the board of directors

51   Which of the following is a disadvantage of a pie chart

    A   They do not show differences in the elements of two different totals
    B   They do not show the relative sizes of elements in a total
    C   The trend line is difficult to estimate
    D   They do not show the absolute sizes of elements in a total

Question 52 refers to the spreadsheet and chart shown below

	A	B	C	D	E
1	**Projected Results for 20X7: New products**				
2					
3		Flipp	Bopp	Mapp	Total
4					
5	Sales units	280	640	320	
6					
7		$	$	$	$
9	Sales	7000	20480	5120	32600
10	Cost of Sales	3360	8960	1600	13920
11	Profit	3640	11520	3520	18680
12					
13					
14					
15					
16					
17	Selling price	25	32.00	16.00	
18	Unit cost	12	14.00	5.00	
19					

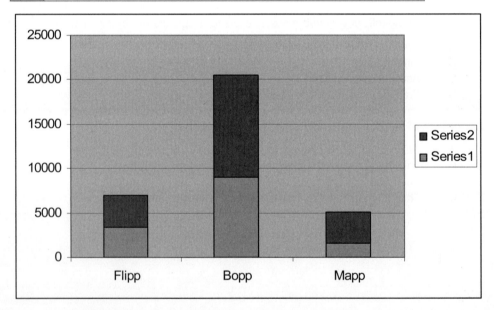

52   The data from which cells were used by chart wizard to prepare the chart?

   A   B3:D3 B9:D9 and B10:D10
   B   B9:D9 B10:D10 and B11:D11
   C   B3:D3 B10:D10 and B11:D11
   D   B3:D3 B9:D9 B10:D10 and B11:D11

1	B	This is the best definition of an office.
2	A	Strict interpretation of instructions will create inflexibility. Manuals can cover induction and training and are not necessarily demotivational. They will have no effect on suppliers.
3	C	The accounts department will not despatch customer orders.
4	C	Real-time systems are updated immediately, so are always up to date.
5	B	Prime entry records prevent a large amount of detail from appearing in the ledgers.
6	C	Good information should be a s simple as possible – remember ACCURATE.
7	D	Only this option refers to internal information.
8	B	Depreciation is likely to be excluded from the management accounts.
9	B	The other three items have been processed in some way to provide meaningful information whereas total sales value per product is the basic data for further processing.
10	B	The graph shows a variable cost since the graph is for cost per unit, not total cost.
11	C	Small consumables such as staples are often treated as indirect costs.
12	C	Motor insurance is a fixed cost.
13	B	Prime cost is the total of all direct material, direct labour and direct expenses.
14	B	The assembly department would be a **production** cost centre.
15	D	Finance lease payments would be the concern of the finance function.

16 C

Asset turnover   =   Sales / Capital employed
                =   40,000 / 20,000
                =   2

17 C

	$
Divisional profit	61,050
Notional interest (555,000 × 0.09)	(49,950)
Residual income	11,100

18	C	The using of letters of the customer name is a form of mnemonic coding.
19	B	An inventory shortage is likely to mean customer orders cannot be fulfilled.
20	B	This is the correct sequence.
21	D	3,000 + 760 -1,250 = 2,510
22	A	The employee's benefit contributions and income tax are deducted from the employees' gross pay and paid over to the tax authorities and are therefore not a cost to the employer.

23 A Total good production 210 – 17 = 193

	$
100 @ $0.20	20.00
93 @ $0.30	27.90
	47.90

| 24 | D | It is the overtime premium which is treated as an indirect cost not the total payment for the overtime hours. |
| 25 | A | Under FIFO the number of units of closing stock (200 + 100 – 250 + 125 – 75) = 100 are all valued at the latest purchase price as more than 100 units have been purchased at that price. |

$100 \times \$4.30 = \$430$

26 D

		$\$$
Indirect workers –	38 hours × $5 × 10	1,900
	6 hours × $7.50 × 10	450
Direct workers – over time premium 6 hours × $2.50 × 20		300
		2,650

27 B This is allocation of overheads.

28 D The insurance cost will be based upon the value of the machinery rather than floor area occupied, number of machines or operating hours.

29 C In marginal costing, variable selling and distribution costs are included in the inventory valuation , fixed selling and distribution costs are included in the profit calculation and deducted after contribution has been calculated.

30 D Products do not need to be homogeneous for job costing to be applied.

31 D $(630 \div 0·9 \text{ hours}) \times \$12/\text{hour}) = \$8,400$.

32 D All units are fully complete with respect to raw materials. 9,200 units are complete with respect to processing and 800 are 75% complete. $[9,200 + (800 \times 0.75)] = 9,800$.

33 B $\$194,860 \div [11,400 + (1,200 \times 0.6) \text{ units}] = \$16.08$.

34 B A flexible budget is adjusted to actual activity levels.

35 A This report will show whether hotel guests are using the facilities which is the objective of the manager. The other reports will not identify if residents are using the catering facilities.

36 A Feedforward does not relate to the setting of performance standards or enable budgeted data to be amended for the next period.

37 A Number of units sold is a non-financial method.

38 A

	$\$$
8,800 units should have cost	44,000
But did cost	44,380
	380 Adverse

39 C Personnel involved should not be relevant to the decision to investigate a variance.

40 B Statement (i) is consistent with a favourable direct material usage variance, because higher quality material may lead to **lower wastage.**

Statement (ii) is consistent with a favourable direct material usage variance, because lower losses would **reduce material usage**.

Statement (iii) is not consistent with a favourable direct material usage variance. If activity levels were lower than budget this would not affect the materials used **per unit** of production. The usage variance would be calculated based on the **standard usage for the actual output.**

41 A

	Units
Budgeted sales volume	800
Actual sales volume	775
Activity variance in units	25 (A)
× Budgeted sales price per unit	× $20
Activity variance	$500 (A)

42 D All three items are important.

43 A The purpose of an ad hoc report should be agreed upfront which will make the purpose clear.

44 C Production should be based on sales orders not sales enquiries.

45 D The matter should be referred to your superior, in this case the head of finance.

46 B A graph can be part of a spreadsheet, but cannot be a cell input.

47 C #VALUE! Is returned when a formula refers to a cell containing text.

48 A I and II only

The formula =C4+C5+C6/3 will first divide the value in C6 by 3 then add the result to the total of the values in C4 and C5. The formula =(C4+C5+C6)/3 will add C4, C5 and C6 together and divide the result by 3.

49 B Ctrl + C is the shortcut for copying cells.

50 D A board report will be created using word processing software, although it may contain charts and tables created in a spreadsheet.

51 D Pie charts do not show the **absolute** size of elements in a total, they do show the relative size and differences between elements. Trend lines are part of scattergraphs.

52 D

Index